Stardom, Film Couples and Love Teams in 1970s Philippine Cinema

International Film Stars
Series Editor: Homer B. Pettey and R. Barton Palmer

This series is devoted to the artistic and commercial influence of performers who shaped major genres and movements in international film history. Books in the series will:

- Reveal performative features that defined signature cinematic styles
- Demonstrate how the global market relied upon performers' generic contributions
- Analyse specific film productions as case studies that transformed cinema acting
- Construct models for redefining international star studies that emphasise materialist approaches
- Provide accounts of stars' influences in the international cinema marketplace

Titles available:

Close-Up: Great Cinematic Performances Volume 1: America
Edited by Murray Pomerance and Kyle Stevens

Close-Up: Great Cinematic Performances Volume 2: International
Edited by Murray Pomerance and Kyle Stevens

Chinese Stardom in Participatory Cyberculture
By Dorothy Wai Sim Lau

Geraldine Chaplin: The Gift of Film Performance
By Steven Rybin

Tyrone Power: Gender, Genre and Image in Classical Hollywood Cinema
By Gillian Kelly

Film Stardom in Southeast Asia
By Jonathan Driskell

Diana Dors: Film Star and Actor
By Martin Shingler

Yul Brynner: Exoticism, Cosmopolitanism and Screen Masculinity
By Susanna Paasonen

Ricardo Darín and the Construction of Latin American Film Stardom
By Clara Garavelli

Stardom, Film Couples and Love Teams in 1970s Philippine Cinema
By Chrishandra Sebastiampillai

www.euppublishing.com/series/ifs

Stardom, Film Couples and Love Teams in 1970s Philippine Cinema

Chrishandra Sebastiampillai

EDINBURGH
University Press

Edinburgh University Press is one of the leading university presses in the UK. We publish academic books and journals in our selected subject areas across the humanities and social sciences, combining cutting-edge scholarship with high editorial and production values to produce academic works of lasting importance. For more information visit our website: edinburghuniversitypress.com

© Chrishandra Sebastiampillai, 2024, 2026

Grateful acknowledgement is made to the sources listed in the List of Figures for permission to reproduce material previously published elsewhere. Every effort has been made to trace the copyright holders, but if any have been inadvertently overlooked, the publisher will be pleased to make the necessary arrangements at the first opportunity.

Edinburgh University Press Ltd
13 Infirmary Street
Edinburgh EH1 1LT

First published in hardback by Edinburgh University Press 2024

Typeset in 12 on 14pt Arno Pro by
Cheshire Typesetting Ltd, Cuddington, Cheshire, and
printed and bound by CPI Group (UK) Ltd,
Croydon, CR0 4YY

A CIP record for this book is available from the British Library

ISBN 978 1 3995 2099 7 (hardback)
ISBN 978 1 3995 2100 0 (paperback)
ISBN 978 1 3995 2101 7 (webready PDF)
ISBN 978 1 3995 2102 4 (epub)

The right of Chrishandra Sebastiampillai to be identified as the author of this work has been asserted in accordance with the Copyright, Designs and Patents Act 1988, and the Copyright and Related Rights Regulations 2003 (SI No. 2498).

Contents

List of Figures	vi
Acknowledgements	viii
Introduction	1
Chapter 1: Theorising the couple: what is a love team?	22
Chapter 2: Building the couple: industry, society and politics in 1970s Philippines	44
Chapter 3: Producing the couple: individual star images	66
Chapter 4: Reading the couple: joint star images	97
Chapter 5: Filming the couple: the teenage jukebox musical genre	137
Chapter 6: Becoming the couple	168
Conclusion	200
Bibliography	218
Filmography	228
Index	231

Figures

1.1	The basic film couple	26
1.2	The second type of film couple possible	28
2.1	Fans attending the premiere of a Nora Aunor film in 1970 (*Graphic*, 13 May 1970, p. 29). Source: from the collection of Nestor de Guzman	52
3.1	This image of Aunor and Doc Perez highlights Aunor's diminutive stature and young age. Source: from the collection of Nestor de Guzman	70
3.2	Portrait of Aunor in the early 1970s. Source: from the collection of Nestor de Guzman	74
3.3	Santos as Imee Marcos in *Iginuhit ng Tadhana* (1965)	78
3.4	Tirso Cruz III with Aunor in the early 1970s. Source: from the collection of Nestor de Guzman	87
3.5	Mortiz in his childhood television career. Left: *Eskwelahang Munti*. Right: *Tawag ng Tanghalan*	91
3.6	A typical image of Mortiz that emphasises his clean-cut looks and gentle nature. Source: from the collection of Nestor de Guzman, scan of *Liwayway*, 3 August 1970	93
4.1	Aunor and Cruz are a physically contrasting couple. Source: from the collection of Nestor de Guzman	101
4.2	Magazine article on the separation of Aunor and Cruz, dominated by the word 'TRIANGLE'. Source: from the collection of Nestor de Guzman	106

4.3	The poster for *Young Love*, featuring all four stars and the two love teams of this research. Source: from the collection of Nestor de Guzman	109
4.4	Santos and Mortiz in *Edgar Loves Vilma*	111
4.5	A typical example of a fashion layout from *Liwayway* featuring Aunor and Cruz. Source: from the collection of Nestor de Guzman	130
4.6	The poster for *My Blue Hawaii*, featuring garlands and carved wooden tiki. Source: from the collection of Nestor de Guzman	132
5.1	A poster for *Guy and Pip*, featuring illustrations of the 'Alphabet Song' and the fantasy wedding scene of the pair. Source: from the collection of Nestor de Guzman	142
5.2	The poster for *The Young at Heart*, featuring the names of Moreno, Lozada and Badiday. Source: from the collection of Nestor de Guzman	151
5.3	The poster for *My Little Brown Girl* shows Aunor imprisoned and crouched over a corpse. Source: from the collection of Nestor de Guzman	153
5.4	A poster for *Guy and Pip*, featuring the crowds at Aunor's birthday party, included prominently in the film. Source: from the collection of Nestor de Guzman	158
5.5	Left: Santos tilts her head and smiles as she sings. Right: Mortiz looks off-screen at Santos and smiles at her in *Edgar Loves Vilma*	163
5.6	Vilma and Edgar dance surrounded by young people and their respective dates (behind and right of Edgar) in *Edgar Loves Vilma*	164
6.1	Aunor on the cover of *Liwayway* for All Saints Day, 1970. Source: from the collection of Nestor de Guzman	175
6.2	Maria Leonora Teresa with Cruz. Source: from the collection of Nestor de Guzman	195
C.1	Richards and Mendoza play Guy and Pip on *Eat Bulaga!* in 2015 on a set that recreates the set of 'Together Again' from the film *Guy and Pip*. Source: GMA Integrated News YouTube channel	208
C.2	Pepot dressed as Maria Leonora Teresa with the fairground impersonators of Guy and Pip in *Pepot Artista*	215

Acknowledgements

My sincere gratitude to:
- My PhD supervisor, Dr Jonathan Driskell, who patiently guided me over the years to achieve the very best. Thank you for your support and dedication.
- My second supervisor, Dr Roland Tolentino, who provided invaluable support and practical assistance on the ground in the Philippines.
- My panellists at my annual milestones for my PhD dissertation, Assoc. Prof. Thomas Barker and Assoc. Prof. Andrew Ng Hock Soon, for their insight and three years of commitment to the progression of my candidature.
- The academic and administrative staff of the School of Arts and Social Sciences who have nurtured my growth as a scholar and a person for years: Prof. Helen Nesadurai, Assoc. Prof. Yeoh Seng Guan, Dr Tan Meng Yoe, Tan Mei Sie, Eswary Sivalingam and many others.
- Nestor de Guzman, and the Noranians and Vilmanians I spoke to in the course of writing this book for their time, assistance, memories and devotion to their stars.
- The kind Filipino academics who encouraged and supported me along the way, among them Professor Emeritus Doy del Mundo, Assoc. Prof. Cheryll Soriano, Jose Javier Reyes, Dr Patrick Campos and Prof. Patrick Flores.
- My friends in the Philippines, Noraisa Simpal Guadalquiver, Katrina Ross Tan and the many Filipino scholars I befriended along the way.
- Abegail Macasing Cutig, who meticulously assisted with translating pages of magazines for me.

- Mithila Narendran, who was kind enough to proofread early versions of this work with good humour and a sharp eye for mistakes in addition to her support throughout my academic journey.
- Sheril A. Bustaman and Esther Ho, who supported and encouraged me through hours of work, despair and triumph in the wee small hours of many mornings.

And chiefly, my love and thanks to my family for supporting, tolerating and facilitating my work in the years of ups and downs during the writing of this book. At least, in of all of this, my uncle got to meet Nora Aunor.

This research was supported by the Monash University Malaysia Merit Scholarship.

Introduction

The Philippines is home to the unique and enduring love team – two stars that work together on-screen to portray a romantic couple, sometimes as a one-off project, and sometimes for multiple films over the course of their career. Love teams are one of the primary ways to achieve stardom and retain it in the Philippines, with love teams and romance films forming the majority of the country's cinematic output over the years, following in the tradition of its earliest domestic film that featured singing lovers (*Dalagang Bukid*, dir. Jose Nepomuceno 1919).[1] Love teams, or the film couple, often form the basis for successful stardom in the Philippines, with nearly every popular star of note (and many more minor stars) belonging in their history to a love team. Rosa del Rosario and Leopoldo Salcedo were first paired together in the late 1930s; Carmen Rosales and Rogelio de la Rosa were a glamorous star couple in the 1940s; Nida Blanca and Nestor de Villa were the dancing Philippine Fred Astaire and Ginger Rogers of the 1950s; Fernando Poe Jr (considered the 'King of Philippine Cinema') had his wife and love team partner Susan Roces in the 1960s; the love teams of this research, Nora Aunor and Tirso Cruz III, and Vilma Santos and Edgar Mortiz dominated the 1970s; Sharon Cuneta (known as the 'Megastar of the Philippines') and Gabby Concepcion worked together and married in the 1980s; Dawn Zulueta and Richard Gomez were the *mestiza/moreno* (fair skinned, mixed ethnicity/darker complexioned) love team of the 1990s; Bea Alonzo and John Lloyd Cruz are the longest-running modern love team in the 2000s at twenty two years of work together; and Kathryn Bernardo and Daniel Padilla were the teenage sweethearts of the 2010s.

The impact of the stars of the love teams of this research (particularly Aunor and Santos) and their fan following remains relevant to the present as a marker of love team and star success. Despite the current stature of the two female stars who continue to work and their devoted fan following, rewriting the rules for becoming a film star in the Philippines and shaping the industry for teenage stars and the Philippine love team to the present, no academic work has examined the beginning of their stardom and the unique genre that produced them. This is perhaps due to the fact that both the love team and the jukebox musical genre of their early fame are considered low culture in the Philippines and are generally dismissed in a pejorative sentence or two on commercial films. This work seeks to fill that gap, examining the love teams of 1970s Philippine cinema as a nationally unique and persisting form of stardom and how it expands current academic work on the star, a concept most commonly shaped by Western stars and ideals. It considers the forces that produced a new type of love team in the Philippines in the 1970s and how socio-political events shaped them in a time of authoritarian rule.

Film couples are presently examined in Martha Nochimson's and other academic work by exploring their joint image, or the unique combination of two individual star images to form a new 'joint image'. Within the wider discipline of film studies as a whole, the role of the film couple is a surprisingly underdeveloped area of study considering their ubiquity in cinemas all over the world. To fully explore the complex levels of identity and meaning contained in the couple, I propose a new vocabulary for considering the joint image derived from James Naremore's three levels of performance: a division of the couple into two or three distinct identities. The first two are common to all film couples and consist of a 'star couple' (the two professional performers) and a 'screen couple' (the two resulting characters portrayed on film). The third is unique to couples who are also in a real-life romance, the 'celebrity couple'. The love teams of this research exist at the confluence of all three couples, with each of the three levels of identity and performance inflecting their joint image. The star couple is informed by the off-screen relationship of the celebrity couple, while the screen couple deliberately conflates the romantic and the professional relationships into its narratives and identity in the 1970s Philippine love team. The resulting blurring of lines between romance, work and fiction combine to make the love team a particularly compelling film couple, one in which 'real' and 'reel' bleed together to form an indistinguishable whole. Authenticity is therefore a key feature of the 1970s Philippine love team, and one considered in detail through the two love teams of this research.

The centrality of the couple in Philippine stardom suggests a different approach to stardom than the individuality described by Richard Dyer in his analysis of Hollywood and Western cinemas (2004: 7–9). While the Hollywood star celebrates the distinct individual, Philippine cinema operates on the principle that two stars are better than one, regularly packaging stars together as a strategy of achieving stardom, of subsequently modifying a star's image and as a guarantee of profit. Philippine culture and the dominant Catholicism reinforces this combining of individuals in narratives of courtship, marriage and family in society. The love team film is similar to the star vehicle film, with the spectacle and pleasure of the film lying in watching a particular combination of stars perform together in a particular way. Stars become something more in being paired together: love teams elevate the star and make them doubly appealing to the audience.

The love teams of this research rose to fame at a unique juncture of Philippine history. They represented a shift in the type of stars made and the audience they were appealing to with the rise of a new global demographic: teenagers. Rising on the back of a global youth revolution that brought fame to Elvis in the 1950s and the Beatles in the 1960s, teenage stars emerged in the Philippines a little later at the end of the 1960s on the television and the radio, bringing to the cinema the music that first made them popular in the new genre of the teenage jukebox musical. The studios of the era were weakening after the First Golden Age of Philippine Cinema in the 1950s, but still held some influence on the industry and were responsible for the early careers of three of the four stars of this research. At the same time, President Ferdinand Marcos came to power in 1965 and began imposing increasingly authoritarian rule on the nation, resulting in the urban educated youth and labourers staging a series of street protests in 1970. In the face of the conflict between youth and authority figures, the family owned and operated studios relied on long-standing methods of star grooming and management developed in the 1950s to manage the new stars, creating a hierarchy of power that mimicked the family with the studio owner as the head, and the stars as the subordinate and obedient family members. Film narratives were also moral and cautionary tales that imparted desirable values and punished negative behaviour via the stars and films produced. At a national level Marcos also leveraged the ideology of family, positioning himself as the Father of the Nation, intent on creating a New Society after the implementation of Martial Law, a movement he described in terms of national discipline.

The love teams of this research represent a significant proportion of the output of popular Philippine cinema during the 1970s, releasing teenage romance films at a rate of fifteen films together in 1970 (Santos and Mortiz) and breaking box-office records with their films, screening in the cinema for six months and earning US$1.24 million with *Guy and Pip* (dir. German Moreno 1971) (Aunor and Cruz).[2] Between the four stars, studios were able to cater to a wide range of people and tastes in Philippine cinema – whether you were from the upper or lower class, whether you sought to identify with the local or the exotic, the two love teams could satisfy your requirements. Aunor and Santos later contributed to the Second Golden Age of Philippine Cinema in more mature and gritty incarnations. Their origins in the love teams that immediately preceded this period (sometimes directed by auteurs) formed their training and set them on track for famous roles in films with Lino Brocka, Ishmael Bernal, Celso Ad Castillo and Mike de Leon among others. In turn, it is precisely their fame earned from love team films that allowed auteur directors to use them effectively and subversively to make what are considered to be some of the greatest films in Philippine cinema (see Aunor in *Himala*, dir. Ishmael Bernal 1982, discussed in more detail below).

The teenage love teams were most active in the first three years of their partnership, shifting to more sporadic work as they sought to move beyond their teenage images towards more mature roles, with their work together slowing by the mid-1970s, a period acknowledged as the beginning of the Second Golden Age of Philippine Cinema (David 1990), born of the discontentment of young auteur directors under Martial Law and a curtailing of freedom. The research is also naturally delimited at its upper end through the very definition of the stars examined: teenagers, who transitioned to their twenties and more adult roles by 1973, when Cruz turned twenty-one, Aunor and Santos turned twenty, and Mortiz was the youngest at nineteen. The period also coincides with the slow collapse of the old studio system that characterised film production in the Philippines from the 1930s onwards. Tracking these love teams in this period yields information about the Philippines in transition at a key moment of national upheaval.

In order to uncover the star images and the joint images of the stars and love teams, I examine filmic and extra-filmic materials available on them such as magazine articles, interviews, images, songs, public appearances and press releases. These items have been archived by various stakeholders including the National Library of the Philippines and a leading collector and seller of old Philippine films, Simon Santos of Video 48. The remaining archives of Sampaguita are presently housed in the ABS-CBN Film Archive, a privately held collection that requires special permission for visiting scholars (Lim 2010). As a result, this research is limited in several ways (especially with regards to the Santos and Mortiz tandem), firstly by what films were available and what publications had been archived – some magazines fared better at the archives than others, and any publishing biases towards or against couples have an impact on the amount of information available. To the best of my knowledge, this work represents the most in-depth use of archival materials in star studies in the Philippines, particularly in terms of the use of contemporary popular magazines to explore star images. These are supplemented where possible with several fan interviews as well as an interview with Aunor. A final note on the limitations of this study is that it is based on the love teams' film careers and leaves out their colourful careers in variety television and radio, equally important sites of locating their images, but prohibitively difficult to access and rumoured by some to be lost after the closure and takeover of radio and television stations across the country on 22 September 1972, the day after the declaration of Martial Law.[3]

Exploring the star image

Star studies has expanded greatly from Edgar Morin's early concept of stars as 'sacred monsters' in *Les stars* (1972 [1957]) to Francesco Alberoni's view of them as the 'powerless elite' – of interest to the public but limited in terms of power (1972) – and Charles Affron's *Star Acting: Gish, Garbo, Davis* published in 1977, which formed the notable precursors to Dyer's *Stars* (1979) and *Heavenly Bodies: Film Stars and Society* (1986). Subsequently, Christine Gledhill's *Stardom: Industry of Desire* in 1991 brought together a collection of works on stardom to create a comprehensive text on stars, including among them Barry King's 'Articulating Stardom' (1985), which examines the star as operating within various 'economies' in cinema. In 2001, Chris Rojek wrote *Celebrity*, examining the broader field of popular culture figures beyond film studies, followed by Graeme Turner's *Understanding Celebrity* (2004). Several collections that take critical approaches to star and celebrity studies have followed, including Lucy Fischer and Marcia Landy's *Stars: The Film Reader* (2004) and Sean Redmond and Su Holmes's *Stardom and Celebrity: A Reader* (2007), while Martin Shingler's *Star Studies: A Critical Guide* (2012) forms a comprehensive introduction to star studies.

The seminal works on stardom are Dyer's *Stars* and *Heavenly Bodies: Film Stars and Society*. Dyer's examination of stars combines the disciplines of sociology and semiotics to uncover star images. To understand love teams, their individual star images must be examined to get a sense of their stardom. Stars are constructed images, 'a combination of visual, verbal and aural signs that constitute the general image' of a star in films and all kinds of media texts (Dyer 1979: 34). The image is found across a range of media texts including films (their primary 'work'), promotion, publicity, criticism and commentaries (ibid.: 60–63). They are simultaneously sociological by virtue of being influential individuals or figures of identification in society (an aspect of film's industrial nature), as well as semiotic because they are part of the way films signify (ibid.: 1). As this work deals with couples as well as individual stars, it will also consider what I will refer to as a 'joint image', that is, a shared image of coupledom to which each star contributes that is unique to their tandem.

Stars are a product of capitalism. They are in the first place capital possessed by the studio, or themselves a holder of a monopoly on their services that they can contract to interested parties (ibid.: 10). In this manner, stars are labour that work to produce a product – simultaneously the product of their image as well as their performance in films. They are then an investment to the studio, 'a guarantee or a promise against loss on investment and even of profit' (ibid.: 11). They are outlay in that they form the major part of a film's budget, and producers are careful to manage their use (ibid.: 11). Stars are a means of managing the market: they are used to sell films, to organise the market, and to estimate and predict audience response (ibid.: 11). Stars are also important as they are the centre of spectacle, with the common construction of narrative to best display the star image, most notably in the star vehicle film (ibid.: 12). The roles of love teams as labour and the studios in controlling, employing and creating their image is explored further below.

To ensure the success of the star system, the industry invests in advertising or manipulation of the market (ibid.: 12). Stars are by no means constants, but people who rise and fall with time and fashion: initially they emerge as a novelty and ultimately they disappear as their popularity fades (ibid.: 14). Stars range from being exceptional, gifted and wonderful to hard-working, humble and lucky (ibid.: 16–17). These phrases reflect how the discourse surrounding stars has shifted from thinking of them as gods or ideals to their becoming figures of identification that embody typical ways of behaving (ibid.: 22). To aid in this impression, stars are frequently thought of as 'types' – a shared and easily grasped image of how people are in society, such as the 'bad boy' and the 'independent woman' (ibid.: 47–59). The medium of film (perhaps because of its more intimate format and use of close-ups) creates and encourages the star phenomenon in a way that the theatre simply could not.

Similarly, love teams are seasonal, exemplified by the rise of teenage stars and love teams in this research. Simultaneously ordinary and extraordinary, they provide figures of identification not just as individuals, but as couples who go through some of the same struggles and triumphs on-screen as their audience does off-screen in real life. They provide examples of love, courtship, romance and marriage that inform the ideas of the public and are in turn informed by the public. Different love teams at different stages of their partnership also tend to fall into types: the sweet young couple next door, the working-class couple who struggles to cope with mundane daily challenges, the forbidden or taboo couple, or the (dis)harmoniously married pair.

Stars are inherently ideological. They embody a multiplicity of meanings, with some foregrounded while others are masked or displaced. Stars are an easily accessible and strong media representation of ideas of what people are and are supposed to be like (ibid.: 20). But at the same time, they exist as persons independent of fiction and are an ideal location to explore the tensions of being an individual in capitalist society and the agency they possess in constructing and negotiating their public identity (Dyer 2004). This concept is explored in greater detail through the familial and industrial pressures brought to bear on Aunor in Chapters 3 and 4. Stars are presented as being simultaneously ordinary and extraordinary (ibid.: 35). This is the quality of being like 'one of us', giving a sense of representativeness and allowing the audience to identify with the star. Equally, there must be a quality of being elevated, or 'apart from us', usually expressed in great talent, beauty or some other distinguishing factor. The attainment of financial security creates the impression that their lives are in order, an impression that is marred by wide media speculation on their relationships and marriages, one of the key ways in which film couples and love teams are encountered in the media, explored in Chapter 4 (ibid.: 45). Love teams reinforce the ideologies of heterosexual unions, both off-screen and on. In the majority Catholic population of the Philippines, they are also representations of acceptable (and forbidden) norms of courtship, love and marriage. An examination of the love team and love team films reveals many aspects of Philippine culture they embody and in turn influence, discussed in Chapter 6.

Stars play characters; they labour to produce constructed representations of persons in their films (Dyer 2004). Star identification allows the audience to draw on their understanding of the star's image to expose some truth about the character they are playing (Dyer 1979: 125), a phenomenon particularly visible in the stardom and filmography of the stars of this research because the star couples played fictionalised versions of their real-life relationships on-screen in multiple films. The work of the star is another important aspect of exploring the love team that is discussed in greater detail in Naremore's *Acting in the Cinema* (1988). Naremore discusses the language and techniques used to frame performances, including gestures, delivery of dialogue, rhythm, tone, emphasis, posture and even a deliberate lack of any overt actions or reactions. In discussing star acting in particular, he agrees with Dyer on the separation of the star into multiple aspects, including the performer playing fictional characters, the public figure playing theatrical versions of themselves (or the image, as Dyer calls it) and the person, or an individual self. This research expands on those three identities with regards to the film couple in the categories of the star, screen and celebrity couple, each speaking to a different level of performance. Stars are involved in several levels of performance: the performance of the self (Naremore argues that all human identities are performances), the performance of their persona (their star image) and the performance of their work (the creation of fictional characters). There exists some form of overlap between all three performances, something that is deliberately emphasised in the love team films of this research to further erase the boundaries between each performance and identity. Star performances are vital to audiences as through watching the star's previous work, a pattern or similarity exists and is recognisable as being the product of that particular star. In this manner, stars come to be known by their 'ideolect', a set of 'performing traits that is systematically highlighted in films and sometimes copied by impressionists' (ibid.: 4).

With love teams, analysis of the performance must additionally consider the way the two performers play off each other. Their familiar rhythms and particularities carried over the course of an entire career working together form a solid aspect of their couple chemistry. A gaze, the pauses in their speech and the quickness of their movements are the result of the interplay between two people performing a story. Long familiar traits become part of their love team performance ideolect – perhaps a tendency for long, drawn-out parting scenes, a tendency to tears, or a song and dance number which viewers come to expect from their films together. Another aspect of their performance is their performance as a love team – the two stars put together in extra-filmic material. They may perform as cordial co-workers or passionate lovers, relative strangers who do not get along outside their films or best friends, bitter ex-lovers or smitten teenagers; each approach conveys a different performance of a love team and achieves very different effects.

Stars perform their work for the studios that employ them. Paul McDonald's work on *The Star System: Hollywood's Production of Popular Identities* (2000) considers the role of the Hollywood studio system in creating star identities and their dissemination, describing the Hollywood studio system at its height as employing 'mechanisms designed to produce and reproduce the star phenomenon by actively working to manufacture and take legal control of star identities' (ibid.: 43). McDonald further details the efforts of studios to control the production of star identities from talent scouting, talent training and development to launching of the star in stages and then producing star vehicles for maximising profit. Early Philippine studios operated in a very similar way but with a twist: studios were family owned and operated businesses with family members taking hands-on roles in the daily operation of the studio, fostering loyalty through a sense of familial gratitude and reinforcing this through familial titles such as 'Mommy' Vera.

The Classical Hollywood studio system was a well-oiled machine that could churn out stars and films efficiently and with a shrewd understanding of what audiences wanted to see. Studios took strong measures to counter competition, developing their own stable of stars and binding them with restrictive contracts that could last for up to seven years. This gave the studio the power to control the star's image and career, a relationship that Dyer notes was not always harmonious. Early Hollywood stardom had its share of contractual disputes and divisions between stars and studio. In response, stars attempted to resist on an individual basis and ultimately, when the system collapsed, became producers themselves. Post-studio, stars are contracted on a film-by-film basis and the contract negotiations between stars and studios have become much more balanced in terms of power (even with an edge in favour of stars who are guaranteed to bring in a strong box-office profit). In the Philippines, the studio system has persisted in one form or another to the present. This is one reason why love teams are a viable product for them: they do not have to pay exorbitant talent fees to put together individual stars in the same way a Hollywood production would have to set aside millions purely for the talent fee for a project with Tom Hanks and Meg Ryan today. A lot of their risks are managed in this way; a box-office hit is certain if you give the audience the stars they like best in the combination they like best, and the content is not always relevant to the success of the film if the tandem is 'phenomenal'. To this end, Philippine studios have developed strategies for scouting for, recruiting, training and using love teams that will be explored in this book. The star system does not work in isolation but exists in tandem with other media producers. During the reign of the studios (both in Hollywood and in the Philippines), studio executives were able to exercise a fair amount of control over the images of stars by careful work and cooperation with various media outlets.

Examining the couple

A natural extension of examining stars is to examine the couples they form in films, not always limited to the romance genre. There has been surprisingly little extended work on screen couples, with the main work on the subject being Nochimson's *Screen Couple Chemistry: The Power of 2* (2002). This work is the first to consider screen couple chemistry and does so by examining several star couples of Classical Hollywood (William Powell and Myrna Loy, Fred Astaire and Ginger Rogers, Johnny Weissmuller and Maureen O'Sullivan, Katharine Hepburn and Spencer Tracy) and couples from 1980s–90s television (Bill Cosby and Phylicia Rashad, Bruce Willis and Cybil Shepherd, David Duchovny and Gillian Anderson).

One of Nochimson's main arguments is that not all partnerships are created equal, dividing them into four main categories: the Synergistic Couple, the Iconic Couple, the Functional Couple and the post-studio category of the Thematic Couple. The Functional Couple is the most easily defined among the four as being 'a simple cog in the wheel of the churning plot, adding little if any screen chemistry to the experience of the movie' (ibid.: 8). The Iconic Couple is on the next rung and the most common kind of pairing, 'making clichés glamorous and established dramatic and comedy recipes that could work for comparatively large numbers of interchangeable star partners' (ibid.: 10).

It is Nochimson's definition of the Synergistic Couple and chemistry that is more complex than the rest. The Synergistic Couple is one whose 'energy tended to disrupt the formulas in interesting ways so as to create highly distinctive perspectives on the social practices embedded in the usual narrative pattern' (ibid.: 9). The task of the Synergistic Couple is to rise above the constraints of a formulaic plot and to disrupt it through their energy, challenging or at least engaging with dominant ideologies. Nochimson's definition of chemistry is vague as she acknowledges that chemistry is unquantifiable and difficult to study, likening it to smoke or clouds (ibid.: 8). Nochimson uses various adjectives to describe chemistry, including 'raging energy' (ibid.: 3) and 'freestanding energy vortex' (ibid.: 4), before discussing the matter in some detail in an appendix titled 'Theorizing Chemistry in Entertainment via Neuroscience'.

In ranking some couples by chemistry and leaving others out, Nochimson seeks to study only the couples that are Synergistic – disruptive and critical of social norms. This excludes the vast majority of couples, which are presumably less than the best in terms of chemistry. It also excludes some couples who had excellent chemistry and popular followings but failed to 'disrupt' dominant ideologies. Rather than discussing a broad variety of film couples for what they are as a whole, the end result privileges what Nochimson perceives as the best narratives (original and disruptive of the status quo) and the best chemistry (synergistic), discussing the couples' weakest work (their formulaic films) as a sort of disappointing postscript to their partnerships. The resulting work prioritises establishing and discussing chemistry in its strongest and finest forms rather than discussing film couples in their various iterations.

I argue that couples are worth studying without category or reserve as they are the heart of the romance genre and a chief attraction to audiences. Whether the couple turns out to have the best chemistry in the world or the most subversive energy, the couple is still a central feature that conveys much about love and courtship in their society – a fact that Nochimson agrees with, but one that her methodology does not fully allow her to explore. In fact, the star couple is such a sure guarantor of success that the plot can be completely irrelevant to the audience's enjoyment of their films. What critics may consider to be 'bad' films do not diminish the status of the couple but rather prove that their chemistry together overrides this and provides them with the ability to weather weak plots and contrivances. An interesting aspect to consider is couples who make films that are generally judged to be mediocre or poor in terms of plot but draw large audiences regardless of this fact. By that measure, many of the films made by the love teams in this research qualify in terms of 'poor' plot quality but unwavering fan support.

If no judgement is made as to the quality of chemistry and narratives, even the poorest Functional Couples say as much about screen couple chemistry as those who are considered the best. I understand chemistry as the dynamics or unique relationship between people. Accordingly, my discussion of love team chemistry is seated in an examination of performance. In the case of love teams, these relationships are romantic and there are several levels of performance that are simultaneously in operation: the performance of the individual persons of their star image, the off-screen performance of the stars as long-standing colleagues in the business of portraying a couple, and the characters (yet another couple) they play in a film. As such, I will seek to understand what these specific performers bring to their performances in their respective star images, their performance of a love team in their extra-filmic material, and their performance as a couple on-screen. One area of interest this research seeks to examine is what these specific couples offer to the audience that is unique to their partnership and their films.

To aid my discussion of couples and ground my discussion of chemistry in more tangible terms, I propose to discuss their star images as offering unique attractions to audiences. Stars provide figures of identification and function on one level as representations of persons negotiating love and courtship on the big screen, a fact which Nochimson addresses in her work. In this respect, my approach more closely resembles the general strategies employed by the writers of several chapters on screen couples in Rutgers University Press's *Star Decades: American Culture/American Cinema* series. Of particular interest are the decades/editions of the 1930s featuring Errol Flynn and Olivia de Havilland, Fred Astaire and Ginger Rogers, and Myrna Loy and William Powell (McLean 2011); the 1940s featuring Humphrey Bogart and Lauren Bacall, and Cary Grant and Katharine Hepburn (Griffin 2011); and the 1950s featuring Rock Hudson and Doris Day (Palmer 2010). *First Comes Love: Power Couples, Celebrity Kinship, and Cultural Politics*, edited by Shelley Cobb and Neil Ewen (2015a), also considers the couple but from the perspective of celebrity or real-life couples such as 'Brangelina' and 'Robsten', referring to the names given to the power couples of Brad Pitt and Angelina Jolie, and Robert Pattinson and Kristen Stewart respectively.

Philippine cinema and stardom

Scholarship on Philippine cinema often examines its auteur directors, such as Lino Brocka, Ishmael Bernal and Mike de Leon (Hernando 1993; Lent 1996; Campos 2006). Their influence on Philippine cinema is immense, and any list of its best films will feature all three prominently. Another prevalent area of study is the history of Philippine cinema. Originally emerging as an extension of American colonisation when American studios set up distribution branches in the Philippines (Deocampo 2011a: 16), post-colonial Philippine cinema and Third World cinema are recurrent themes in academia (Tiongson 1983; del Mundo Jr 1998; Capino 2010). National and transnational cinema is also a subject which has been explored (Tolentino 2001; Campos 2016). More recent work considers topics such as influential films, directors, genres, ideological questions, post-colonial cinema, the place of the Philippines in global cinema and stardom. Gender in film has become a particularly popular subject that examines the shift in the traditionally male gender role as provider to the female and the new screen men and women that result, and this is one of the lenses through which stars have been discussed in Philippine film scholarship.

In terms of stardom, scholars tend to focus mainly on Nora Aunor (by far the most researched star), with scattered works on other stars such as the 'King of Philippine Cinema' Fernando Poe Jr, Dolphy and even Weng Weng. Fernando Poe Jr was the alpha male champion of the underdogs in the 1960s action films and westerns (Velasco 2009), Dolphy was a comedic icon, bringing laughter to the screen for over sixty years (Ancheta 2006), and Weng Weng was a 'Filipino midget James Bond' with transnational cult film stardom (Smith 2013). Writing on Nora Aunor focuses on her stardom as being unusual in the line-up of Philippine stars: her petite stature, dark skin and poor background marked her as being different to the usual tall *mestiza* (mixed ethnicity) beauties that Philippine cinema privileged. Neferti Tadiar explores Aunor's stardom as containing a subversive or 'heretical' potential in her 2002 work examining Aunor's threat to patriarchal power (religious and political) in her role in the iconic *Himala*, while an earlier work explores the 'Noranian imaginary', with reference to Aunor's fans (2000). Patrick Flores writes that Aunor's star image has been linked to a patient 'sufferance' through recurring narratives of pain in her film roles read in conjunction with her background of poverty (2001). Bliss Cua Lim's 2004 work on Aunor explores her relationship with gender, religion, class and the cult-like following Aunor possessed through a close reading of her role in *Himala*. Aunor's unprecedented and passionate fandom is explored in Lim's subsequent 2012 work on fan consumption of Aunor's star image and the resulting 'Noranian collectivity', particularly how Aunor and her fans negotiated the politics of the era. Another article by Bliss C. Lim explores how a 1980s *mestiza* star mimicked Aunor's rags-to-riches biography in her film narratives, resulting in a 'Noranian turn' that boosted her career (2015). In 2015, Joel David wrote a history of scholarship on stardom in the Philippines, considering in particular Aunor-as-auteur and why the magnitude of her fame and stardom may be inhibiting broader work in star studies in the Philippines.

Despite Aunor's centrality to any work on stardom in Philippine cinema, there is no work that concentrates on her beginnings and early stardom, or how she earned her status as 'Superstar' of the Philippines – through her love team with Tirso Cruz III. It is this early tandem that put her in the spotlight and broke box-office records, some of which are still competitive when adjusted for inflation to the present. Her rival Vilma Santos is likewise absent from much of the literature on Philippine stars. She is mentioned in work on other subjects, as in Rolando B. Tolentino's work on overseas Filipino workers (OFWs) in contemporary women's films (2009) and in Johven Velasco's chapter on 'Star Texts' (2009), commenting on her versatility and ability to change her image (which earned her the title 'Star For All Seasons'). This work in turn draws from Cesar D. Orsal's article 'Vilma Reads Her Fans' (2000). There are some books on both Aunor and Santos written and published by fans, which are a rich source on their early careers and their star image as perceived by their fans, such as Baby K. Jimenez (a celebrity and entertainment reporter), *Ang True Story ni Guy* (1983); Nestor de Guzman, *Si Nora Aunor sa Mga Noranian: Mga Pagunita at Pagtatapat* (2005); and J.B. Garcia, *Queen Vi: An Intimate Biography* (1984). The male stars of the love teams are similarly reduced to a footnote in the stardom of their more famous love team partners.

The contemporary stars of the Philippines have not been explored in great detail but are a growing field in current Philippine scholarship. The main English language text on the subject is entitled *Huwaran/Hulmahan Atbp.: The Film Writing of Johven Velasco* (Velasco 2009). The book deals mainly with the icons of cinema mentioned above (and their contemporaries) but also examines some current stars such as

Piolo Pascual and Jericho Rosales. One of the chapters, previously published in another book, deals with changing gender roles in contemporary melodrama (Velasco 2008). The other main source on stars in Philippine cinema is written in Tagalog by R.B. Tolentino, titled *Richard Gomez at ang mito ng pagkalalake, Sharon Cuneta at ang perpetwal na birhen at iba pang sanaysay ukol sa bida sa pelikula bilang kultural na texto* (2000). Orsal also considers female stars in his Tagalog work *Movie Queen: Pagbuo ng Mito at Kapangyarihang Kultural ng Babae sa Lipunan* (2007). Elsewhere, stardom tends to be mentioned in work concerned with gender or genre, such as an analysis of films on the OFW as portrayed in contemporary melodramas (Tolentino 2009) as well as a study of Judy Ann Santos as an icon of gender and sexuality (Santiago 2006).

Most recently, Philippine scholars have begun to examine the love team in their writing. When I first began my research on love teams in 2013 (Sebastiampillai 2022), there were no academic works available on them, nor were there any when I embarked on the thesis that would result in this book in 2015. Since then, emerging scholars have focused their analysis on recent love teams, interested particularly in love teams created and consumed across social media and their respective fandoms. Richard Bolisay's article on the 2010s love team JaDine (2019) is the first academic work to set out a considered definition of what a love team is, and explores how the James Reid and Nadine Lustre love team are consumed by their contemporary online fandoms (discussed in greater detail in Chapter 1). An earlier work of Bolisay (2016) participating in a roundtable on the AlDub love team with two other scholars (Del Campo and Brugada) explored the Alden Richards and Maine Mendoza love team that emerged from a popular television programme and how the couple performed in their subsequent films together. In 2021, Samuel Cabbuag published an article that closely examines the AlDub fandom, and how fans negotiate their fandom and what might be deemed being an 'authentic' fan. While Bolisay's 2019 article refers to star studies theory through Dyer's 1979 work (chiefly in terms of the star as an ideological figure of representation, and raising the question of authenticity in love teams), star studies is not a primary theoretical framework used in his work.

Outside academic writing, recent years have produced several coffee table books of interest. B.M. Carballo has written a history of Philippine cinema in terms of the notable directors and studios over the years in *Filipino Directors Up Close: The Golden Ages of Philippine Cinema, 1950–2010* (2010). Kathy Almajose and J.V. Ramos wrote *Kakaibang*

Tingin, Kakaibang Titig (2013), a book on the Sampaguita studio and its stars. There has been no significant work about more recent studios (such as the television studio) except for coffee table books commissioned by studios themselves. These consist of two biographical works on the Lopez family, the owners of ABS-CBN (Rodrigo 2010, 2006), and a book on the history of the television network (Sioson-San Juan 1999). Most recently, a how-to book on stardom was written by talent manager Noel Ferrer, titled *Sisikat Din Ako!: Your Guide to Making Your Mark in Show Business* (2015), containing his advice and observations on the industry and requirements for stardom. Any other writing on the subject originates from the press or fans on their internet forums and blogs.

Summary of research

The first chapter examines the Philippine love team, considering the meanings and significance contained in the concept and how it relates more broadly to film couples as a whole. The love team typically consists of a male star and a female star who work together primarily in the romance genre (and other genres which feature a romance subplot) to depict romantic couples on-screen. Love teams complicate the individual-centric Western stardom because of the sheer popularity and ubiquity of the film couple, a primary strategy of stardom in the Philippines to the present. The film couple (just like the individual star) functions as a promise to the audience about the quality and specific elements of the romance portrayed on film, whether it is a tendency towards comedic plots or particularly passionate romances. This in turn works as a subgenre of sorts, with the couple's films representing specific things to the audience. Pairing stars elevates the stardom of single stars through their combination into a new joint image, and most popular stars in Philippine cinema have an associated partner in their history. This chapter also examines the film couple as it is presently understood in order to contextualise the Philippine love team in this broader context of film couples.

Chapter 2 establishes the industrial and political atmosphere of the Philippines in the 1970s, examining the material conditions that produced the 1970s love team, and how the studios and President Marcos were able to leverage the film industry to reproduce authoritarian values. It first explores the prevailing studios and star system in place immediately prior to the stars of the 1970s love teams, looking in particular at the role of the studios in sustaining a hierarchy of power that adopted the ideology of the family in the daily operation of the studios, with stars' discipline and behaviour governed by patriarchs and matriarchs of the family-run studios with consequences for unacceptable behaviour. A close examination of the political couple of Ferdinand and Imelda Marcos suggests that Marcos worked with the film industry to further his political ambitions and relied on the generic conventions of the melodrama to connect with the masses (Espiritu 2017). An analysis of his biopic, *Iginuhit ng Tadhana: The Ferdinand E. Marcos Story* (dir. Conrado Conde, Jose De Villa and Mar S. Torres 1965), demonstrates the cooperation of Sampaguita Pictures in giving Marcos the spotlight in the run-up to his first election as President, with key personnel of the studio associated with popular love teams working to produce the film, which is regarded by Marcos himself to have been key in winning him the election.

Chapter 3 examines the individual star images of the four stars in the two love teams of this research. In this chapter, several of the main features of stardom in the 1970s are explored including the class divide in the audience and among the stars, and the prevailing preference of *mestizo* or mixed ethnicity stars. It also considers the changing nature of the film industry in the 1970s, with teenage stars and films emerging as a distinct consumer category. The four stars took different paths to fame, some relying on the established means of achieving celebrity – through proximity and connections within the industry – while others were modern stars of a modern medium, television. Television also shifted fame from something that was conferred by the studio to something that could be earned through merit in the televised singing contest. While the stars of the 1950s studio discussed in Chapter 2 were distant and glamorous, the 1970s teenage stars were much more accessible and relatable, with Aunor being particularly representative of the poor *masa* (masses). Aunor's star persona contained a mixture of a Cinderella narrative and a localised version of the American Dream – an ordinary young girl of noble heart is lifted out of poverty through her extraordinary talent and hard work, becoming representative of the poor, dark masses she originated from. She performed in her songs and films the suffering of the poor, given voice for the first time through her person. Comparatively, Aunor's rival Vilma Santos was the 'Glad Girl' (de Manila 1990). As a fresh-faced *mestiza* child star with relatives working in Sampaguita, Santos fulfilled the requirements of traditional star material under the studio system. Cruz was similarly proximate to the industry through his famous musical family. Cruz was tall, *mestizo* and musical, all key features for attaining fame in the 1970s teenage jukebox musical. Both Cruz and Mortiz marked a shift in the hypermasculine roles of Philippine cinema during the era – leading men were commonly men of action. Mortiz represented a gentler masculinity, the kind of boy that mothers loved. He came to the film industry through the same televised singing contest as Aunor, resulting in his voice being a defining aspect of his image.

Chapter 4 discusses the joint images of the love teams of this research, getting to the heart of their discovery, development and career trajectory as planned by their studios and what made them unique as film couples. Love teams in this generation were the result of trial and error from amongst the pool of teenage musical stars to test the right combination through the television variety show and radio. The two love teams complemented each other in the differences found in their joint love team images. Aunor and Cruz possessed a stormy dynamic, one brought by Aunor's image of drama and struggle and born of a nation with class division that spilled into the population's consumption of popular culture. Opposition is in the very definition of their image, with Aunor representing the subversive or unconventional star in her petite, dark-skinned, poverty-stricken origins and new entrance into the film industry, while Cruz represented the establishment in his membership of the upper class, his *mestizo* heritage and close relationship with the industry. Santos and Mortiz were the opposite of this image, becoming known for their even-temperedness and dependability, earning them the title 'Proven to be Stable, proven to be Strong'. Santos and Mortiz were the model love team for the studio: talented, with a unique chemistry and popular following, compliant, professional and grateful, and from families that supported a strong work ethic and emphasised the importance of work and career. A key factor in understanding the 1970s love team is the distinction between 'real' and 'reel', a fine line that love teams in the Philippines often do their best to blur or at least leave a sense of hope in fiction becoming fact.

Chapter 5 discusses the genre of the 1970s love team, performance, the relationship between star and genre and its recurring settings. The teenage jukebox musical is a film in which 'there is no original music score, and which uses existing well-known music', often associated with low culture due to its lack of originality (Knapp et al. 2013: 1277). The genre is under-explored not only in the Philippines, where related scholarship is non-existent, but more broadly in film studies, with a fair proportion of the scholarship on the genre coming from the theatre rather than film. The chapter discusses a subgenre that is associated particularly with the love team of Aunor and Cruz: the semi-biographical teenage jukebox musical, which is the (re)telling of Aunor's life story and attainment of success through her extraordinary talent. One key way in which the Philippine jukebox musical differs from other musicals is where it locates the spectacle – in the stars rather than in intricate and grand ensemble musical numbers. Love team films function as star vehicles, allowing them to 'do their thing' and working to blur the lines between the stars and the roles they play, marking their performances as a site of slippage between real and reel. Love team performances are analysed to explore the unique attractions they offer the audience as well as being one of the primary sites for studying the love team's chemistry. One key aspect of *mise en scène* that influences the love team is the settings of the films they star in. The real and imaginary spaces that the love team are set in reflect the image of the society that the studios were intent on (re)producing. In the subgenre of the semi-biographical teenage jukebox musical, the studio becomes a rich site of meaning. Television variety show cinematographic techniques are brought to bear in the film, highlighting intricate and themed sets. The studio in teenage jukebox musicals both functions as a backstage glimpse into the industry with the star at work as well as symbolising an aspirational stage that offers success and liberty.

Chapter 6 looks at the love teams as being uniquely shaped by society and shaping society in return through their images and films in the 1970s. Love teams of the era were built at the confluence of youth culture and authoritarianism, and regularly negotiated between tradition and modernity in their images and films. Both love teams performed the work of becoming the couple in their filmic and extra-filmic work, naturalising coupledom in popular culture. The couple is the basic framework for becoming the family, another concept that love team films embody. The family is achieved in a literal sense by Aunor and Cruz through the 'person' of their doll 'daughter', Maria Leonora Teresa, a visual representation and barometer of the relationship between the stars, conceived immaculately and representing the purity and innocence of their love. Santos and Mortiz also performed the work of becoming the family in their filmic and extra-filmic work, through the narratives of combining their individual families to form a single family through their relationship. Marcos recognised the power of the media and the family and used it to his benefit in a popular teen magazine profile, in which he positioned his family as the Father and

Mother of the Nation pushing for discipline in the New Society he championed in the wake of Martial Law. The new love teams of the era were in a constant negotiation with authority figures over their identity, taking a middle path that gave new freedoms within acceptable boundaries. The Church in the majority Catholic Philippines confers an authenticity to the romance of the teenagers in their films and in real life. But the Church also acts as another form of authority, performing a key function in teaching submission to the will of God, particularly in female stars known as *babaeng martir* (Tadiar 2002), or 'female martyrs' – a common type of self-sacrificial female character in Philippine culture. In a final conflict between modernity and tradition, Aunor and teenage musical stars were criticised during their era as being agents of 'neo-colonisation' because of the use of English in their films and their foreign cultural values, reflecting a nationalist fear built around protecting the new national language. Aunor was condemned both for her attempts to engage with the upper class through English as well as for her 'tacky' Taglish films, despite other stars not being held to the same standard.

Conclusion

This research exists at the heart of a disconnect between academia and the popular audience, the upper class and the lower class, and is an ongoing point of struggle over what Philippine culture should be. For those in the camp that privileges social commentary plots that enlighten the audience, the love team film falls short. Love team films viewed in this light are an embarrassment to Philippine cinema, the aspects of local culture that some wish would disappear in order to make room for better, more realistic and educational films. Criticisms of commercialism and mass culture have thus far precluded a study of the local star system that drives one of the most vibrant cinemas in Southeast Asia, and also one of the most fascinating aspects of Philippine cinema from the perspective of an outsider. Philippine cinema is known more for its edgy auteur films of the Second Golden Age of Philippine Cinema, the aspect of 1970s Philippine cinema that is significantly better researched and more positively acknowledged by critics and those in the academic field, both locally and internationally. Such an approach ignores the appeal that popular stars and genres have to Filipinos, who continue to enjoy the love team more than a century after the first film couple in the first domestic film production appeared on the screen. An account of a century of Philippine cinema surely must consider its most popular stars and films, and it is my hope that this research on love teams honours 100 years and counting of lovers on the silver screen.

Notes

1. Star Atang de la Rama sang live backstage during every screening in Manila accompanied by a violinist, a trumpet player and a pianist (Abunda 2007).
2. Adjusted for inflation, this figure comes close to PHP560 million (Video 48 2009), or almost US$12 million, a profit that is not readily attained by local films even at present.
3. ABS-CBN claims that 'the musical records and radio dramas accumulated by ABS-CBN in a span of twenty-five (25) years and stored in its library were now gone', as stated in a legal decision from the Supreme Court dated 15 October 2008.

Chapter 1

Theorising the couple: what is a love team?

Introduction

This chapter will discuss couples in film and introduce the love team, a film couple unique to Philippine cinema and the subject of this research. I will begin with a simple etymological discussion of the term 'love team' and follow with a brief review of the literature that focuses on couples in film. There exists an ambiguity in the discussion of film couples, a gap that this chapter will address through the introduction of three subtypes of possible couples: the star couple, the celebrity couple and the screen couple, referring to various aspects of the stars' work, personal relationships and fictional portrayals on-screen. Each subtype of the couple acts independently and in conjunction with each other to create the resulting couples in films. Slippage between the various aspects of the couple work to erase the construction of the couple and the boundaries between real and reel, conferring a sense of authenticity to the couple.

Love teams complicate the individual-centric Western stardom that Dyer discusses in his work on the stars of Hollywood cinema, with Philippine screen couples indicating a tendency towards combining stars rather than treating them as individuals, particularly in the early stages of their career. This can be seen in the branding of the couple, which shows them to be inextricably linked by their names and their films. The role of the audience in influencing the decisions of studios and stars in their personal lives and careers is also of interest, as well as what aspect of the love team's coupledom they place importance on – a factor that may be influenced by the source of their fame. This chapter will address questions of what a love team is, how they fit in with current academic understanding of the couple in film, and how the love team helps clarify and expand work on the couple and stars in film studies.

In plain language

The phrase 'love team' is one that tends to raise eyebrows when I explain my research, often politely followed by the question, 'You mean love theme?', a more logical combination of words in the romance genre. Unique to the Philippines, 'love team' conveys a range of meanings, which will be discussed over the course of this chapter in order to arrive at a vocabulary and theoretical framework for discussing the couple in the subsequent chapters on two 1970s Philippine love teams. It will discuss the current academic work on the couple and identify gaps which will be explored and discussed with regards to the Philippine love team and how this relates to the concept of the couple and stars as a whole.

I will begin with a simple English language discussion of its two root words, 'love' and 'team', followed by an investigation of the concept of love teams in the Philippines. Love is at once a simple and complex thing to define. Common meanings include a strong feeling of affection, a great interest and pleasure in something, and a specific kind of love, *eros* – passionate or romantic love. The last meaning is at the heart of the love team and romance genre, the quest for love between two compatible people that is universal. Further examination will demonstrate that its other meanings also come into play in the concept. 'Team' is the more unusual of the words, and one usually reserved for more practical pursuits than love. There are several generally accepted meanings. Firstly, 'team' refers to the act of two or more people working together to achieve a common goal, or a group of players in a competitive sport. Secondly, it is to match something together to create a desired effect, or to harness together two or more animals to pull a burden. While at first glance the word 'team' may not seem to be the most fitting to describe stars working in the romance genre, the word actually conveys many of the love team's different aspects.

Firstly, the love team consists of two stars who work together primarily in the romance genre (and other genres which feature a romance subplot) to depict romantic couples on-screen. This definition refers to the people involved in the love team – specifically the professionals. The use of the word 'team' to match something together refers to the act of deliberate sorting through options to reach a specific combination. It implies a sense of purpose and calculated thought in the arrival at a final pairing. This highlights the constructed nature of the love team, a carefully considered pairing arrived at through matching two people together to produce a combination that is pleasing to the audience. Then there is the harnessing of two stars together to guarantee profit and pull the weight of the project at hand. The final meaning is competitive, and refers to sporting teams, which love teams can be said to be. There is competition between stars for success, a goal won by securing a successful partner, and competition between love teams for the strongest following among the public.

This meaning implicates the fans, another vital component of the love team. Teams must have supporters, and Philippine fans in the 1970s were a vocal and well-mobilised group, forming clubs around their favourite stars and partnerships. The fans also contribute another meaning to the word 'love' in their passionate devotion to their favourite love team. This translates to a fierce protectiveness and rivalry among other fan groups, each rooting for their love team to be both on-screen and off. This desire to make the fictional real is a key part of the love team's appeal and provided useful publicity for 1970s stars off-screen, feeding an industry that featured love teams in *komiks* (comics magazines that featured stars), youth magazines, television, radio, concerts and other live appearances. The films of these love teams can be read in part to be fantasy fulfilment, a fictional outing for a real couple that fans long to see together on-screen, or conversely for a non-couple in real life to be together at least on-screen for the duration of the film.

Working towards a definition

A love team is a pair of stars who may or may not be a couple in real life that work as a couple in films (or television) and the accompanying promotion of those films in the romance genre, or in films which have an element of romance in their plot. They are native to Philippine cinema and stretch back to the indigenous theatre form of *sarsuwela* (musicals with romance plots) (Lumbera 1989: 172). The first locally produced film, *Dalagang Bukid* (1919), featured a love team that had first performed the roles in the theatre before bringing them to cinema (Tiongson 1983: 87). There is no equivalent concept in other major popular national cinemas such as Hollywood or Bollywood, these cinemas instead featuring the 'screen couple' (a term that I will explore in greater detail below). To understand the concept of love teams, it is first necessary to examine the different elements that constitute a love team. Present literature tends to discuss the stars of the romance genre using the terms 'star couple', 'screen couple' and 'celebrity couple' interchangeably. Here, I find it useful to differentiate between the three kinds of couple in the hopes of establishing a clear distinction between the three types as well as to show that there are no universally understood terms to convey these distinct meanings.

The main literature on screen couples is written by Nochimson (2002), whose work discusses iconic screen couples of the past. These include such stars as Fred Astaire and Ginger Rogers, and Katherine Hepburn and Spencer Tracy. Her book chiefly discusses the subtypes of the screen couple, ranging from Functional to Iconic and Synergistic (discussed in the Introduction). Nochimson refers to the characters in the film merely as a 'couple' or by their character names, while at various points she refers to stars working together as 'captivating acting pairs', 'onscreen pairs' and 'star couple' (ibid.: 3, 6, 9). Cobb and Ewen's edited collection *First Comes Love: Power Couples, Celebrity Kinship, and Cultural Politics* uses 'celebrity couple' and 'star couple' interchangeably to refer to stars in personal relationships off-screen, which their book is largely interested in (2015a: 10). In a 2015 poll conducted on the British Film Institute (BFI) website to find the greatest screen couples of all time, the term 'screen couple' referred to characters (not off-screen couples) that included Scarlett O'Hara and Rhett Butler in *Gone with the Wind* (dir. Victor Fleming 1939), Buttercup and Westley in *The Princess Bride* (dir. Rob Reiner 1987) and Han Solo and Princess Leia of the *Star Wars* saga (1977–) (BFI 2015). In order to clearly distinguish between these three different types of couple, I will use the terms 'star couple', 'celebrity couple' and 'screen couple' to signify the professional relationship, the personal relationship and the fictional relationship respectively.

Star couples, celebrity couples and screen couples

The film couple is the site of multiple performances of identity. I derive this understanding of identity and its three broad divisions from Naremore, who divides star performances into three levels: the self, or the person; the star, or the star image; and the character, or the fictional person created for the film. Film couples at their most basic are divided into two: the star couple, or the two professionals working together to portray a couple, and the screen couple, which is the resulting fictional characters (sometimes based on real historical couples) in their films (see Figure 1.1).

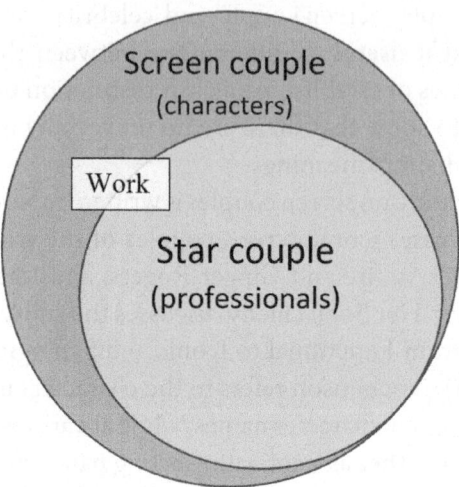

Figure 1.1 The basic film couple

The screen couple is at the heart of romance in films, and the film couple necessarily hinges on the existence of the screen couple. All star couples play screen couples, and the relationship between the screen couple and the star couple is one of work. The star couple of Tom Hanks and Meg Ryan, for example, produces a specific kind of screen couple, and one that has been informed by their long professional association and multiple films made together. Specifically, their joint image of wholesomeness and ordinariness contributes to the nice-guy-meets-girl-next-door roles they portray in *Sleepless in Seattle* (1993) and *You've Got Mail* (1998), both directed by Nora Ephron (who also in turn influences the kind of screen couple they portray, which typically happens with star couples who are associated with a particular director).

The professional output of the Hanks–Ryan star couple is dwarfed by the records of the Philippine star couples of this research as well as another Southeast Asian star couple of the 1960s. Mitr Chaibancha and Petchara Chaowarat are known as the most celebrated star couple of Thai cinema, working together in 150 films from 1962 until Chaibancha's untimely death in 1970 at the age of thirty-six in an on-set accident (Jimenez-Varea and Expósito-Barea 2015: 153). These 150 films represent more than half of the films made in Thailand during that period (ibid.), demonstrating the popularity of the star couple. In India, Shah Rukh Khan and Kajol have appeared together in seven films, winning them the title of 'Most Romantic Bollywood screen couple of all time' in a 2013 online poll conducted by Sanona, the UK's largest online Pay-Per-View Indian movie portal (Press Trust of India 2013).

However, not all screen couples are played by star couples. Important issues to consider when classifying a screen couple as a star couple include: are they stars? Do they work 'together'? Are there other significant contributors to the screen couple? This becomes particularly clear in the case of animated films in which voices for the characters may be provided by relatively unknown voice talents (for example, Batman, voiced by Kevin Conroy, and Wonder Woman, voiced by Susan Eisenberg, in *Justice League, the Animated Series*, 2001–2004). Both voices are instantly recognisable to the audience (particularly Conroy, who voiced Batman between 1992 and 2022), but most of the audience are also unlikely to recognise the faces behind the voices and may even be unaware of their names. Voice talents also work to create the couple, but cannot be said to be a star couple, particularly if they are unknown, and they never interact with each other as the voice recording process often entails recording artists separately. In the case of a silent animated film, the human element of providing a voice is removed, and the professionals involved in animating the couple and the screenplay writers who shape the narrative thus become primarily responsible for creating the screen couple.

A second configuration is also possible with the inclusion of the celebrity couple, an element that comes into play when the stars have a present or prior romantic or other sort of personal relationship that informs the reading of the couple through the additional aspects of the stars' real-life relationships. South Korean stars Son Ye-jin and Hyun Bin were brought together by a film they co-starred in, the 2018 film *The Negotiation* (dir. Lee Jong-seok). This first pairing ignited speculation about the stars during the publicity for the film and a rumoured 2019 vacation together in Los Angeles. The two would work together again in the globally successful television drama *Crash Landing On You* (dir. Lee Jeong-hyo 2019–2020), playing the star-crossed South Korean businesswoman Yoon Se-ri and the North Korean soldier Ri Jeong-hyeok respectively. Their romantic relationship was exposed by the tabloid magazine *Dispatch* in 2021 before the pair made an announcement of their engagement soon after, referring to the iconic roles in *Crash Landing* that brought them together in their social media official announcement posts (*L'OFFICIEL Vietnam* 2022).

Their professional work as the star couple created the celebrity couple, adding a sense of interest to the screen couple and the chemistry of both *The Negotiation* and *Crash Landing*. Of particular interest to the audience is the collision between real and reel – when did fiction become fact? The film and the drama become curiosities, the opportunity to witness the birth of such a high-profile celebrity couple. The press would go on to cover their wedding, honeymoon and the subsequent birth of their first child, driving interest in the pair (dubbed the 'Bin-Jin couple') locally and internationally. Vanessa Diaz's chapter in Cobb and Ewen (2015) explores the blended name phenomenon of celebrity couples through Hollywood couple 'Brangelina', consisting of stars Brad Pitt and Angelina Jolie, along with several other chapters that also consider film couples that blur the lines between fact and fiction through their romantic relationship in addition to their star and screen couple identities (Negra 2015; Leonard 2015). The celebrity couple is a well-established phenomenon internationally, with another example from the Golden Age of Malay Cinema being the iconic celebrity couple of P. Ramlee and Saloma who sang together in a series of musical films, marrying in 1961 (Yeoh and Begum 2014). These couples all exist at the intersection of the professional, the fictional/representation and the personal, demonstrated in Figure 1.2.

Some celebrity couples are fictionalised or represented on-screen, and thus become screen couples, such as Queen Elizabeth II and Prince Philip

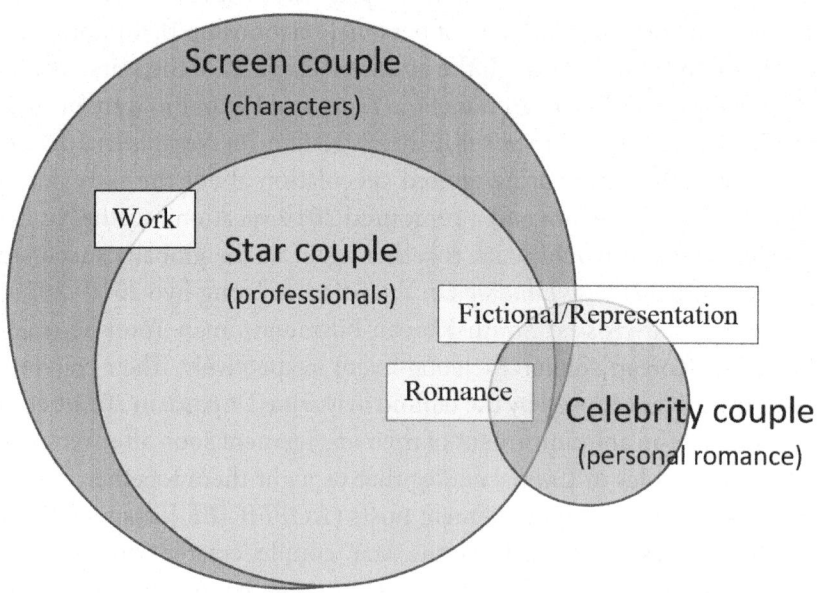

Figure 1.2 The second type of film couple possible

in *The Crown* (2016–2023) (discussed further below). Alternately, celebrity couples may exist as screen couples without a star couple presence (for example, archival footage of Queen Elizabeth II and Prince Philip in a documentary).

The 'star couple' refers to the professional relationship between star performers – two stars who work together to create couple characters. Within this category are several subtypes such as the television star couple, a star couple that works together over the course of a television series. A good example of the television star couple is Gillian Anderson and David Duchovny, who worked on *The X-Files* (1993–2002, 2016, 2018) for a count of 213 episodes in eleven seasons spread over the course of twenty-five years to create the fictional characters, or screen couple, of Scully and Mulder. Another subtype of 'star couple' is the one-off pairing frequently featured in the romance genre. Some of these go on to become iconic one-off pairings, such as Julia Roberts and Hugh Grant, a star couple made iconic through their roles in *Notting Hill* (dir. Roger Michell 1999). Another kind of star couple is the sequential pairing, where a star couple is called upon to repeat their roles in a sequel or franchise. An example of this is Rachel Weisz and Brendan Fraser in *The Mummy* (dir. Alex Kurtzman 1999). The franchise's third film performed badly after Weisz did not return, resulting in a re-cast for her beloved character, Evie. This subtype of star couple is crucially linked to its screen couple: beloved stars are firmly linked to their roles, and films may suffer as a result of the star couple being re-cast in the event of one star's unwillingness or inability to reprise their role.

The final subtype is the recurring non-sequential collaboration. This is the rarest kind of star couple in post-studio era Hollywood: stars that recurrently work together to create couples who are not linked to previous performances by narrative or franchise. Usually considered iconic in terms of their unique chemistry and performance style, these star couples tend to become increasingly expensive as the individual star's profile rises (or those of both stars do). They may be increasingly expensive, but they are also increasingly guaranteed to draw a profit at the box-office due to their track record together. Such stars include Tom Hanks and Meg Ryan in their four film collaborations, *Joe Versus the Volcano* (dir. John Patrick Shanley 1990), *Sleepless in Seattle*, *You've Got Mail* and *Ithaca* (dir. Meg Ryan 2015); and Drew Barrymore and Adam Sandler in their three collaborations, *The Wedding Singer* (dir. Frank Coraci 1998), *50 First Dates* (dir. Peter Segal 2004) and *Blended* (dir. Frank Coraci 2014).

The second type of couple is the 'celebrity couple', which refers to the personal romantic relationship: two celebrities who are in a romantic relationship in their personal lives off-screen. There are of course many kinds of celebrity couples, but in this instance, I am referring to a specific subset of celebrity couples who achieve their fame or work within film or television. The 'celebrity couple' is separate from the 'star couple' because it is indicative of a personal romantic relationship between two celebrities rather than the professional working relationship that the latter implies. Contemporary examples include married celebrity couples Daniel Craig and Rachel Weisz, John Krasinski and Emily Blunt, and Javier Bardem and Penélope Cruz, while a younger couple (but unmarried couple) is Zendaya and Tom Holland. All these couples have also starred together in various films, which means that their status as celebrity couple not only informs their star images but also the screen couples they create. As the means of becoming a celebrity diversifies and expands over time, the film celebrity couple is no longer as common as they once were, with stars now able to date a wide list of other celebrities such as the more traditional musician celebrity pairings and the newer reality TV celebrities and social media influencers.

The final type of couple is the 'screen couple', which refers to the fictional relationship: the fictional characters created on-screen who are in (or are headed towards) a romantic relationship with each other and are either fictional or representations of real individuals or celebrities. These characters range from the forgettable to the iconic, fading from memory as soon as the film ends or living on as iconic fictional characters of popular culture. Nochimson (2002) deals with this matter in depth in a sort of cross-section between the screen and star couple. And it is the screen couple that the BFI contest addressed in its public poll that received thousands of votes worldwide. The success of the screen couple is often contingent on the chemistry between the stars playing them along with a skilfully written script. In some cases, however, the screen couple dominates the project, eclipsing even the star couple chosen to portray them. This is most often the case where the screen couple is based on historical figures or characters and stories that are well established in other art forms of popular culture, such as literature, folk tales or song. Examples of such couples include Queen Elizabeth II and Prince Philip in *The Crown*, the various versions of Robin Hood and Maid Marian, and in the Philippines, Ferdinand and Imelda Marcos in their two biopic films made in the 1960s. All these films are driven by their screen couples rather than the star couples, though care is certainly taken in the casting to ensure that the correct image and level of skill are present in the performers. Equally, some aspects of the star couple make their way into the screen couple, with performers leaving their mark on their fictional characters as Harrison Ford and Carrie Fisher did with the tempestuous relationship between Han Solo and Leia Organa in the *Star Wars* franchise – a combination that is impossible to replicate by substituting other stars in their place.

Analysis of these three types of couple and their hybrid relationships illustrates several of the binary oppositions discussed in Dyer's work such as the public/private, the ordinary/extraordinary and authenticity/constructedness (Dyer 2004). Star/celebrity couples, for example, resolve the opposition of the private and the public by making public through their work as a screen couple that most private of relationships, romantic love. Their work together in films can be read by fans to be a series of fictional episodes of their real love. Conversely, fans can also infer from the fictional episodes perceived 'truths' about the celebrity couple's 'real' off-screen relationship, as happened with speculation about the lack of real-life chemistry between husband and wife celebrity couple Tom Cruise and Nicole Kidman when they portrayed a screen couple in *Eyes Wide Shut* (dir. Stanley Kubrick 1999). Suzanne Leonard refers to these relationships as a state 'wherein the boundaries between performance, intimacy and sexuality are forever blurred' (2015: 261). Similarly, the star couple exposes the construction of the couple on-screen as a commodity by making explicit the work of portraying a screen couple. Conversely, the existence of a real relationship between a celebrity couple can mask the construction of the screen couple and conceal the commodity of the star couple through the appearance of authenticity; that is, the 'realness' of the relationship that the celebrity couple possesses legitimises the star and screen couple. Nochimson refers to the relationship between fiction and fantasy in the minds of the audience as 'slippage':

> Their too great impact on moviegoer sensibilities imperilled the public's social grounding in reality, often blurring the boundaries between actuality and illusion, as in some part of the audience's mind the real personhood of the actors slipped into the identities of the onscreen lovers, and chemistry slipped into history. The public imagined the screen couples as offscreen intimates, without actually marking the place where slippage had taken place. (Nochimson 2002: 4)

It is worth noting however that Nochimson here is speaking of the strength of the chemistry between a star couple that is so strong that it is able to suggest a sense of reality rather than an actual coinciding of star and celebrity couples in an off-screen relationship.

Aside from being constructed and commodified, stars (and couples) are also inherently ideological. Stars convey popular norms and values of their society, positioning themselves either in support of or in opposition to them. Couples in particular are in a position to reconcile sometimes opposing ideological positions in their two persons. These often include discourses on class, religion and the family. Heterosexual couples in the romance genre reinforce heteronormative ideals, promoting a monogamous heterosexual relationship as the prerequisite of the family unit, vital for reproduction within a society. Diane Negra, in discussing the celebrity couple, describes the ideological reinforcement of heteronormativity, writing that the 'couple is the privileged and pre-eminent social unit' in our contemporary cultural belief (2015: 313–314).

A brief history of love teams and their studios

The strategy of the large early studio giants of the Philippines such as Sampaguita and LVN is described as follows by David: 'first, launch some young stars, preferably in compatible pairs; then, when they're not so young anymore, combine them with old stars to draw in the mature moviegoers' (1990: 128). Bienvenido Lumbera considers love teams and stars not purely an import of Hollywood cinema, but rather a pre-existing feature of Philippine theatre, particularly the *sarsuwela* (musicals with romance plots), where *sarsuwela* artists were 'idealized and lionized' in the press, much like film stars are treated today (1997: 172). Nicanor Tiongson writes that the first locally produced film in the Philippines, *Dalagang Bukid* (1919), was an adaptation of a *sarsuwela*, starring the same love team that performed in its theatrical version (1983: 87). In his account, *Dalagang Bukid* brought to the silver screen the first instance of the many subsequent love teams of Philippine cinema.

According to Nick Deocampo, 'The main attraction of a *sarswela* film is the pair of famous singing personalities, later called the "love team"' (Deocampo 2011b: 283). Deocampo ties the first native couple of Philippine cinema, Atang de la Rama and Marcelino Ilagan (of *Dalagang Bukid* fame), to Nora Aunor and Tirso Cruz III in a genealogy of the *sarsuwela*, citing Tiongson's connection of Aunor to the *sarsuwela* (ibid.: 282) and his own argument that Aunor and Cruz, and Santos and Mortiz were responsible for preserving the spirit of the *sarsuwela* until the early 1970s (though 'modified in content, form and presentation') (ibid.: 283). In his 2011 work *Film: American Influences*, Deocampo considers the love team and the star system to carry influences of both Spanish and American colonisation of the Philippines, claiming, 'The creation of love teams, heroes and anti-heroes, deployment of special effects and many other aesthetic conventions has Hollywood as their model' and describing the star system as 'one of the longest-lasting traits that the Tagalog movie industry inherited from Hollywood' (ibid.: 580, 526).

Tiongson, Deocampo and Clodualdo del Mundo Jr are united in identifying love teams as carrying over from the theatre to cinema in the Atang de la Rama and Marcelino Ilagan love team. The pair strongly showcased their *sarsuwela* roots with songs interspersed with obstacles faced by the young lovers. While their first film was made in 1919 when cinema was still silent, de la Rama's singing and the musical aspect of the film were considered so important that she sat behind the screen during Manila screenings and sang along, accompanied by a live band.

Becoming famous in the 1930s was matinee idol Rogelio de la Rosa (whose birth name was Regidor Lim de la Rosa), who began as a villain in regional *sarsuwela* performances and was cast at the young age of thirteen in his first film opposite Rosa del Rosario in *Ligaw na Bulaklak* (1929) (Almajose and Ramos 2013: 27). De la Rosa is an example of a star who became famous before the intervening years of World War II, which would disrupt early Philippine cinema and see him return to theatre before making a comeback to cinema after the war, regaining dominance of the box-office with the title 'Golden Boy of Philippine Cinema' (ibid.: 28). He is described by Almajose and Ramos as 'faithful, dependable, reliable, trustworthy, and sincere; a true gentleman', professional and without scandal attached to his name (ibid.: 29). De la Rosa was partnered with multiple leading ladies such as Rosa del Rosario, Corazon Noble, Paraluman, Mila del Sol and Carmen Rosales until he shifted into a political career in 1957 (ibid.: 28). His most enduring love team partner, however, was Carmen Rosales, with whom he made at least twelve films. They worked together between 1939 and 1956, initially at Sampaguita and later across multiple studios.

Rosales, by contrast, came to cinema at twenty-one years old, later than de la Rosa, after she had already married and become a mother.

Born Januaria Constantino Keller, Rosales joined the guerrilla movement as a sharpshooter against the Japanese Occupation to avenge the death of her husband at the hands of the Japanese, and would later appear in films about the Occupation (Fernandez 2013: 10). Prior to World War II, the large studios in power included Malayan Movies, Del Monte Pictures, Sampaguita Pictures, Parlatone, Filippine Films, Salumbides Brothers, X'otic and Excelsior Pictures in the mid-1930s, which were joined by LVN in 1938 (Mercado 1977: 9). Rosales was launched in 1938 by Excelsior Pictures after she was turned down without a screen test by LVN matriarch Doña Sisang because she had 'no profile' (ibid.: 10; Mercado 1977: 29) although she was already popular, performing in *sarsuwelas* on radio. She would subsequently move to Sampaguita Pictures, launching her popular love team with de la Rosa and working with him steadily until he moved to LVN, a time during which she was said to have a feud with him and refused to speak with him for many years before starring with him in *Kampanang Ginto* (dir. Gregorio Fernandez 1949), produced by LVN (Mercado 1977: 29). Rosales was paid 40,000 pesos, making her the highest-paid female star of the era.[1] According to Fernandez, the reason behind the feud was revealed to be de la Rosa's higher talent fee than hers in their early projects, which Rosales deemed unfair (2013: 53).

The stars of the First Golden Age of Philippine Cinema were in this manner closer to the glamourous, out of reach 'sacred monsters' described by Morin (1972 [1957]). De la Rosa and Rosales (known as Roger and Mameng) are amongst the most memorable love teams of Philippine cinema. Rosales's spark paired well with de la Rosa's penchant for formal wear (for which Rosales called him 'Mr Society') and together they embodied the glamour of the era, their performances often featuring them singing in each other's arms, her soprano voice blending with his deep baritone in famous love songs such as 'Ang Tangi Kong Pag-ibig' in the 1955 film of the same title (dir. Mar S. Torres). Taking over from Roger and Mameng were Nestor de Villa and Nida Blanca, the dancing love team of the First Golden Age of Philippine Cinema. Nestor and Nida's stardom indicated the later turn to television that would soon become another venue for stars, appearing in their own television show, *The Nida-Nestor Show*, which ran from 1960 to 1964 on ABS-CBN. Their extended and intricate dance sequences earned them the title of the Fred Astaire and Ginger Rogers of the Philippines; in addition to their dancing prowess, this love team carried a strong association with comedy. Both love teams have their origins in the studio system that also produced Nora Aunor and Tirso Cruz III and is discussed in detail in Chapter 2. The teenage love teams of this research would rise next in the late 1960s and dominate the first few years of the 1970s as the large studios declined and new, smaller, independent studios stepped into the breach.

Andrew Leavold writes that the 1980s saw the introduction of 'brash, youthful players' who would take over mainstream filmmaking (2014: 145). Regal Films was set up by the Monteverde family and headed by 'Mother' Lily Monteverde, who ran the production company with a firm hand, overseeing her crop of stars that were known as 'Regal Babies' (ibid.: 145). Viva Films, run by 'Bos Vic' Vicente del Rosario Jr, would emerge in 1981 and would be followed by Seiko, run by 'TF King' Robbie Tan (ibid.: 145). While this new 'Big Three' started as independent studios, their takeover of the mainstream included a return to some of the hallmarks of the earlier studios, including maintaining a stable of stars and directors, as recorded by Joel David (2018) in an interview with Bienvenido Lumbera in the 1990s. It was in this setting that Sharon Cuneta emerged in 1980 as the 'jukebox princess' who would likewise cross over into film stardom and attempt to appropriate Aunor's popularity with the massive lower-class audience despite being from a privileged *mestiza* background (Lim 2015: 174). Lim writes that aside from sharing musical talents, Cuneta and Aunor also shared a wholesome star persona characterised by suffering – or the perpetual virgin, as described by R.B. Tolentino (2000) – against a backdrop of sexploitation films (2015: 175).

Gabby Concepcion, meanwhile, was a Regal Baby and was paired with Cuneta in the 1981 film *Dear Heart* (dir. Danny L. Zialcita), followed that same year with a sequel, *P.S. I Love You* (dir. Eddie Garcia). The pair would make eight films together, going on to marry in 1984 and having a daughter together before separating three years later. Jeline Malasig writes that the charm of the couple's films and joint star image lay in their '"aspirational" love story', or how the pair were rich young lovers whose only problems came from their rich parents (2018, quoting Ramos). This provided a good contrast to the other popular love team of their era, the 'inspirational' Maricel Soriano and William Martinez, who both came from humble backgrounds (ibid.). Undoubtedly, their on- and off-screen relationship was also a key draw for the audience. When asked about their success in a 2019 interview,

Concepcion theorised that they were probably popular due to a combination of fewer love teams during the era – he reckons there were only about four – and their marriage and child together (Asilo 2019). The pair would be reunited twenty-six years after their final film together in a 2018 McDonald's advertisement that features the pair as exes who run into each other after a long time, smiling and exchanging shy glances for most of the 90 second advertisement.

The history of the rise of television network studios as the dominant force in star and film production begins with ABS-CBN. In the early 1990s, the ABS-CBN television network faced the significant hurdle of securing talent that either belonged to established film studios, such as Regal Films and VIVA Films, or were established freelance stars, to produce content for its own television shows. This arrangement was fraught with difficulty as it was subject to the willingness of those studios to allow their stars to work for ABS-CBN. It also meant that ABS-CBN was paying top dollar for that talent (Paredes 2012). The solution that ABS-CBN came up with revolutionised the star and studio system in the Philippines (Sioson-San Juan 1999: 164). Freddie M. Garcia, then the ABS-CBN executive vice-president and general manager, decided that the best course of action was for the network to build up its own stable of talent working exclusively for ABS-CBN and to pay wages that ABS-CBN would control. To this end, the ABS-CBN Talent Development and Management Centre (now known as Star Magic) was set up in 1992, headed by director Johnny Manahan with the assistance of Lino Brocka before Brocka's untimely death. A process was set up whereby candidates would audition before a panel of judges (which included Manahan, and sometimes Garcia and Charo Santos-Concio, then president of ABS-CBN and award-winning actress). If selected, actors joined each year's Star Magic Circle Batch and were groomed to become stars for ABS-CBN, first on television and then on the big screen (Paredes 2012).

Operating on similar principles as those adopted by early Hollywood studios, Star Magic and its system of talent production proved to be hugely successful in several ways: firstly, it gave the studio access to reasonably priced home-grown talent. Secondly, the big stars of the screen found that they could no longer charge the high fees that they had previously, resulting in a more manageable talent fee for even the biggest stars. Thirdly, the abundance of affordable and home-grown talent coupled with existing recording infrastructure meant that ABS-CBN could make its own films rather than pay to redistribute the films made by the film studios. This led to the establishment of Star Cinema, the filmmaking arm of ABS-CBN which dominated contemporary film production into the 2010s. GMA (the main rival of ABS-CBN at the time) soon followed suit, and so in short order, television studios had taken control of the production and deployment of stars, once the sole domain of film studios. ABS-CBN launched popular love teams such as Claudine Baretto and Rico Yan in the late 1990s, Piolo Pascual and Judy Ann Santos in the early 2000s, and John Lloyd Cruz and Bea Alonzo, who were popular from the mid-2000s onwards (discussed in detail in the Conclusion). The 2010s would bring the popular teenage love team KathNiel, consisting of Kathryn Bernardo and Daniel Padilla.

Writing in 2019, Bolisay examines the love team through a cultural studies lens, applying Theodor W. Adorno and Max Horkheimer's work on the culture industry to explore a popular contemporary teenage love team and their online fandom. Bolisay does not offer a single comprehensive definition of the love team within his work; rather, he astutely presents the various definitions and analogies made by Filipino users on the internet trying to explain the concept to cultural outsiders, likening them to various Hollywood couples. In this manner, Bolisay also demonstrates through the online posts the continued colonial connection between Philippine cinema and Hollywood cinema, a theme that runs through many discussions of Philippine cinema.

In his abstract, Bolisay (2019) does offer this shorter definition: 'a pair of good-looking stars launched by a mainstream studio to appear in a succession of films, TV series, adverts, mall shows, etc.', which covers some of the more modern transmedia aspects of love team extra-filmic work. Notably, this definition as well as some of the online definitions in this article point to love teams as being a recurring partnership between two stars. In the course of my research, I encountered various articles in modern media that list one-off pairings as love teams and rank them in the same lists as recurring partnerships. Bolisay identifies several of the concepts that will be examined closely in this work on love teams, namely, their historical ubiquity within Philippine cinema; how love teams are constructed and commodified for a specific audience by studios; the slippage between the stars' performance and reality in the eyes of fans; and how love teams are grounded in heterosexuality and thus promote heteronormativity (2019: 42–46, 57).

Love teams and the couple

The 'love team' is the Philippine term for (at the minimum) a star couple and screen couple combined, but sometimes combines all three couples in one irresistible popular culture product. The love teams of the 1970s discussed in this book are an example of the combination of all three types of couple, and specifically the recurring non-sequential collaboration subtype of star couple. But even in the event of a lack of real-world romance, Philippine love teams are encouraged to give the impression of being a couple or at the very least to be coy about the possibility of becoming a couple at some point in the future (or having been one in the past). With the 1970s love teams that form the case studies in the following chapters, the studio deliberately worked to reinforce slippage between the real, the fictional and the professional couples, giving fictional characters the same names as their stars, and plots that closely resembled their real lives and fame. The love team is ubiquitous in Philippine cinema and a vital component of the film industry. Where the recurring screen couple in Hollywood has largely died out with the studio system and subsequent independence of stars, the Philippines has maintained the concept to the present since the inception of its domestic film industry.

The love team in the Philippines complicates the Western concept of the individual which Dyer wrote is a key factor in understanding the star (Dyer 2004, 1979). The Hollywood star celebrates the individual: 'the whole structure of celebrity is built on the construction of the individuated personality' (Turner, cited in Diaz 2015: 280). The achievements and success of the star are the celebration of the individual, the extraordinary talent of the ordinary person. The prevalence of star couples in Philippine cinema suggests a trend away from the individual and towards the couple – the cornerstone of the family unit. The goal of romance films is to join a suitable couple and move them towards a socially sanctioned happily ever after, which in the majority Catholic Philippines is matrimony. This celebration of the couple, whether in the romance genre, horror or comedy, suggests that couples that lead to marriage are the natural destination of personhood. The tendency of love teams to span all age groups also supports this theory: whether featuring children of eight years old or adults of sixty years old, love teams often define their careers and plots.[2] The popularity of love teams in the press and popular culture also suggests that the couple is a valuable commodity in the Philippines, possessing double the attraction and success of a single star.

The love team is particularly useful as a strategy with middling talent, where stars fare better packaged together than individually. But in the case of a particularly strong talent or superstar, oftentimes the love team works to showcase the individual's powerful charisma which carries the love team. In most cases, in fact, there is usually one partner in the love team that clearly outshines the other, in terms of either performance or star power, and usually that star is the one to have the lasting career post-love team or to have particularly successful work away from the partnership. This would suggest that the individual still is central to the understanding of the star. The tendency to combine individuals into couples in Philippine popular culture, however, suggests that even in the case of an extraordinarily talented individual, pairing elevates personhood and is a desired status, that is, that the identity of the 'self' is understood through membership of the family unit and one's place in it. This will be discussed in detail in the following chapters on the love teams and a subsequent discussion of the sociological importance of love, courtship, coupledom and marriage in 1970s Philippine society.

With love teams, instead of the self, two selves combine to form a new entity, which is seen in the naming conventions of the tandems, specifically the 'and' that joins the stars' names. The names are used in popular discourse, in print, radio, film and television so that the sight and sound of the particular combination becomes natural and permanent. Individual names are associated with certain qualities and ideas, and similarly, the combination of two names also becomes laden with meaning. The combining of two stars' names also combines aspects of their star personas into a joint star image. This modifies, enhances and suggests new qualities and ideas native to a particular combination. The combined name (the star couple) becomes its own brand, immediately recognisable and understood in specific ways coded by familiarity with the love team's professional work, the characters they play (screen couple) and their personal lives (possible celebrity couple).

In the naming conventions of the love team, nicknames perform an important function: they represent a means of intimacy, authenticity, validity and permanence. The use of a nickname is generally reserved for those nearest and dearest to a person and indicates a close relationship between the speaker and the subject (Cobb and Ewen 2015a: 283). The ability of fans to address their favourite couple by their nickname indicates an intimacy, but also a sense of authenticity in the relationship between the stars and the fan: the fan knows who the stars 'really' are, and calls them by their nickname, placing them in a privileged place of affection and genuine closeness. Thus, the stars of this research are affectionately known as 'Guy and Pip' and 'Vi and Bot' to fans and the entertainment industry. The authenticity that nicknames convey also works to mask the industrial and ideological construction of the couple; if fans think of them as their intimate friends, they are less likely to think of them as products.

The love team's name is featured prominently in the media, from their professional collaborations to their public appearances, endorsements, interviews and images. The recurrence of the couple's names across the media and popular discourse confers a validity and permanence to an otherwise unofficial pairing that might be purely in the early stages of dating, or even just working together. Since their names are married to each other, the relationship is publicly acknowledged and given tangibility. Marriage may not be forthcoming, but their names are inextricably linked in print, language and films. If they are an off-screen couple, their relationship confers authenticity to their screen adventures: the couple can be read as being always somewhat in character (Negra 2015: 308), or their characters as always somewhat reflective of the 'real' couple. The films act in this instance as fantasy fulfilment, where the beloved couple is able to fall in love and marry on-screen again and again even if they never do in real life.

The love team also serves to reinforce or brand a specific stage of a star's career. Love teams and the films they star in are reflective of their age group and appeal, or the age group they are targeting. Similarly, star couples and celebrity couples are a means of branding a star's image. Linda Ruth Williams (2015) explores this through the image of Jane Fonda and how her three off-screen relationships reflected different stages and points of change in her star image over the years. The same can be said of an industry of love teams, with different tandems coming to represent different stages and aspects of a star image. Contemporary love teams fall into roughly three stages: teenage stars in innocent romances; adult love teams; and veteran or iconic love teams, known for their long partnership and ability to convey nuanced narratives and ideas of romance. As a star ages and passes through the various stages of life, they may shift from a teenage love team to an adult one with a different star, or mature with their teenage love team, making the transition together to the next stages.

The audience plays a major role in the success of love teams, particularly fans. The entertainment industry relies on fans who are interested enough to purchase not just the films of their favourite stars, but a variety of other media texts such as magazines, records, concert tickets and other memorabilia. The industry relies on fan interest to decide which love teams to prioritise on covers and stories, corporations rely on fan interest to decide which stars to feature as endorsers, and studios rely on fans to formulate their plans for the studio and stars in the upcoming year. Sometimes fans are able to disrupt these plans, and even override the agency of the stars themselves. Fans fiercely protect their love team for a variety of reasons, among them the preservation or contestation of the romantic notions of 'true love' and 'happily ever after'. The commitment of fans to their love team often outlasts the existence of the actual partnership, with fans refusing to accept a parting as final, retaining hope even through other relationships and marriage. However, it is equally true that the industry is able to shape the audience to some extent through the films it produces and in its choices of which love teams to prioritise, how many films that tandem releases in a year, and the narratives of their films together.

Applying Nochimson's (2002) ranking of disruptive or Synergistic Couples would miss the point entirely in Philippine cinema with its proliferation of Functional and Iconic (by Nochimson's definition) love teams and slippage between different types of couple. It is not always about what the star couples achieve on film (and therefore if they are able to 'disrupt' dominant ideologies); it is sometimes simply about what the celebrity couples are doing this week on film. The off-screen life and relationship may be perceived as the real text while the films are screened interludes of drama, song and dance. Fans place more emphasis on the hoping, waiting, visiting and devotion to the off-screen than to the cinematic image, with the drama of the everyday superseding the screened drama. Where the celebrity couple's off-screen relationship takes precedence in the minds of the fans, it may be the case that love teams are not a kind of star, but rather a kind of celebrity that happens to star in films.

It is instructive to ask the question of what fans are actually consuming in the love team, and what they place their greatest emphasis on – the screen couple, the star couple or the celebrity couple? The origin of the star also complicates the perception of the star, especially with multiple routes to stardom sometimes originating from outside the film industry. Do fans view the couple as being film stars? Or do they see instead a beloved celebrity that happens to star in a film from time to time? Rojek's definition of celebrity is 'the attribution of glamorous or notorious status to an individual within the public sphere', a concept he further elaborates through the distinction between three different kinds of celebrity: those who 'achieved' celebrity through the merits of their talent, those who are 'attributed' celebrity by the media, and those who are 'ascribed' celebrity through blood relations (2001: 10–17). These different routes to stardom have an impact on how star images are perceived by fans, and perhaps on how they should be examined. Philippine love teams have taken different routes to film stardom in the past. Traditionally, the film star achieves celebrity through their talent of performing, or in some cases music, while for others celebrity is ascribed through family dynasties.

The primary medium of the love team also has a strong bearing on how their star images are perceived. The love teams of the 1970s were sold primarily through an association with music, whether through singing or dancing. Off-screen encounters with fans were also a primary site of meaning, as discussed above. Through a combination of gossip, behind-the-scenes access to their work at the studios, photos of public appearances, posters, themed editorials and photoshoots, comics features, and positioning the love team as icons of fashion, magazines also shaped the love team through the celebrity couple, rarely addressing the screen couple in their content. The most privileged medium for stars is the star vehicle film, or the love team film, built around the particular combination of the star couple and their strengths to appeal in specific ways to fans. Where each couple appeared in these media, how they were represented and to what extent they existed in each medium helped shape the love teams' primary site of meaning, different in the case of each couple.

Conclusion

This chapter has focused on the theory of couples and how it relates to love teams. Introducing the terms 'star couple', 'screen couple' and 'celebrity couple' to the vocabulary of couple analysis allows the different aspects of their personas and work to be discussed in a more specific and accurate manner. The love team also challenges and builds on various ideas of star studies, such as the centrality of the individual in Western culture and stardom, the authenticity of the star and couple, the relationship between the private and the public aspects of the star and how this is connected to the relationship between the reel and real. The Philippine love team builds on this in a specific national context, unique to its methods of star production and cultural context. The love teams of this research are specifically of the 1970s, and the next chapter situates them in their era, firstly in terms of their production by the studio and prevailing industrial conditions of the 1970s, and then in the socio-political climate of Martial Law in the Philippines.

Notes

1. Fernandez (2013: 53) lists 45,000 pesos instead of 40,000.
2. A popular love team in the Philippines of the 2010s was a child tandem consisting of an eight-year-old boy and a six-year-old girl, Zaijian Jaranilla and Xyriel Manabat, who first starred together in the 2009 ABS-CBN television series *May Bukas Pa*.

Chapter 2

Building the couple: industry, society and politics in 1970s Philippines

Introduction

The love teams of the 1970s were the culmination of about fifty years of domestic Philippine cinema and about three generations of prior love teams. The period between the height of the studios' power and the new media 1970s teenage stars was an eventful and tumultuous time, covering the newly independent Philippines' early steps and an increasingly liberated youth and media, soon to be arrested by the rise of a new authoritarian rule under President Ferdinand Marcos and the subsequent Martial Law. This chapter explores the state of the nation and the industry that produced the love teams of the 1970s, including the pre-existing but weakened studios of the 1950s, the film industry and the steps taken to regulate it before and during Martial Law, and the Marcoses, their public image and struggle with the youth of the era.

First, the chapter discusses the 1950s industry of stars and studios that laid the groundwork for the 1970s through the example of Sampaguita Pictures, the studio responsible for discovering Vilma Santos as a child star and the home studio of the love team of Aunor and Cruz. What were the prerequisites of stardom and what kinds of stars did the 1950s studios produce? How did studios go about the process of star-making and management? And what sorts of films did those stars and the internal policies of the studios create? I will then discuss the political celebrity couple of Ferdinand and Imelda Marcos and their skilful crafting of their images that extended to mythmaking and fictional retellings of their romance in popular films and other media. It also explores Marcos's difficult relationship with the Philippine youth of the 1970s, who formed the greatest challenge to his leadership in staging a series of street protests and embracing subversive new films such as *bomba* cinema, which led Marcos to control the media through his New Society initiative after imposing Martial Law in 1972. The relationship between the studio and the industrial policies introduced by Marcos, and the studio's relationship with the Marcos family itself will also be investigated. Finally, it will establish the industry that the 1970s love teams inherited, and briefly outline the path towards the Second Golden Age of Philippine Cinema and the celebrated auteur cinema of the 1970s, starring familiar faces in new roles.

Stars and studios of the 1950s

The 1950s were known as the Golden Age of Philippine Cinema, named for its remarkable output of 350 films per year by four main studios. Films released in the 1950s are considered to have combined high quality and audience appeal (Almajose and Ramos 2013: 1). The 1950s were also known for their crop of glamourous stars, uniquely positioned as being among the first stars of Philippine cinema, born of it and in combination with the Philippines' pre-existing popular art form, theatre. This section will explore the industry inherited by the teen stars of the 1970s: the studios and personalities that governed filmmaking, the stars that captured the imagination of the nation, and the general trends of filmmaking that formed the history and backdrop of 1970s love teams.

The film industry of the 1950s consisted of four large studios that produced the bulk of the output of the era. The two biggest rivals, Sampaguita and LVN, were particularly known for their quality and star-making prowess.[1] The large studios brought several benefits to the system: firstly, there was a sense of security and discipline about the process, with a retained in-house staff that worked on films from start to finish. Secondly, facilities, equipment and resources that were dedicated to the art of filmmaking were invested in and continuously researched. Thirdly, a sense of competition and friendly rivalry existed between studios, which kept quality and quantity high. All these factors ensured that the costs inherent in film production were kept in the control of a central body – the studio – which could plan out and budget the year's entertainment with a tight schedule and emphasis on quality.

The studios were large, family-run businesses, often with a matriarch or patriarch at the head with children, in-laws and extended family members occupying positions such as producer, costume and set design, supervision, choreography and whatever other jobs needed doing. As a result, studios developed a family-like atmosphere, with emphasis placed on obedience, loyalty and hard work:

> One of the best examples for this [good work ethic] is the family-like environment present in Sampaguita Pictures and LVN Pictures. The Filipino's high regard for family was basically extended to the workplace, making studio owners take care of their stars like they were their own children, and the star respecting and obeying the former like they were their own parents. (Almajose and Ramos 2013: 4)

Sampaguita was owned and run by the Perez family, while LVN was run by the de León family. Both families ran the operations with a focus on profit, propriety and vision, raising and training successive batches of employees for the film industry. Patriarchs and matriarchs of the studio commanded the loyalty of stars and enforced discipline, ensuring that stars behaved well and films were family friendly. The role of matriarchs in the studio stood out in particular, a position that required them to play equal parts mother, disciplinarian and business manager:

> Dolores Honrado Vera, or more popularly known as Mommy Vera, was given the task to be the administrator of Sampaguita Pictures; and just like any other mother, she treated the studio like it were her own home and everyone else were her own children. (Ibid.: 10)

Administration of the studio later passed to her son-in-law, Doc Perez, who is described as a paternal boss: 'Doc Perez handled the studio with a father's hand and a mother's heart. He treated his talents like they were his own children, He set the rules, and everyone else lovingly obeyed' (ibid.: 11). The result was a stable of stars and studio employees that were bound into the chains of hierarchy that the family dynamic of the studio encouraged, each knowing their rank in the system and respecting the order it represented. Clear lines of authority and responsibility were demarcated and enforced, with stars retaining a loyalty and affection to the studio in multiple interviews even years after the studio's collapse (Almajose and Ramos 2013).

The contract system by which stars were retained involved several provisos designed to protect star and studio, such as a maximum of four or five films a year per star to avoid overexposure, and a contract for the first two years of a star's career on a four- to five-film basis that would be replaced by full star remuneration in the event of attaining success (Mercado 1977: 11). Studios were on the constant lookout for new stars, either from among the family or social circles of the stars or the studio executives, or from among the ranks of the extras they employed (ibid.), or in the earliest days of Philippine cinema, from the theatre. The industry prized a particular kind of star that underwent a rigorous training process, had a strong sense of discipline, loyalty and work ethic, and was a larger-than-life figure that appealed to the audience through their potent star presence. In her book on Doña Narcissa de León of LVN, Monina A. Mercado refers to potential talent as requiring 'screen personality', explained as an 'undefinable something that causes the audience to rivet its attention on him when he is on screen' (ibid.: 10). One of the most iconic stars of the 1950s was Rogelio de la Rosa, the dashing leading man of the famous love team with Carmen Rosales who starred in a variety of films over the course of his career, which began in the late 1920s during silent cinema and thrived through to the 1960s when he left filmmaking to become a senator. He began his career playing the villain in countryside fairground productions of *sarsuwelas*, a singing drama popular in the Philippines and the recruiting ground for talent and stories adapted for film in early Philippine cinema (Almajose and Ramos 2013: 27). Stars like Gloria Romero entered film through the recommendation of an uncle who worked in the industry and introduced her to Doc Perez (ibid.: 24).

Once recruited, stars would undergo a rigorous training process, which included, among other things, table manners and etiquette, formal dinners with famous personalities, lessons on walking and standing with poise, elocution and attending formal events to learn other aspects of proper comportment (ibid.: 11). Sampaguita and LVN took great pride in the good conduct and appearance of their stars and would show them off during these formal events as well as at smaller studio events such as the birthday of the matriarch, which required all stars to be in attendance and on their best behaviour (Mercado 1977). Rogelio de la Rosa is described as the epitome of a gentleman of the era:

> faithful, dependable, reliable, trustworthy, and sincere; a true gentleman; and that is how he is even off camera. No scandal has ever stained his career and good name. He knows how to draw the line between his public and private life. He maintained a low profile. (Almajose and Ramos 2013: 29)

Good morals, values and public behaviour was demanded of stars, with the studio matriarchs monitoring star behaviour and correcting those stars deemed unruly. According to Almajose and Ramos, quoting an entertainment journalist of the era:

> Danny Dolor was straightforward in saying that the scandals of today were also present back then in the '50s. 'The big difference today is that they did not flaunt these scandals. Producers were very protective of their stars; unlike today, where in these scandals seem to be something that people are proud of. Now negative publicity could be used to make the stars popular.' (Ibid.: 83)

On-screen, the standards were just as high, with studio executives being careful to maintain their stars' good images. One resulting early idiosyncrasy of romance films in the Philippines was the suppression of kissing scenes. Almajose and Ramos note:

> In the 1950s, fans felt that kissing corrupted their idol's image. Manuel de León once shared that viewers would write to LVN studio complaining about such scenes, and so producers had to make sure that expressions of love onscreen were limited or done within marriage. (Ibid.: 54)

The anger of the fans also extended to concern for their favourite stars and dislike of the villains that challenged them, which is why 'box-office stars usually had storylines with happy endings, and why villains were looked at differently' (ibid.). Indeed, the designation of *bida* (hero) and *kontrabida* (villain) remain in casting and guiding the development of star images to the present.

This jealous protection of their stars' good character was an extension of how fans felt about stars of the era. The love teams of the 1950s were a very different type of film couple, and indeed a very different type of star. Studios looked for the tallest, fairest and most exotic people – the *mestizos* of the country's colonial past and Hollywood influence. The emphasis on fair skin is an abiding colonial legacy imprinted during the five centuries of colonial rule of the Spanish and Americans. This privileging of the *mestizo* (which means 'mixed blood') has a long history in the Philippines. Traditionally referring to a person with both Filipino and Spanish heritage, *mestizo* is now more loosely applied to any Filipino of mixed ethnic heritage and is socially constructed to include lighter skin tone and class in its usage. Historically, *mestizos* occupied a privileged socio-economic position somewhere between the ruled masses and the ruling Spaniards (Rafael 2000: 165). More recently, *mestizos* have come to symbolise modernity (Rafael 1995: 105). Philippine cinema is one of the primary sites of reproduction of *'mestizoness'*, evidenced by its proliferation of *mestizo* stars (ibid.: 118).

The earliest stars of Philippine cinema would not have looked out of place in Hollywood, with screen names such as Paraluman (which means 'muse' in Tagalog) and Tita Duran working to indigenise the more foreign-sounding names of Sigrid Sophia Agatha von Giese and Teresita Durango respectively, or – more often than not – transform them into a more familiar foreign sound: the Spanish names their colonial past had given them. The era's films were shot in black and white and lovingly framed luminous screen goddesses and towering screen gods that stood apart from the people they entertained. Remote and out of reach, these stars maintained a careful distance from their fans, as evidenced by the quote referring to de la Rosa above. Knowing when to be public and when to be private and maintaining a dignity in both spheres of their life factored in their success. This is also where the rigorous training by the studios on comportment, dressing and etiquette came into play: stars were figures of glamour and refinement and were expected to maintain that image at all times. Mercado writes that there was an unwritten law that required stars to 'speak, dress and conduct themselves like the glamourous figures that they were supposed to be, that the public expected them to be' (1977: 51–52). To this end, advances on salaries or special budgets were set aside by studio heads to ensure that their stars were always attired in the finest fashion of their day, both on-screen and off. Glamour was a key aspect of the era's stars, and the subject of an article titled 'The End of the Glamour Stars' (Fuentes 1970). Remarking on the shift from glamorous stars to the new ordinary stars characteristic of the 1970s, Eduardo C. Fuentes writes:

> They were a beautiful set. They had class and glamour and perhaps a little talent and a lot of earth-shaking box-office appeal. There was something exciting and mysterious about them and the colourful lives they led, almost reminiscent of a life-style exemplified by the jet-set. (Ibid.: 29)

Comparatively, the new generation of stars that would come were 'plain stars' (ibid.: 31):

> But an entirely new crop of stars are making an entrance in a boisterous way and no less sensational than the earlier

> generation . . . They have set a new trend, a new mood, a new style for the very young superstars who are expected to be both singers and dancers . . . The young stars are not in any way different from the crowd that adores them. They speak a common language and dress like anybody else. They're part of the crowd and they've got what any previous generation of stars didn't have – a sense of being real, a sense of identification and belonging to a much larger mass of movie-goers. (Ibid.: 30–31)

Aunor particularly is a powerful figure of identification, something which will be explored more fully in the following chapter in a section on her star image.

Another key difference in the stars of the 1950s and the stars of the 1970s was the means of their discovery. As discussed above, the stars of the 1950s were products of a carefully regulated studio system. Successive stars such as Aunor became famous through other avenues such as radio and television. Reflecting on the difference between a studio-bred star and one discovered through other means, 1950s matinee idol Leopoldo Salcedo said, 'Stars now are created by the media. We were reliable, punctual and responsible, even in our actuations in public. We were always aware that whatever we did or said reflected on the entire industry' (Mercado 1977: 52). Salcedo points out that new stars are created by the media, and not the strict gatekeepers of the studio system. He also suggests that the studio system was a better one because it inculcated a strong work ethic that reflected both on-screen and off, something that he finds missing in the successive stars. This will be discussed in greater detail in the following chapter on Aunor and her control of her work and star image, a unique relationship that contrasts with Salcedo's experience of agency under the studio system.

The influence of the studio heads was also key with regards to what films they chose to make and the values that they screened. Studios were known for emphasising films with moral lessons contained within and viewed themselves to a certain extent as moral gatekeepers for the audience, choosing to produce films that would reflect this. The daughter of Sampaguita owner Doc Perez, Marichu Vera-Perez Maceda, explained the 'morality clause' that ensured that films were driven by clearly distinguishable good and bad characters:

> 'My father and my family believe in black and white. White denotes good; black denotes bad; and always, good triumphs over evil,

white over black ... there is no room for any shade of grey because that will be confusing to the simple minds of film viewers.' (Quoted in Almajose and Ramos 2013: 8)

This simplification of characterisation meant that there were clear villains and heroes, and the audience was left in no doubt about who they were meant to cheer for and despise. It also takes a paternalistic and (perhaps more damaging) patronising approach to the studio's dealings with the audience, framing the studio as the gatekeeper of public morals and thought.

The Philippine film industry is considered to have been in a period of decline after the Golden Age of Cinema in the 1950s. These films fizzled out in the 1960s and gave way to local versions of popular foreign films such as the secret agent film, the Philippine western and martial arts films. The 1960s also marked the rise of the *bomba* or pornographic film, leading Lumbera to write of the period under the following subheading: 'Rampant commercialism and artistic decline (1960–1975)' (2011: 39). The 1960s also saw the beginning of the slow decline of the major studios in the face of increasingly expensive talent fees and labour, and competition from star-owned independent studios.

The tumultuous year of 1970 marked the first films of the two love teams at the centre of this research. The contrast between teenagers singing love songs in cinema and on the television and radio with the increasing violence towards youth on the streets and the rise of a middle-aged male authoritarian figure could not be any stronger. Nestor de Guzman, a fan of Aunor who has published a book on the star, commented on the early 1970s, saying there were only two reasons large crowds could be seen on the streets of Manila: student demonstrations against President Ferdinand Marcos, or Aunor's fans headed out to watch her latest film (see Figure 2.1) (Llanes 2008b). Lumbera describes the fans and what they were looking for: 'Young audiences made up of vociferous partisans for "Guy and Pip" or "Vi and Bebot" [sic] were in search of role models who could take the place of elders whom the youth revolution had taught them to distrust' (2011: 11).

There was little crossover between Aunor's fans and those protestors, a matter that will be discussed in detail in Chapter 4 on the Guy and Pip love team. During the era (and to the present), fluent English was a clear marker of the educated and upper class. The students of the universities in

This is what happens whenever Nora Aunor attends the opening day of one of her pictures, in this case, "Three For The Road," which paralyzed traffic along Quezon Boulevard and Yeba I recently. Will she also attend the opening of "Young At Heart"?

Figure 2.1 Fans attending the premiere of a Nora Aunor film in 1970 (*Graphic*, 13 May 1970, p. 29). Source: from the collection of Nestor de Guzman

the capital were more interested in consuming popular culture products in English, seeing foreign films as containing an element of quality that local Tagalog films did not provide (a subject discussed in greater detail in Chapter 4) (Lacaba 1970).

The love team of Santos and Mortiz worked with Tagalog Ilang-Ilang Productions (TIIP), one of the newer independent studios that emerged to challenge the Big Four, producing several secret agent films in the 1960s and releasing its last film in 1991. TIIP gained the reputation of attracting stars by paying higher talent fees than those offered by the big studios (del Mundo Jr 1999: 40). Owned by lawyer Espiridion Laxa, who would go on to become influential in the film industry, TIIP was also responsible for the Darna film trilogy, the adaptation of a popular Philippine comic book heroine that starred Vilma Santos. The studios of the Golden Age of Philippine Cinema in the 1950s remained in power though increasingly weakened through the birth of the independent star-owned studios of the 1960s and the emergence of television as a new star-making force in the 1970s. The techniques and ethos of the studio's film and star-making process would continue in the new stars of the 1970s. The two love teams represented a new kind of film couple: teenage stars who worked in films geared towards a teenage audience, the first time a distinct market and genre had arisen for this demographic in the Philippines. The 1970s heralded new times in the Philippines, not least in terms of its politics, marking the decade in which Martial Law replaced democracy in 1972.

Couples were already prevalent in the late 1960s, with love teams such as Fernando Poe Jr and his wife Susan Roces, and Amalia Fuentes and her husband Romeo Vasquez featuring as the most popular love teams immediately prior to the teenage love teams of the 1970s. These stars were joined by another celebrity couple: the presidential couple of Ferdinand and Imelda Marcos, whose marriage and family were regularly featured in the media during the era. As a prominent media couple, the Marcoses also shaped public discourse on marriage and coupledom in specific ways and were able to leverage romance and domesticity to suit their purposes. The following section considers how Ferdinand and Imelda Marcos appeared in film through their 1965 biopic, the influence exerted on their films, and how the film industry participated in circulating the Marcoses' image. It also explores the strategies of relatability and authenticity that the Marcoses used in their public romance and coupledom, including prevailing methods of promotion and generic conventions of love teams and romance in terms of their fictional selves in films (the screen couple) and their public appearances as celebrities (the celebrity couple).

The Marcoses' joint image in film and other media

Another very different couple in the Philippines during the 1970s was the presidential couple of Ferdinand and Imelda Marcos. The pair possessed public personas that hinged on spectacle and destiny, a strategy that was in places almost identical to that of the film stars of the day. The similarities ran to their origin stories, their performance styles and musical talent, a brush with film stardom and the maintenance of larger-than-life, god-like images supported by the very mythology of Philippine primordial stories. The origins of the couple have been told in authorised biographies in terms of destiny and mythology. The word 'destiny' was even used in the film made to support Marcos's election bid in 1965, *Iginuhit ng Tadhana* (Destined by Fate). Marcos made every attempt to connect his life and ascendance to the presidency as a matter of destiny, fated from birth with every event in his life leading naturally to the moment of his becoming president (Rafael 2000). Vicente L. Rafael's chapter on the

Marcos couple is particularly interesting as he analyses their images in a manner similar to a star studies approach. Where Marcos was inevitable, Imelda was a triumph of luck against the odds, rising from relative poverty to becoming the wife of the president (ibid.: 128). In fact, the author of one of her biographies, Carmen Navarro-Pedrosa, explicitly calls Imelda's life a Cinderella story, complete with fairy godmother and magic wand that led her to Ferdinand Marcos (ibid.).

As a political couple, the pair were a potent combination. Marcos was a brilliant lawyer and orator, known for his deep booming voice and virility. Imelda possessed a good singing voice, which she used to entertain crowds whether in the city or the barrio, often to warm up the crowd before Marcos spoke (ibid.: 124). The highlight of the event would be a duet between Ferdinand and Imelda, which Rafael describes as making 'their private lives into public spectacle, staging a stylised version of their intimacy' (ibid.: 124). This could just as easily be a description of the Guy and Pip tandem, with their real romance a spectacle played out on stage across a variety of locations and plots. In using the power of music to hold the attention and entertain a crowd, 'Ferdie and Meldy' were no different than Guy and Pip in their strategy for attaining popularity. Rafael quotes a particularly descriptive paragraph on Imelda's performance of a song on stage:

> She bends and barely sways, beating time glancing at the guitar and then lifts her face to point with her chin at the night bright with neon lights and a moon – the old charisma, with its look of suffering, potent tonight as never before, the brilliance of beauty commingling with the brilliance of pain, the haunted, agonized, tragic look encircling the plaza and holding her audience in thrall. (Polotan 1969, quoted in Rafael 2000: 129–130)

Power, Rafael writes, came to Imelda in 'her ability to turn herself into an image recalling a sense of shared "suffering" among those who watch her', a 'fantasy of loss' that she plays out in song on the stage (2000: 130). The similarities in the passage above to the descriptions of Aunor's star persona and sufferance are startling; where Aunor performed the suffering of the masses (to be discussed in Chapter 3), Imelda appeared able to simulate such a suffering and connection in song, earning her the honour of being Marcos's 'secret weapon'.

Rafael begins his section on the Marcos couple by referring to a painting the pair had commissioned that hung in the presidential residence, Malacañang Palace, depicting Ferdinand and Imelda as *Malakas* and *Maganda*. This refers to the Filipino primordial myths of the first man and woman, respectively Strong (*Malakas*) and Beautiful (*Maganda*) (ibid.: 122). The portraits depicted the presidential couple as embodying these traits, with Marcos emerging shirtless and muscled from a patch of bamboo while Imelda also emerges clad in a diaphanous flowing cloth with long, voluminous, shiny, black hair flowing around her body. Where Marcos's painting is sunny and bright, Imelda's has a darker background with a rainbow behind her. Marcos's painting features sturdy bamboo dominating the frame as well as the mythical bird that split the bamboo, allowing the couple to emerge. In Imelda's, there are flowers and the single split bamboo of her birth. Virility, strength and vitality characterise Marcos's while beauty, daintiness and a dark, mysterious background contrasted by the pure white robe define Imelda's painting.

The choice of myth by Marcos is no coincidence – *Malakas* and *Maganda* are the Filipino Adam and Eve. In this painting and in their commission of a rewriting of the tale to feature themselves, Marcos and Imelda cast themselves as the parents and origin of the Filipino people, embodying gender ideals of strength and beauty (ibid.). Rafael explains:

> To the extent that they were able to mythologize the progress of history, the First Couple could posit themselves not simply as an instance, albeit a privileged one, in the circulation of political and economic power; they could also conceive of themselves at the origin of circulation itself in the country (ibid.).

This appropriation of the myth of the Filipino progenitors was extended into an ideology of family and the hierarchy of obedience and power through which the pair ruled the Philippines, a concept explored further in Chapter 6.

Their meeting has been immortalised and rewritten in many biographies, interviews and articles over the years and characterised as a whirlwind romance. As the official story goes, Marcos saw an image of Imelda in the newspaper, met her, spirited her away to Baguio (a popular mountain resort city) and married her, all within a matter of eleven days. The story is made even more appealing by the near brush of Imelda with stardom: just a matter of days before meeting Marcos, she had auditioned at Sampaguita and attracted the attention of the studio, only to be thwarted by their courtship and her subsequent marriage to Marcos (David 2008:

230). Their meeting was also depicted in *Iginuhit ng Tadhana*, an analysis of which reveals many similarities to that of the conventional romance films of the era. Marcos recognised the power of the popular cinema and used it to his advantage several times over his career. Sampaguita played a vital role in showcasing Marcos's image in film through a connection to the Perez family through Doc Perez's son-in-law, and husband of Marichu Vera-Perez, Senator Ernie Maceda, who along with Doc Perez recruited noted director (and love team collaborator) Emmanuel H. Borlaza to write the screenplay in consultation with Marcos (Babao-Guballa 2011). In *Iginuhit ng Tadhana*, no fewer than three directors were employed in order to best depict the three different acts of the film: the first, a courtroom drama in which a young Marcos ably defends himself against a charge of murder; the second, a wartime drama which outlines his exploits against the Japanese Occupation (an account that has been challenged and found to be without historical basis); and the third, his romance with Imelda. The romance was directed by Mar S. Torres, an able and frequent director for successful Sampaguita romance films, who would go on to direct several of the love team films of this research in the 1970s (*Star For All Seasons* 2015). Several elements of the traditional romance film found their way into *Iginuhit ng Tadhana*, including the meet cute, the humorous but earnest pursuit, and the montage of the couple in love against a backdrop of nature and the garden (discussed below).

In *Passionate Revolutions: The Media and the Rise and Fall of the Marcos Regime* (2017), Talitha Espiritu details several elements of the film. Espiritu writes that the arrival of Imelda (played by Gloria Romero) marks a clear change in the narrative, which up to that point was focused entirely on the person of Ferdinand Marcos (played by Luis Gonzales) and building his mythical and charismatic persona. Imelda's arrival disrupts the narrative, immediately drawing the gaze of Marcos, who is shown staring openly at her, and leading the audience to fix their gaze on her person. She is shot in a series of medium shots which draw the gaze to her beautiful face and loveliness, a key element of Imelda's charm to the Filipino people. Espiritu writes that Imelda's introduction combines two disparate elements of her image: the aristocratic woman of the Marcos official biographies, as well as the victim of the *Untold Story*, an unauthorised biography that positioned Imelda as an impoverished woman of noble descent who was relegated to the garage of her home by the children of her father's first wife, and thence to the countryside, where she remained in limbo until brought to the city to be discovered and shaped by Marcos through her connection as first cousin to the respectable Senator Daniel Romualdez (ibid.: 70).

Espiritu's work discusses the Marcos romance as a melodramatic text and locates much of the source of melodrama in Imelda and her performance as wife and star accompanying Marcos on public appearances in the poorer parts of the Philippines, where the audience was susceptible and well trained in the art of reading the melodramatic text through their cultural consumption of native songs, *sarsuwelas* and films. The Marcos couple relied on these melodramatic cues to code their coupledom in an instantly recognisable and relatable manner. This in part explains the continued popularity of the Marcos couple among the lower class of the Filipino people, a class of people they appealed to most and conversely least resembled. The film plays on Imelda's brief and surface membership of the very class they are targeting by clearly marking her person as being out of place in the opulence of Congress, wearing a plaid blouse and mismatched slippers as she eats dried watermelon seeds (a working-class food) in a large, white canteen while simultaneously clearly demonstrating her noble birth through her cousin, a senator she is waiting to meet (ibid.: 70–71). This scene positions Imelda as spectacle, with Marcos's saviour gaze soon to transform her from shabby to feminine perfection and civility (*Maganda*). Ferdinand is thus introduced in the film as a patriarchal transformative figure who will uplift the nation, as he uplifted the noble suffering Imelda (ibid.: 70–72).

The introduction of Imelda in *Iginuhit ng Tadhana* comes late, in the last hour of a film with a running time of 2 hours 17 minutes. In the scene where she is introduced, Marcos is already very much a presence marked by his absence – his deep commanding voice is heard booming in authoritative English over the speaker system in the cafeteria, condemning the spending of the government of the day. Imelda, sitting with a female chaperone, discusses the owner of the voice long before he appears on-screen, with her companion remarking that it is a pity that the speech has ended as his voice is attractive to listen to. The camera cuts from medium shots of the women to a close-up of the loudspeaker, announcing the importance of the voice and framing it in relation to Imelda before Marcos arrives. When Marcos finally enters, he is arrested in the act of taking his seat by the sight of Imelda across the room. He begs her cousin, Senator Romualdez, to introduce him to her, demonstrating the force of will he becomes famous for, and is ushered to her table where the camera and his and her gaze draw attention to her mismatched shoes framed in a close-up.

This scene functions as their meet cute and conforms to all the conventions of the romance genre, with shy glances, quirky music to highlight the comedy of her shoes, and her discomfort in trying to conceal them, all meant to win the audience's empathy for this sweet and unfortunate girl with the mismatched shoes. The pair are awkward and communicate more in quick glances and hasty speech, with the moment over quickly after Marcos's intense gaze registers his interest and signals Imelda's destiny to the camera and audience. As in real life, the courtship proceeds at a whirlwind pace, with Marcos informing his mother immediately after that he has met the woman he intends to marry. There are only six scenes between their meeting and their marriage, divided into his pursuit of her, signified by his earnest delivery of many bouquets of flowers to her workplace, several phone calls made to her at work and at home, which she awkwardly fends off by either claiming to be busy (in English at work) or a maid (in Tagalog at home), and his civil marriage to her in Baguio. A prerequisite church scene in Baguio sees the pair kneeling in prayer after he waits for her to arrive at the empty church. Whether through propriety or genuine anger, she does not engage with him beyond a quick, haughty glance, returning thereafter to praying. Another typical romcom moment comes for the pair in Baguio when he jumps out from behind a pillar to surprise her, causing her to drop her drink and giggle with her female companion.

By accident or design, Imelda appears to be a reluctant party at all junctures, looking awkward, outrightly uncomfortable and forced, especially in the scene where Marcos compels her to sign marriage papers. Several times, Imelda gets up to leave, and each time Marcos takes her by the arm and pulls her to sit down again, pushing the papers into her hands. His friend tell her that Marcos is unable to eat or sleep without her, which Marcos solemnly tells her is true, quietly declaring in English, 'Imelda I want you to be the mother of my children. Please, Imelda.' Perhaps the narrative is attempting to protect her reputation by making her fight for her honour, but the result is a deeply uncomfortable woman who is begged by Marcos several times, has the papers and pen pushed into her hands, and desperately tries to retrieve the papers after she signs them, only to be thwarted by Marcos. Despite this, 'Dahil Sa'yo' (Because of You), a popular Filipino romance song closely associated with the couple, plays in the background, an audio cue of their many later public appearances when

Imelda would serenade him and the crowd with the song. The wedding of the couple is shown a mere 20 minutes after the introduction of Imelda and is filmed first from behind and then in a series of medium shots while a woman sings 'Ave Maria' off-screen, with no other diegetic sounds audible. If Imelda has appeared uncomfortable before this, she is shown to be liberated, joyful and smiling in the montage of the honeymoon that follows, with the pair walking hand in hand through various locations, including public gardens. The church and the public gardens are key settings in love team films that signify specific things (divine blessing and freedom), discussed in greater detail in Chapter 5. The film continues to show their early marriage, three children and a heart attack that Marcos suffers before running for political office, with Imelda now the picture of grace and elegance, a loving wife and mother who dotes on her family.

The film was released at a crucial time, immediately before Marcos ran for his first presidential election. Imelda was said to have taken a close interest in the casting of the film, particularly in the casting of a screen Marcos, who was required to have the charisma, stature and deep voice that he was famed for. The casting of Luis Gonzales and Gloria Romero was a skilful use of an already established and popular love team that began working together in the mid-1950s and eventually made around thirty films together. Gloria Romero was known for her regal bearing, a poised woman of grace and beauty, tall and fair due to her American mother. Romero also possessed a reputation as a strong dramatic actress. Luis Gonzales was a leading man of versatile talents, appearing in action, comedy, drama, musical and romance films in the 1950s and 1960s (GMA News 2012). Gonzales was a strong choice as a leading man, and his deep voice won him the role when auditioning to match Marcos's famous baritone (San Diego Jr 2012). Given the casting of popular stars and strong directors, the film would undoubtedly help Marcos during the election. Ironically in the end, it was his opposition, sitting President Diosdado Macapagal, who handed him the sympathy of the public when the film was suspended by the Board of Censors for Motion Pictures (BCMP) on a technicality (Yambot 1965). Public sentiment favoured Marcos, perhaps allowing him to win the election, a fact that he himself acknowledged, reportedly saying, 'You movie people are very close to my heart, because if it were not for your film maybe I would not be president' (Babao-Guballa 2011).

The Marcos couple are a good example of a screen couple that relegates the star couple playing them to a smaller detail than the standard star couple usually are in films where the entire plot must hinge on their believable chemistry or combined star power. In this instance, the screen couple are a fictional representation of a real and charismatic celebrity couple, a couple that would go on to rule the Philippines together legitimately and then under the famed 'conjugal dictatorship' for about twenty years. In this instance, casting the screen couple remained vital in terms of ensuring that a handsome and reputable pair would play the presidential couple so that the characters were given the appropriate on-screen presence, but the real people that the characters were based on far outweighed anything else that the star couple could bring to the table. In such a scenario, it is reasonable to assume that the main draw to watching the film is the celebrity couple that is to be fictionalised (or perhaps more accurately 'mythologised') in the film. However, the appeal of the star couple cannot be completely dismissed, as a mismatch in terms of casting would reveal the film to be of inferior quality and potentially distract the audience. The casting of a veteran love team draws in a wider audience and adds value to the film's prestige: not only are we watching the story of Ferdinand Marcos, we are also watching a film of the highest quality with strong and favoured performers. It would also be prudent to avoid casting a love team that has too much sensational value as there would be a risk of the screen couple (especially if the star couple were also a celebrity couple) being upstaged. A balance was struck with Gloria Romero and Luis Gonzales – a good-looking veteran love team that performed well at the box-office without a hint of scandal, known for a long-term platonic professional working relationship that could be relied upon to get the job done well without imposing themselves onto the story.

That Marcos chose to make a film that skilfully used melodrama to promote his image is no accident. Espiritu's work examines the couple as drawing on melodramatic codes and conventions to make the nation into a family that they led via a conjugal dictatorship, thus securing their legitimacy as its rulers (2017: 4–5, 67). The appellation 'conjugal dictatorship' was coined by a close aide, Primitivo Mijares, who grew disillusioned about the couple and subsequently wrote *The Conjugal Dictatorship of Ferdinand and Imelda Marcos* (1976). The heart of the melodrama is the female victim of circumstances, and Imelda played this role ably, serving as a spectacle that the crowd could gaze at while Marcos spoke (Espiritu 2017: 74). To appeal to the audience, Imelda chose as her uniform the national dress of the Philippines, the *terno*, with its distinctive butterfly sleeves, which along with her charming persona and strong resolve earned her the title 'Iron Butterfly of the Philippines'. Espiritu writes that Imelda's success lay in her ability 'to create a homology between her own melodramatic persona as the victim-heroine of the Marcos romance and the collective imaginary of the folk as victims of history' (ibid.: 75). The Marcoses' skilful use of the beloved star couple of Gloria Romero and Luis Gonzales to depict their romance at a crucial moment in the run-up to the elections allowed them to leverage the melodrama inherent in their images and disseminate it on a nation-wide scale, widely seen to be a key factor in winning Marcos the presidency. Marcos thus formed and remade Imelda (and through her person, the people of the Philippines) into the image of his choosing. Before Marcos, she was artless and wretched, but beautiful. Under his power, he made her glamorous and assertive, a seductive, melodramatic spectacle and his vision for the Philippines.

While Marcos had a relatively easy time disseminating his image via the media in the 1960s, the 1970s would bring him challenges, specifically in terms of his relationship with the urban university students and labourers. Accordingly, Marcos took several steps to regulate the media, and specifically the film industry, during the stormy period. The internal studio policies of the era are of interest in determining how the industry interpreted and abided by the regulations Marcos imposed. Additionally, the state's general attitude towards the youth during an era that increasingly made films that specifically catered towards teenagers as a new demographic reveals the fraught relationship between the youth and government of the era.

Ferdinand Marcos and the Youth of the Nation

The Romero–Gonzales love team was called upon once again to reprise their roles in a sequel for Marcos's 1969 re-election campaign, *Pinagbuklod ng Langit* (Heaven's Fate) (dir. Eddie Garcia 1969). The year 1969 was an unexpectedly difficult one for Ferdinand Marcos with the Philippines in debt and facing inflation due to heavy spending for his re-election campaign (Celoza 1997: 26–27). During the year, Marcos faced increasing pressure and criticism from the youth as well as farmers and labourers struggling in the difficult economy. The youth would turn out to be Marcos's biggest problem, but a very specific youth at that: an urban, middle-class, university-educated youth brought together in two major universities in the capital, the University of the Philippines Diliman and Ateneo de Manila.

The First Quarter Storm refers to the series of 'demonstrations, rallies and strikes spearheaded by the student movement' during the opening months of 1970 (Brillantes 1987: 47–48). Marcos perceived the ranks of students as having been infiltrated by radical leftists to bring about a revolution, and so the response was swift and brutal, resulting in the injury and death of several students over the course of the year (ibid.: 48). The catalyst for the Storm was a demonstration by about 20,000 students, workers and farmers during Marcos's State of the Nation address (titled 'National Discipline: The Key to Our Future'), which saw stones, bottles and other debris hurled first at Marcos and then at the police on 26 January (Celoza 1997: 26–27). Subsequent rallies sparked headlines such as 'Rampaging Youth Stormed the U.S. Embassy after a Mass Rally' in *The New York Times* (ibid.: 27). The net result was a hardening of the government and police against the youth, who were branded as radicalised Communist sympathisers and denounced by Marcos.

Also in 1970, Marcos faced an embarrassing national scandal when his former mistress, American actress Dovie Beams, released an audiotape of his distinctive voice singing to her in bed, a blow to his carefully crafted image of the presidential family leading the Philippines in domestic accord to a better future (Espiritu 2017). For a time, Dovie Beams shared the headlines with Nora Aunor on the front pages of *Taliba* on 12 November 1970 and 15 November 1970 as the scandal unfolded in the national press.

Sex was a matter of national contention at the time between Marcos's scandal, the thriving *bomba* cinema and the subsequent crackdown on it that he led, partly in retaliation for his embarrassment during the scandal. *Bomba* films, or the pornographic film, mainly consisted of 'melodrama heavily laced with sex' (Lumbera 2011: 12). According to Espiritu, *bomba* cinema also began attracting youth and members of the educated urban middle class at a time when *bomba* films were a breeding ground for subversion and merely watching them provided the thrill of breaking the law (2017: 104).

The groundwork for Martial Law was laid by 1970 through the administration's response to the First Quarter Storm and its subsequent events, including the Plaza Miranda bombing in 1972, officially named as the catalyst for the imposition of emergency rule. Having served two full terms, Marcos was constitutionally prohibited from extending his presidency. Proclamation 1081 made on 23 September 1972 effectively declared Martial Law and would keep him in power for a further fourteen years. One of Marcos's vital means of maintaining his power was the media, which was controlled by the introduction of several new policies geared at censorship and the promotion of a New Society. In regulating the film industry, he took two main measures: firstly, a requirement that a complete script be submitted to the BCMP before commencing production; and secondly, the issuance, six days after the declaration of Martial Law, of Letter of Instruction No. 13, s. 1972, which listed seven guidelines for the BCMP to ban certain films. These guidelines were designed to 'safeguard the morality of our society, particularly the youth, against the negative influence of certain motion pictures' (Official Gazette 1972). The intended effect of this policy was to block unwanted content from the public, but also to guide studios in their production of films, thus regulating future content and promoting the desired values of Marcos's New Society. The seven guidelines covered among other things the *bomba* industry; the unruly students and intellectuals Marcos sought to contain by blocking the screening of potentially subversive films; and crime, specifically prohibiting crime from being portrayed in a 'cool' manner.

In their book covering the 'Golden Period in Philippine Cinema' (which they define as the 1950s), Almajose and Ramos (2013) list seven taboos that the Big Four avoided in their films, a list that bears a remarkable similarity to the seven guidelines Marcos issued in 1972. In fact, it departs in two main instances: the introduction of the prohibition of films that contain 'Disrespect for the parents and elderly' and 'Portrayals of sexual liberation or the glorifying of unfaithful spouses and broken homes', while combining other guidelines thematically in their list (ibid.: 9). The two taboos introduced arguably fall under article (7) of Letter of Instruction No. 13, s. 1972:

> Films contrary to law, public order, morals, good customs, established policies, lawful orders, decrees or edicts; and any or all films which in the judgment of the Board are similarly objectionable and contrary to the letter and spirit of Proclamation No. 1081. (Official Gazette 1972)

It is uncertain how the authors derived this list, and perhaps it is based on Letter of Instruction No. 13, which would mean that it was created retrospectively after both the 1950s and Martial Law for the purpose of the publication. However, it is also true that Sampaguita films were moral tales, as confirmed by Doc Perez's daughter, Marichu Vera-Perez Maceda (and MOWELFUND president at the time of the book's publication[2]) in an interview with Almajose and Ramos, and reinforced by the foreword she wrote for their book:

> Philippine Cinema in the 1950s served as a Teaching Instrument then. The movies during that era was [sic] a clear reflection of the values prevalent in that society. Values such as honesty, hardwork [sic] and decency were generally the themes presented in the films. The Producers then always made it a point to include in their projects basically 2 objectives: encourage use of our National Language, Pilipino as a medium of communication and inculcate in the minds of the audience that in whatever endeavour, 'Good triumphs over Evil.' (Almajose and Ramos 2013: iii)

Thus, Sampaguita and the major studios as a whole were already producing films that taught and reinforced authoritarian values and were compatible with the New Society that Marcos sought to create before he even rose to power in 1965. The films of the popular studio required little regulation and made them an ideal site for teaching values that encouraged obedience and submission, circulated by an industry built on the principles of hierarchies of power, and made palatable through the ideology of the studio 'family' with patriarchs and matriarchs at its head.

Conclusion

The stars and studios of the 1970s had shifted conclusively since the 1950s, with stars of the 1970s being made by television rather than the monopoly of the Big Four. Ferdinand and Imelda Marcos married in 1955 and set about crafting a couple image that appealed in specific ways to the nation, playing on melodramatic codes and conventions to appeal to a national audience that understood the melodrama intrinsically, a mode of story-telling that is ultimately very similar to those of 1970s teenage jukebox musical stars. As the 1970s loomed, Marcos came into direct conflict with the youth of the nation, with his increasingly authoritarian ways becoming a source of strife between them. This is the industry and society that the love teams of the 1970s inherited and would come to shape and be shaped by in turn.

The next chapter explores the individual star images of the new love teams of the 1970s, considering four of the new teenage star images (the stars of the love teams of this research), and how they differed from he stars of the previous era. It considers how they were they discovered and developed, and the kinds of new images of masculinity, femininity and youth that they represented on-screen and off. As young adults, they were also in the position of negotiating questions of personal and professional freedom within the industry with different results.

Notes

1. The remaining two being Lebran and Premiere Productions.
2. The Movie Workers Welfare Foundation, Inc. (MOWELFUND) is a non-stock, non-profit social welfare, educational and industry development foundation organised and established in 1974 to serve marginalised workers in the Philippine motion picture industry.

Chapter 3

Producing the couple: individual star images

Introduction

The four stars of the two couples of this research are representative of the pathways to and prerequisites of Philippine cinema stardom during the late 1960s and early 1970s. All four were teens with an association to music that found early success in the genre of the teenage jukebox musical. Their ascent to fame covers various modes of celebrity, defined by Rojek as 'the attribution of glamorous or notorious status to an individual within the public sphere', including Rojek's 'ascribed' celebrity (which is derived from bloodline) and 'achieved' celebrity (which is attained by personal achievement) (2001: 10–17). Each star's success pivots on different themes raised by Dyer in his formative works *Stars* (1998) and *Heavenly Bodies* (2013), including, amongst others, concepts such as the binary oppositions of the ordinary/extraordinary and the private/public, and narratives such as the dream (a democratic narrative of achieving personal success through the values of working hard first explored in the Hollywood-specific concept of the American Dream). Ideological questions of class, gender and ethnicity in particular distinguish the success and images of the four stars and their negotiations of these identities in 1970s Philippine society.

This chapter will explore the individual star images of Nora Aunor, Vilma Santos, Tirso Cruz III and Edgar Mortiz. It discusses their paths to fame, their individual negotiations of class, gender and ethnicity, and their unique appeal to their contemporary society. It will also consider their relationship with the studio and their agency in their stardom, questioning the extent of their control and power in their early careers. It explores the technologies of their early fame, which vary from one star to another – achieving success on the silver screen, radio or television, from the ground up (approachable and relatable), or from the heavens (separate, distant and out of reach), echoing Dyer's titular *Heavenly Bodies* and Edgar Morin's mythical 'sacred monsters' (1972 [1957]). In particular, the chapter will contextualise their star images in Philippine cinema and society, considering how their star images fit within the larger narrative of stardom in the Philippines, and what their images both joint and individual say about their place in 1970s Philippine culture as a whole.

Nora Aunor

I will first discuss Nora Aunor's image and her revolution of the entertainment industry in the late 1960s through her unlikely stardom and vast following. Discussion of Philippine cinema (academic or otherwise) has been dominated over the years by the petite figure of the Superstar of Philippine cinema. The unique and unrivalled stardom of Nora Aunor includes, among other things, her representativeness of Filipinos, her embodiment of the suffering woman of Philippine literature and religion, her dramatic voice of the oppressed, and her large and devoted fan following. The film industry in the 1970s privileged several factors in filmmaking and star-making alike. The first is *mestizaje*, or mixed blood, a preference for lighter skin and Eurasian features in the stars chosen for the cinema. This tends to be a visual marker of class in the Philippines, with darker-skinned individuals perceived as being from the lower class, a class previously excluded from leading roles in cinema but regularly used to portray domestic helpers (Realuyo 2014). In this context, Nora Aunor was able to leverage a *Sinderella* (Cinderella) narrative to rise from the lower class, win a televised singing contest and win the support of the very class she emanated from, giving them a voice and pride in the petite star who represented them.

For studios, Aunor represented direct access to the *masa* (masses) she came from, a rich market that consisted of a large segment of the Philippine population. Her stardom was the product of television, a democratic medium more accessible to the *masa* and in a format that was irresistible to her audience: a singing competition that combined the love of music Filipinos have with the global youth revolution sweeping the music and film industry. Worldwide, a crop of younger and musical stars was taking over from their predecessors, who had relied on maturity and sophistication in their star image. Nora Aunor and Vilma Santos were the two new female stars with a rivalry that followed in the footsteps of Susan Roces and Amalia Fuentes, two refined *mestiza* stars a decade senior that they had idolised. While Roces and Fuentes had dominated the headlines in the early 1960s, by the time Aunor and Santos had arrived as teenagers on the screen, they had started families with their spouses, both of whom were also popular stars (Fernando Poe Jr and Romeo Vasquez respectively).

Sinderella: extraordinary because of her ordinariness

Aunor's narrative is one of triumph against the odds. The aura of Cinderella's rags-to-riches story is evident from the very start, and even told in fairy-tale style:

> Once upon a time there was a little girl who seemed to have been born under a very unlucky star. She was born small and weak, a sickly baby. Again and again, she would shake with convulsions and fix her eyes in a dying stare. One night, soon after she was born, she fell so ill, burning with fevers and shaking with chills, that her mother rushed her to church and had her baptised in a hurry, late at night ... What she suffered from was the cruel sickness called poverty, a disease endemic in her country. (de Manila 1970: 6)

Key elements of Aunor's persona are foregrounded: poverty, triumph against odds, and the quasi-religious image Aunor would come to have for her fans. National Artist and journalist Nick Joaquin (Quijano de Manila is his pen name) writes that Aunor was born 'under a very unlucky star', and follows it up with consultations of herb healers, witch doctors and magic, all of which could not heal her because 'a bad wind' had got into her (1977: 1–2). These words connect Aunor to the pre-colonial Filipino customs of the poverty-stricken *masa*, but also the fairy-tale style that his writing emulates. Ultimately, Joaquin offers an earthly explanation for her sickliness – poverty. It is not magic or some otherworldly power that ails Aunor, but her own ordinariness, which will one day save her. A commonly held notion of stardom that Aunor subverts is that of being particularly lucky, or special (Dyer 1979). In fact, she was among the unluckiest, and among the commonest. The romance of her persona is derived from her ascent to superstardom and extraordinary heights. This is explored below, in the words of fans interviewed for a newspaper article: 'Nora is poor, we are poor ... we are alike. She is brown, and so are we. How could we be enticed by others if Nora is like one of us?' ('The Appeal of Nora' 1972).

Her ordinariness is also emphasised in these articles: Aunor was not a star that fell from the heavens, but rather one that emanated from among the poorest, darkest and most ordinary Filipinos. Her humble start as a barefoot water vendor along the Iriga railway tracks located her firmly within the poor *masa* of the Philippines, struggling to get by and unable to buy rice on credit from the *sari-sari* stores (small grocery stalls). This depiction of Aunor as a small, frail little girl is one that followed her into her teens and characterised her early stardom. Aside from being petite, Aunor was also dark-skinned, or *kayumanggi*. Early in life, her classmates and other villagers would taunt her with the phrase 'Nora *Negra*!' (Black Nora). Ordinariness made Nora Aunor a powerful figure of identification among the largest segment of the population – the poverty-stricken common Filipino. Aunor herself recognises this in a CNN profile: 'I grew up in poverty, maybe they see themselves in me' (Jaucian 2016). Her physical attributes spoke to a long-suppressed longing within the *masa* for representation amidst a sea of mythical superior stars that were out of reach and out of touch. Where the stars in the cinema were tall, fair-skinned and sharp-featured *mestizas*, Aunor had plain 'native' (Lim 2004: 66) features that were pleasant (though no match for her competition in show business), stood a diminutive 4 feet 11 inches tall, and wore a second-hand dress hastily altered to fit her for the fateful singing competitions first in Naga and later in Manila that would lead to her becoming the Superstar of Philippine cinema (see Figure 3.1).

In the 1970s, stars in the Philippines fell into several categories: the new young teenage idols popping up in musical films, which Aunor was a product of; the action stars of the Philippines (such as Fernando Poe Jr and Joseph Estrada); the comedy stars of the Philippines (such as Dolphy and Nida Blanca); leading ladies who worked primarily in romance or melodrama (Susan Roces and Amalia Fuentes); and, of course, bold stars who worked in softcore sex (*bomba*) films (del Mundo Jr 1999: 42). Aunor was a clear outsider in this collection of stars, with the exception of Dolphy, whose everyman persona and humble origins came closest to resembling Aunor's; Estrada would build a career on a working-class hero persona which lacked any connection with his real upper-middle-class background.

Of the women, Aunor again is the outsider – all three women were prized for their refined physical beauty and mixed ancestry. In comparison, Aunor's fame was premised on her exceptional singing voice, and came at a time when musical films were popular in the Philippines. Hers was

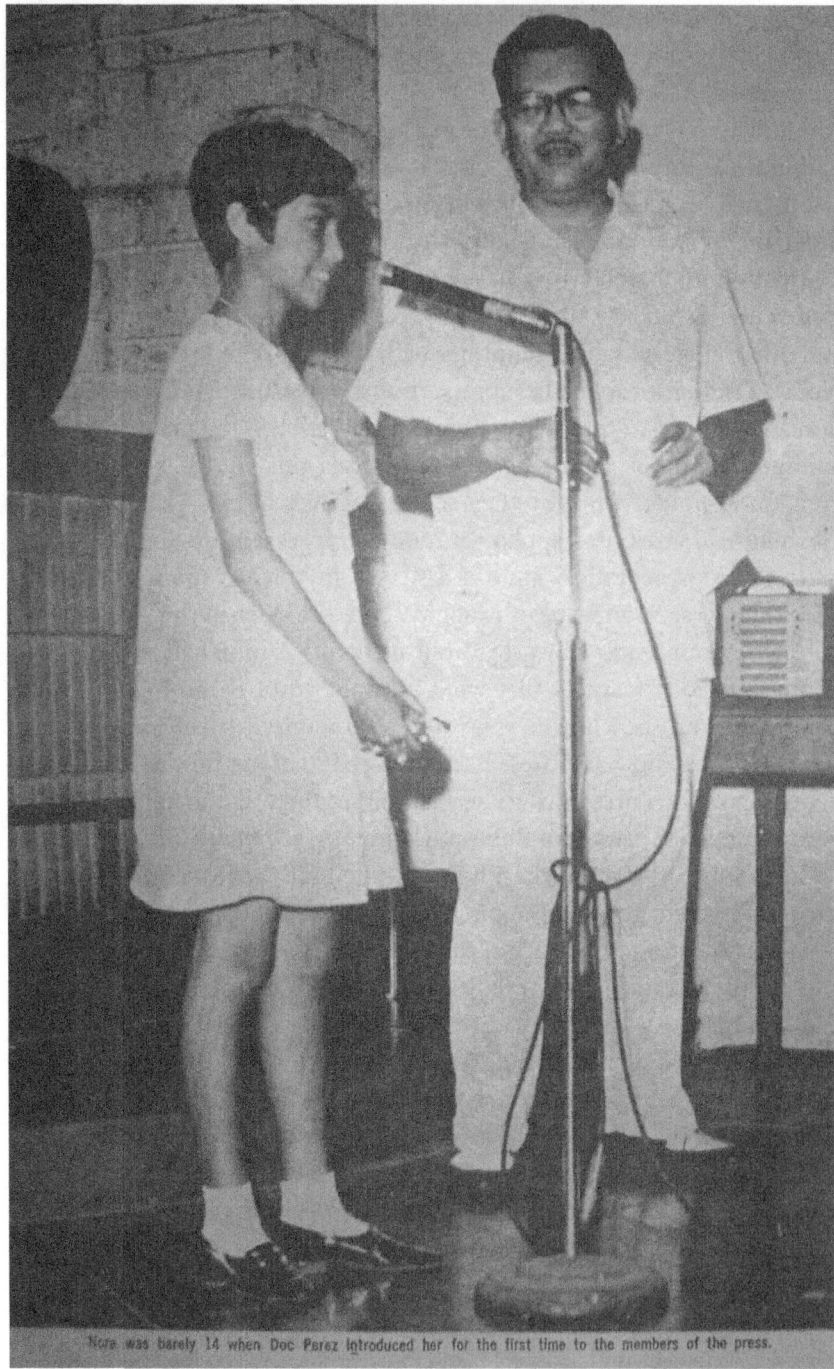

Nora was barely 14 when Doc Perez introduced her for the first time to the members of the press.

Figure 3.1 This image of Aunor and Doc Perez highlights Aunor's diminutive stature and young age. Source: from the collection of Nestor de Guzman

a truly multimedia stardom, with fans acquired from her voice on radio and her face on television and then film. Aunor also marked a different and more modern path to stardom than these predecessors: she rose to fame from a televised singing contest, only later being head-hunted by the film studios seeking to capitalise on her stardom. In this context, Aunor proved to be different and unique among the types of stars that Philippine cinema had been producing.

Aunor's extraordinary voice differentiated her from her peers, distinctive and easily recognisable. Writing in *Graphic*, a nationally circulated English language magazine, Mercado wrote of her voice:

> 'It's unbelievable,' [her husband] said, 'that such a big voice could belong to such a little girl'... She was only 13 or 14 then, but she had this POW in her voice, not really volume but projection, the same lung power which makes Janis Joplin so electrifying. (Mercado 1970)

For such a young girl, Aunor's voice was low-pitched and possessed a mature tone incongruent with her young age. Her voice won her several local competitions and carried her to Manila, where she competed twice on *Tawag ng Tanghalan* (Call of the Stage), a national singing contest which she was immediately eliminated from on her first try, but won on her second in May 1967, aged only fourteen years old. In her essay '*Himala* (Miracle): The Heretical Potential of Nora Aunor's Star Power' (2002), Tadiar discusses the significance of Aunor's voice as being the genesis of her fame. Tadiar ties Aunor's extraordinary voice to the giving of a voice to a traditionally voiceless people, specifically referring to an earlier 1997 work on Filipina domestic workers reduced to 'mute instruments' of labour – merely existing and functioning for others (ibid.: 717; Tadiar 1997: 181). In Aunor, the *masa* found a cathartic means of speaking where previously they were silenced. Aunor made them heard and bestowed upon them a sense of worth; not only were they worth listening to, their voice was soulful and sang of their sorrows and joys.

A new star of a new medium

Aunor's vocal performances provide an early glimpse of what would become her famously restrained acting style. Aunor's delivery is simple, restrained but full of heart and known for her lower contralto tone. Her song selection leans towards the simple and emotive, covering classics such as 'Moonlight Becomes You' and 'Windmills of Your Mind', songs that emphasise her *forte* at the lower end of the vocal spectrum. Her voice transported her from Iriga to Manila and equipped her with the means to compete with *Manileños*. Despite her shabby dress and low social class, she was extraordinary. Her voice was not working in isolation, however. The televised singing competition that she won, *Tawag ng Tanghalan*, was an ideal venue for someone like Aunor. Modern reality and talent competitions regularly emphasise the Cinderella narrative for building a new star: a raw and undiscovered talent waiting to be found, overcoming great adversity to achieve great heights, remaining humble and grateful in the face of overwhelming success with the purest of motivations and alleviating the family's poverty. Aunor fulfilled all of those criteria – she originally participated in a regional singing contest in order to win PHP20 (about US$5 then) for her older sister's school tuition fees (Hernando 2011). Such a combination would win modern competitions easily, but in the Philippines in the 1960s, Aunor was an anomaly that appealed to the public. That television was the medium that made Aunor a star is no accident. A 'mass' medium at heart, the television provides a window into different worlds, and Aunor brought a familiar face and plight to a medium that the *masa* loved but was traditionally excluded from. For some in the Philippines, a movie ticket was a luxury and for many a television was out of reach. But the communal nature of watching television often meant that people gathered wherever a television set was, and thus many were able to witness the birth of Nora Aunor, the star that was born amongst them. This forms part of the reason that television was vital to Aunor's early fame.

Another key aspect of Nora Aunor's stardom was that it was born from a unique youth movement of her teenage peers, all of them searching for their place in society and the world. Her films dealt with the specific anxieties of youth: searching for love, struggling for independence from their elders and yet respectful and loving of them. Her stardom was one that was of the people and for the people. This is reflected in the path of her stardom – television, radio and the singing contest in the Philippines, all popular media and the chosen media of the young. Aunor was a new star, made in a new way for new people. The radio and television are particularly democratic media, closer to the people and their daily lives than the imposing and intimidating big screen that Philippine cinema traditionally built its stars on.

Popular culture in the Philippines at the time of Nora Aunor was a divided world, with the rich and cultured preferring foreign cultural products while the poor, or *bakya* (a derogatory phrase for the lower class, so named for their wooden clogs which marked them as being common and uncultured), adored Nora Aunor and local films. English language newspapers wrote about Gina Lollobrigida, Doris Day and Brigitte Bardot; local newspapers covered Nora Aunor and Vilma Santos. The elite rejected the stars of popular cinema in favour of what they perceived as more sophisticated cultural products exported by their former colonial power and European cinemas (to be explored in the next chapter). At the same time, another popular figure in the Philippines was drawing crowds and using the mass media to win the public – President Ferdinand Marcos.

Another defining aspect of Aunor's star image is her features. The most extraordinary thing about her dusky skin, her thick, shiny, long, black hair, dark arched brows, prominent mole on her left cheek next to her nose, rounded face and features dominated by large, expressive eyes is that they are almost entirely ordinary (see Figure 3.2). Aunor certainly does not look like any other stars of her stature before or after her fame. With the exception of supporting roles or comic figures, Aunor is by far the darkest star of the Philippines.

After winning *Tawag ng Tanghalan*, Aunor began appearing on musical variety shows on television, where her regular singing performances paired her up with several young male stars. From television, recording deals and radio shows, Aunor transitioned to film, a career she thought unlikely because of the prevailing conditions for stardom, believing she would be used mainly as a singer (de Manila 1977). Aunor was proved right in her first run of roles, which cast her in musical numbers which would have her singing, but along the way the box-office success of these roles and the fan following that Aunor generated sealed her reputation as a profitable star 'in movie box-office returns of [sic] which are described as unprecedented in the history of Philippine movies' (Centina III n.d.). Between September 1969 and August 1970, a total of 197 films were made locally, with Aunor appearing in twenty-two films during that period (Torre Jr 1970). It was at this time that she made love team films as a natural progression of her acting career. These films became very successful, most notably with Tirso Cruz III and a brief period with Manny de León. Also during this time, Aunor became the site of several power struggles between

Figure 3.2 Portrait of Aunor in the early 1970s. Source: from the collection of Nestor de Guzman

both her guardians and studios. Still a minor, Aunor was caught in a legal proceeding brought by Sampaguita against Tower Productions that hinged on conflicting contracts signed by her mother (with Tower Productions) and her aunt (with Sampaguita Pictures), who for a time acted as her legal guardian and from whom she took the stage name 'Aunor'. Aunor had gone for some time without an exclusive contract, appearing in multiple studios' releases, but her stardom had reached a point where studios were competing to have exclusive rights to what they viewed as a vital guarantee of profit.

Nora Aunor's early stardom reflects the unusual personal leverage she had with studios. Unlike the majority of teenage stars who submissively accepted roles and orders on the path to stardom, Aunor disrupted the power relations between star and studio, working simultaneously with Sampaguita Pictures and Tower Productions. When a studio demanded too much or took advantage of her, she simply stopped cooperating; one source describes her taking the controls of a train and travelling past her stop in order to avoid returning to the set that day (Francisco n.d.). Her unpredictable behaviour on set was tolerated largely due to her significant fan following. Any film with Aunor in it was guaranteed success, even if several were running simultaneously. The quality and plot of the film was tertiary at best, perhaps her screen partner coming in at secondary importance. Such was the strength of Aunor's star power that she boosted the career of several performers associated with her, among them love team partner Tirso Cruz III, their doll Maria Leonora Teresa, and long-time friend and mentor German Moreno.

Drama and sufferance

One of the chief attractions of a star and a puzzle that fans are constantly trying to solve is the question of authenticity. How authentic is a star? Is she 'really' as nice as her persona and roles portray her to be? Nora Aunor is often considered one of the most authentic stars in the Philippines. She often refers to her humble origins and her status as one of the common people, the *masa* that she represents. This authenticity is reinforced by her unusually open and close relationship with her fans, whom she allows to visit her in her home, call her on the phone and accompany her to all her public engagements, among other things. This policy has been in place since her teenage years and is borne out by fans testifying that she is a down-to-earth person, just like one of them. One fan speaks of Aunor as a simple person who helps out with the washing and cooking, wearing casual clothes and having a close and informal relationship with her staff (Dolor 2016).

The element of melodrama that characterises Aunor's narrative over the years forms part of her appeal to fans. News columns are perennially filled with her highs and lows, and they are nearly always extremes.

Aunor's chaotic and dramatic star image marks her out as a particular type of star. Some stars are characterised by a perfect professional demeanour; some by a sense of blandness that cannot be shaken no matter how hard they try. With Aunor, drama forms a central appeal to her fans, who rally around her in times of need and provide the support to reach new heights. An unattributed quote on a fan website sums it up perfectly:

> Nora Aunor, in the course of her turbulent history, has been in constant trouble, and it seems her audiences have always been there, a presence always summoned by crisis and the spectre of the star's perdition . . . No other actor in Philippine cinema is as transparent as Nora Aunor as her life is an open book. This is one of the reason [sic] why her fans love her, from past until the present her admirers are all the way in supporting her. (Airhernaez 2011)

Fans look forward to the drama in the life of Aunor as a star as much as the drama in her work in film and television. This can be tied back to the popularity of melodrama as a genre in the Philippines, itself linked to the literary genre of the *pasyon* (the Passion of Christ), a tale of suffering and redemption. Like the Mater Dolorosa (the weeping, bleeding Mother of Christ, Our Lady of Sorrows[1]) and the martyrs of Christianity, Aunor suffers just as her fans do. This links Aunor to a sense of authenticity – because she suffers like us, she is *really* like us. In his work on Aunor, 'The Star also Suffers: Screening Nora Aunor', Flores writes that 'When seen in the context of Aunor's history, the utterance of pain, the politics of making it known and acknowledging it in public, assumes authenticity; the star's folklore and filmography could affirm this assertion' (2008: 71).

The persona of Nora Aunor is rooted in her representativeness of the ordinary Filipino, made extraordinary by the paradox of her voice and silent gaze. She is the Cinderella of the Philippines, the fairy-tale Superstar that often falters but always rises again to new heights. In the drama of her life, she reflects the hysterical devotion of her fans and re-enacts the model women of Philippine folklore and faith, or the *babaeng martir* (female martyrs) – the martyrs and the suffering Mother of Christ. The face and voice of the masses became appropriately one of the faces of the Second Golden Age of Philippine Cinema. Nora Aunor remains unchallenged as the Superstar of Philippine cinema, full of heart, following, suffering, character and drama.

Vilma Santos

Appointed from childhood for success

Vilma Santos's rise to stardom adheres to long-standing models of stardom in the Philippines. Coming from a middle-class *mestiza* background with relatives working in show business, Santos was proximate to the industry, claiming Carmen Rosales (popular star of the 1950s) as a grand-aunt on her father's side, but also an uncle who was a cameraman at Sampaguita Pictures. It was her uncle who took her to audition for a role aged just eight years old, bringing her to the attention of studio head Doc Jose Perez (Francisco 2017). Impressed with her personality, looks and talent, he cast her in several films, launching what would become a long-lasting show business career in the Philippines. While her first role in *Anak, ang Iyong Ina!* (dir. Mar S. Torres 1963), starring veterans Lolita Rodriguez and Luis Gonzales, was granted without an audition, she auditioned days later for the role of the titular little girl in *Trudis Liit* (Little Trudis) (dir. Jose De Villa 1963), ultimately beating 800 other children for the role. The role would set her on course for stardom as well as win her the first FAMAS award of her career – for Best Child Actress (Juan 1971).[2] Santos was born Maria Rosa Vilma Tuazon Santos, but Doc Perez chose to use her middle name Vilma rather than Rosa, due to what he considered to be a glut of stars named Rosa at the time.

Aside from being proximate to the industry, Santos also fulfilled another long-standing requirement of stardom in the Philippines: she was a *mestiza*, with Chinese heritage on her mother's side. As a result, she resembled the famous Chinese *mestiza* Carmen Rosales, and represented a familiar yet exotic beauty. As an eight-year-old, Santos possessed a round, chubby face without sharp angles (see Figure 3.3). Her lips, nose, cheeks and brows all arched smoothly into a softly curved face. Her eyes dominated, with the epicanthic fold of skin on the upper eyelids, and sparkled, full of life. Her hair was prone to a loose wave, and soft, short wisps frame her face in a series of large, C-shaped curls. Her mother's surname of Tuazon and her mixed-heritage looks conveyed the suggestion of money and a certain class that is assumed about Chinese *mestiza* Filipinos.

The net result was that young Vilma Santos represented the old star system of the Philippines: young, beautiful *mestizas* of a privileged background with proximity to the industry, similar to the prior Glamour Queen

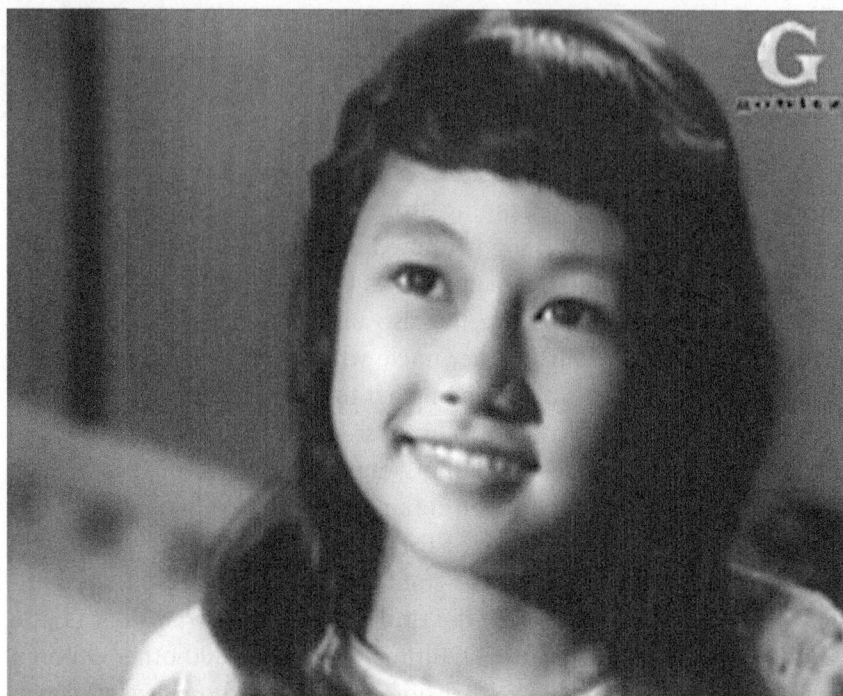

Figure 3.3 Santos as Imee Marcos in *Iginuhit ng Tadhana* (1965)

of the Philippines, Susan Roces. Another factor that played to her advantage was her young age. Child stars in the Philippines are truly beloved, and especially prized for their ability to convey strong emotions. Santos certainly fit this bill, with detractors of her later career describing her performance style as 'over-acting' and 'hysterical' (Gorospe 2018). This evaluation misses a crucial point: Santos's performance style is reflective of the era of Philippine cinema she was brought up in, as well as the conditions of her early stardom. When Doc Perez auditioned Santos, she was asked to cry and laugh on cue, and it is these key emotions, exaggerated to a perfect extent, that marked her as the ideal child star and melodramatic actress after a specific style of performance in Philippine cinema.

During this time, Santos worked on many successful films, starring with all the leading stars of her era, including Luis Gonzales, Gloria Romero and Dolphy. She was also given prominent roles based on historical figures, such as that of playing Imee Marcos in *Iginuhit ng Tadhana* and its sequel *Pinagbuklod ng Langit*. This role cast her as one of the privileged, as Imelda Marcos took a close interest in the casting of the film, handpicking Luis Gonzales for the role of her husband and approving Santos in the role of her child. At the time, Santos was the most attractive and popular child actress, a distinction that won her the role as daughter to the self-styled 'First Family of the Philippines'. Santos's beginnings as a dramatic child star meant that she had already made a name for herself before her transition to teenage jukebox musical films.

After several successful years as a child star, Santos was directed by her parents to return to focus on her schooling, which she briefly did. But Philippine cinema was taking off in a new and exciting direction; it was the era of the teenage jukebox musical, and as a previously already beloved child star, Santos was in a unique position to be particularly successful in this genre, bringing with her an already established audience from her earlier work. During this time, she was managed by an American, William Leary, who recognised the musical direction of the era and sought to include Santos in it. Under Leary's own label, Wilear's Record, Santos released in 1969 an album titled *Sixteen*, featuring the eponymous hit song that would come to define her teenage career. The song would prove to be an iconic moment of Santos's stardom, recreated almost fifty years later on a popular 2018 children's game show by a young Korean child seeking to win in the Philippines. The move to release an album also built on her early star persona as seen in *Ging* (dir. Cirio H. Santiago and Teodorico C. Santos 1964), where she played the street child with a golden singing voice. 'Sixteen' (the single) became an unexpected anthem for teenagers in 1969, offering something that the popular singer Nora Aunor did not have at the time: an original and relatable song in English about being a teen. The melody and lyrics were relatively simple, about teenagers walking and making out in the park, something that featured often in teenage jukebox musical films.

As simple as the song was, it was unable to hide one important detail, namely, that Vilma Santos could not sing. In an industry full of songbird rivals, Santos was at best competent, but prone to sour notes. Her voice was high-pitched and thin, like a child's, where her rivals' voices were full-bodied, mature and capable of sophisticated nuance despite their young age. Despite this setback, Santos's album sold well, chiefly relying on four original songs that would reach her audience rather than good covers of already famous English songs that her peers were making. One of the songs on the album was 'Then Along Came You, Edgar', featuring her love team partner, Edgar Mortiz, to whom she was already being linked in a series of television and film ensemble performances. To distinguish herself from her peers and become competitive in the teenage jukebox musical era, Santos turned to another strategy of the musical: dancing. In this aspect, she would prove to be much more adept, and dancing would become part of her ideolect throughout the 1970s, 1980s and 1990s in various films and television shows she starred in, including her iconic role in Burlesk Queen (dir. Celso Ad. Castillo 1977) in which she plays a young woman who turns to burlesque dancing in order to support her quadriplegic father. This role is often described as marking a conclusive shift in her image from sweet to mature and came a mere five years after her teenage love team career began.

Model of female virtue

As a teenage female star, Santos was the model of good behaviour, being invariably demure and polite in the press and interactions with her fans. Her star image lent itself to the narrative of a good and dutiful daughter, even as magazines debated whether she was having relationships with her various leading men. In interviews, she was carefully circumspect about relationships, choosing to speak generally about the leading man of her current film, or Mortiz, a safe and constant companion during that period.

During this era, Santos had a number of sponsorships that relied on her young and lively persona, such as Glad Rainwear, a raincoat maker that featured an image of Santos on set with her name printed prominently on a director's chair. Santos became the face of a completely unexpected product when she was eighteen – Tanduay, a brand of locally produced rum in the Philippines. How could a teenage girl with a star image of impeccable goodness and virtue sell a brand of alcohol typically associated with adult men in the Philippines? The answer was simple: through her father and ideal man. A picture of her sweet young face appears before the headline 'What do I look for in a man who drinks?' and features a short interview with her, in which she shares a saying her father has about alcohol for her brothers to ensure the respect of peers ('Keep liquor in your belly, not your head!') and reasons that drinking is unavoidable in social settings, such as the presidential residence of Malacañang Palace when entertaining foreign dignitaries. This neatly ties the alcohol to a family practice that is policed by a loving father, and associates the drink with the glamourous diplomats, politicians, respectability and honour of serving the nation (where it is implied that Tanduay is consumed as a local brand that is sophisticated, respectable and a source of national pride). Noting that her ideal man must know how to drink, Santos then reveals that her father is the ideal man she speaks of, and that his drink is Tanduay – a strategy necessary for a girl who was only recently legally allowed to purchase alcohol and of sterling character whose love team partner Mortiz was not legally old enough to drink yet. The other drink Santos promoted (personally) at the time was Coca-Cola, the internationally associated drink of the youth – fun, refreshing and age-appropriate. Santos in this example and in other interviews is the good girl – the biddable, compliant and filial daughter. She is professional in her dealings with the press, and her character is above reproach. This image extends to her screen roles as well, playing the young woman whose innocence and goodness shine from her eyes, set in a young, fresh face.

Santos shared with Aunor a key attitude towards their fans that earned them a truly devoted following during the era: they made themselves accessible to fans in a way that prior and subsequent stars did not. There are many accounts of fans visiting the two teenage stars in their homes at this time, arriving at all hours of the day, often when their star was fast asleep and with their parents allowing them inside to wait till they awakened. *Liwayway* (a leading Tagalog weekly magazine) notes that during a visit to Santos's house the editorial team got lost but found their way there by following teenagers walking inside the Quezon City subdivision towards it. Once awake, Santos demonstrated 'a close relationship with them', greeting those who were familiar, smiling and signing autographs (Juan 1971). Fans of both Aunor and Santos were given the opportunity to be proximate to their stars, to have them accessible and relatable. As a result, their devotion took on legendary status, with fans calling themselves 'solid Vilmanians and Noranians', the word 'solid' in the Philippines being used to indicate the level of devotion of fans; a solid fan is devoted, unswayable and committed to their star (ibid.).

Rival female stardom

Becoming famous in the same era as Nora Aunor came with its share of drawbacks, one of them being that Santos has consistently played second fiddle to Aunor in critical and academic circles (with these two distinct categories oftentimes overlapping in Philippine cinema due to academics also being members of a critical and award-conferring body called the Manunuri ng Pelikulang Pilipino, or the Filipino Film Critics). In comparison with Aunor's atypical and subversive image, Santos represented the establishment – the same *mestiza*, rich, beautiful women that had come before her and would come after her. Every aspect of their images, from performance to looks, was compared and Santos's found inferior to Aunor's. As a result, while there is no shortage of scholarship and articles to be found on Nora Aunor, Vilma Santos remains unwritten, and there are no academic articles to be brought to bear in this section on her star image. Even journalists would turn to discussing her much later, as Joaquin finally did in 1990, in sharp contrast to his 1977 piece comparing Nora Aunor to Cinderella that forms the introduction to the section on her image earlier in this chapter.

And when Joaquin *did* write about Santos, it was in terms of durability, an analysis that benefits from the intervening thirty years between her child star days and her award-winning adult performances. Her famed durability was already on display by the time Santos was nineteen and had spent ten years in show business. Starting out at the tender age of eight, Santos was known as a sweet, round-faced child star, the face of the street urchin turned singing star in *Ging* and her regular four-year-long role as *Trudis Liit*. Joaquin comments that she was particularly lucky and adaptable in the following years, saying that she 'never suffered an ugly-duckling phase of no-longer-a-child and not-yet-a-teener' (de Manila 1990). He goes on to discuss the '13–14–15' period as being a difficult age for a star in the public eye, one that Santos surmounted with ease in her roles such as playing Imee Marcos on-screen in *Iginuhit ng Tadhana* and *Pinagbuklod ng Langit*. By sixteen, she was being featured in the many teenage musical variety shows and films that were slowly doing the work of setting up long-term love teams, such as the tandem she would make with Edgar Mortiz.

A matter of three years later, Santos would begin to move away from love team films towards the next stage of her career – the more critically acclaimed and daring roles she would become famous for under the direction of auteur directors of the Second Golden Age of Philippine Cinema. These are just three of the metamorphoses that Santos would undergo during the course of her career and were followed by at least three further phases: her steady work with television studio ABS-CBN following the end of Martial Law, where she would build upon her dancing image (a strategy adopted early in her career to differentiate herself from Aunor); her transition towards critically acclaimed leading matriarchal roles with the same studio; and finally her shift towards politics, only infrequently starring in films to appease her still passionate fanbase once in a while.

Already within the lifetime of her love team career, three clearly observable steps took place: from child star to teenage love team jukebox musical star, transforming into young adult star beginning to explore more complex dramatic roles, before fully severing the ties with her love team partner.

Joaquin's piece is titled 'Vilma, the Glad Girl', and runs with a subheading declaring a clear comparison with Aunor: 'Unlike Nora la Dolorosa, the durable Vi Santos has made happiness her career' (de Manila 1990). 'Vilma the Glad Girl' is a fairly accurate phrase to describe Santos, known for her smooth, round-cheeked smile, with lips often commented upon by Mortiz, who describes them as 'kissable' and 'irresistible' in an article (Liza Jr 1970a). This is not to say that Santos's roles were that of a perpetually smiling girl; indeed, her performance style has often been labelled 'hysterical' or 'over-acting' (Gorospe 2018) by critics and academics alike. Her crying and shouting in confrontational scenes during the climactic act of her films are so famous as to have passed into her ideolect, oft parodied and imitated by others to evoke her style in popular culture. Her performance style harks back to the older, more melodramatic style found in the native *sarsuwelas* and other theatre forms in the Philippines, and ties Santos with the old gods of Philippine cinema. In contrast, Aunor's style was said to be unusually restrained and quiet, which distinguished her from older stars and show business styles. Santos's more exuberant style may not just betray her roots in the cinema and star system of the previous generation of stars, but could also perhaps be a deliberate strategy to differentiate herself from her main competition in Aunor. Santos was also perhaps referred to as the Glad Girl because of her sunny nature in her public appearances and work outside of film.

As Joaquin notes, Santos would go on to reinvent herself several more times in her career, earning her the title of 'Star For All Seasons' (de Manila 1990). Her teenage career was the platform that earned her the loyal following of Vilmanians, who would follow her throughout her career, remaining as loyal as the Noranians and steadfast throughout the challenges that came her way. Santos defined herself almost in complete opposition to Aunor in these early years, cultivating an image of professionalism and even-temperedness where Aunor posed a challenge to studios and possessed an inherently dramatic star image that rendered her unpredictable. Though Santos had come to stardom naturally, she worked hard to remain relevant as she and the industry grew, proving adept at the work of being a lasting star – a fate that the male stars of their love teams did not share.

Tirso Cruz III

Proximate star

Tirso Cruz III was one of the most popular male teenage stars of 1970s Philippine cinema. During his heyday, he was one half of the most popular love teams in Philippine cinema with Nora Aunor, capable of filling stadiums and theatres with each performance, selling magazines and records by the tens of thousands, and starring in back-to-back blockbusters. But beyond his teenage years and love team, Cruz's stardom faltered and faded along with the costumes and hairstyles of the era – a nostalgic memory of good times past. Cruz seemed forgotten in comparison with Aunor, the more successful star of their love team, until his reinvention as a character actor in the 1990s. There is no academic work on Tirso Cruz III, with work on that era consisting instead of examinations of the phenomenon of Nora Aunor or the films of the Second Golden Age of Philippine Cinema. Working in the shadow of Nora Aunor and in the immediate run-up to the Second Golden Age, Cruz was a casualty of a changing cinema and his age; beyond his teenage fame, he never quite found his place in Philippine cinema.

Tirso Cruz III was born into a family of performers and raised in the family business. The Cruz clan is a sprawling, multi-generational group that comprises musicians, singers and actors. The patriarch of the clan was his grandfather, Tirso Cruz Sr, known as 'Dr Rhythm of the Philippines', the foremost band leader of popular music in Manila in the 1930s and 1940s (Walsh 2013: 272). Offshoots of the Tirso Cruz Band included Danny Cruz and the 747 Band; Joe Cruz and the Cruzettes; as well as a younger brother, Carding Cruz Sr, with his own popular orchestra (ibid.). With so many famous Cruz members, Tirso's stardom seemed inevitable. Indeed, his first role was playing the baby Jesus in *Ang Pagsilang ng Mesiyas* (dir. Carlos Vander Tolosa 1952) aged just six months old (Umerez 1970: 4). Notably, the credits for the film on IMDb include character names for only Cruz and Norma Biancaflor, despite the fact that it starred more famous actors of the time in more active roles than the infant Cruz. Proximity to stars and star-makers always aided Cruz: his role as the infant Messiah was a result of living in the same neighbourhood as Lebran Productions (ibid.).

As a third-generation musician, Cruz started his career singing in the lounges and on the stages of his family's trade by the age of thirteen

(Balbuena 2010). Given the nickname 'Pip' at birth by his father, who had seen a film version of *Great Expectations*, he soon became known in his teenage career as Pip rather than the more formal Tirso of his father and grandfather before him. By age seventeen, he had appeared in his first film, another boy in a crop of upcoming musically talented teenage stars that included among others Edgar Mortiz and Eddie Peregrina. He was managed at the start of his career by the influential Douglas Quijano, for whom Cruz was his very first talent. Quijano later became responsible for many of the most popular stars, such as Aga Muhlach and Richard Gomez, working with and acting as producer for many of Mother Lily Monteverde's Regal Films productions (Santiago 2009). In 1969, aged just seventeen, Cruz starred opposite Nora Aunor in their first tandem film *D' Musical Teenage Idols!* (dir. Artemio Marquez 1969), an immediate box-office hit and the start of both his popular career as a teenage star and the love team that would come to define his stardom.

Tirso was not the sole member of the Cruz clan to become an actor. His cousin Ricky Belmonte was six years older than him and started appearing in films three years earlier in 1966. By the time Tirso came along, Ricky had become one of the leading matinee idols of his generation, aided by his love team with Rosemarie Sonora (sister of Susan Roces). Together, the two were the love team to beat before the new tandems of Guy and Pip, and Vi and Bot seized the crown in the early 1970s. Born Jesus Cruz, Ricky took on the stage name of Ricky Belmonte to deliberately distance himself from the Cruz name (Valdez 1969). He soon rose to become a star talent of Sampaguita Pictures, and his tandem with Rosemarie was a box-office success. As with any famous family connections, rumours of feuds and rivalry followed the cousins and were the subject of many gossip columns and magazine covers. The cousins appeared in *Ricky Na, Tirso Pa!* (dir. Jose Wenceslao 1970) and *The Young at Heart* (dir. Danny Holmsen 1970), released within six months of each other at the height of the popularity of both cousins. In order to capitalise on the fame of the cousins, an uncle put in motion the film *Ricky Na, Tirso Pa!*, a Cruz family production – fully financed by and starring the extended clan, who all sing in the film (Valdez 1969). They also shared the screen in several other projects including *YeYe Generation* (dir. Artemio Marquez 1969) and *Oh, Delilah* (dir. Osorio P. Consuelo 1969).

Establishment star

Tirso Cruz III fulfilled many criteria of stardom in the Philippines in the 1970s: he was young, handsome, from a dynasty of popular entertainers and had the fair *mestizo* looks in demand for the screen. Physically, Cruz's defining characteristics were his thick dark hair that flopped into his eyes with a long curl from his sideburns reaching below his ears, a stern expression and his unusual height, which had him towering over most of his peers (see Figure 3.4).

His family background and profession meant that Cruz moved in the right circles and rubbed shoulders with people that could help him in his chosen profession. Certainly, he did not lack any advantage whether in terms of his education or career. Combined with his already famous cousin, the Cruz boys looked to be the reigning princes of Philippine cinema in the early 1970s. His *mestizo* features and family dynasty are all markers of privilege in Philippine society, a privilege recognised and promoted by the film industry in a dual reinforcement of the colonial hold of both the US and Spain and the influential Hollywood cinema that continued to exert an American influence on its former colony. A particularly class-obsessed article describes Cruz as follows:

> Tirso, more than anything else, is a cleancut [*sic*] young man without airs, without eccentricities, certainly without oddities. By this we mean he is one boy any mother can be proud of. There is no hippie in him like a few young movie stars we know. No long hair, no mannerisms, no pot. Just a good-looking face, a very good singing style, a talent for music. No excessive sex, no violence, certainly no brushes with the law . . . And here is the frosting on the cake: he comes from a distinguished family of music lovers. Anybody who had finished at least the first two grades in school knows that where there is music, there are no savages. (Amurao 1970: 24)

Notably, this article prefers Cruz with Vilma Santos, the *mestiza* star, rather than with Nora Aunor, the *kayumanggi* star, perhaps more closely associated with the unschooled 'savages' the author speaks of.

The 1970s saw Cruz in teenage musical films, concerts and albums. The demand for songs in films favoured Cruz's particular brand of stardom, and his early films required little more from him than the ability to sing and follow the director's instructions in front of the camera. The oftentimes naturally stern expression that he has lends itself to moody

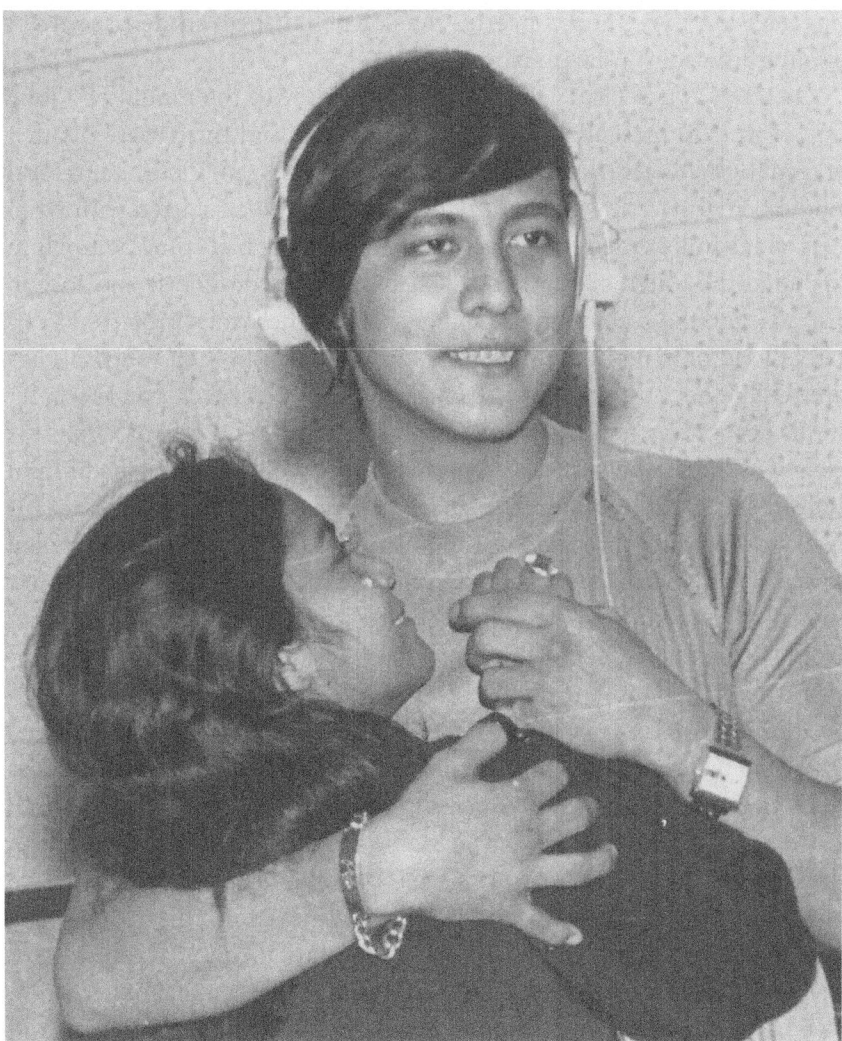

Figure 3.4 Tirso Cruz III with Aunor in the early 1970s. Source: from the collection of Nestor de Guzman

and passionate characters. His skin tone and refined features also make him suitable for playing snobbish upper-class characters that initially are cold and conceited but warm up over the course of the film to become the redeemed and devoted lover. These roles are combined with songs that allow Cruz to cover a range of 1970s pop and love songs with his leading ladies. His family background and stage performances as a singer also gave him an added talent for the screen – his ability to play the guitar, which he sometimes showcased in his roles and during live appearances on television shows and concerts. Outside of film, he recorded a series of albums both solo and with Nora Aunor.

As a star, Tirso Cruz III theoretically fit in with the mould of a long line of *mestizo* masculine men. His main peers and rivals were his first cousin Ricky, Edgar Mortiz, Manny de León, Ed Finlan, Victor Laurel and Eddie Peregrina. All were teenage heartthrobs, and all starred with Nora Aunor at some point in their careers. The stars that had come before him included the tough action heroes, such as Fernando Poe Jr and Joseph Estrada, and the comic genius Dolphy. Each of these men projected a different kind of hypermasculinity, the former two with their tough bodies and willingness to fight for those they chose to protect and the latter in his reputation as a ladies' man on-screen and off. Perhaps Cruz was caught in the shadow of these hypermasculine men, because his star (and indeed the stardom of all the teenage boys listed above) faded after his teenage years and the genre of the musical passed him by, and he failed to transition to any kind of accepted mature male persona. In an attempt to maintain his stardom, Cruz turned to releasing songs and albums that would bolster his career by keeping him on that much more common and democratic medium, the radio.

The genre of romance films in the 1970s was not a forgiving one, especially for male stars. Where female stars would go on to build success from their teenage stardom (such as Nora Aunor, Vilma Santos, Susan Roces and Hilda Koronel), male stars often faded into insignificance. This suggests that there was no place for leading men who did not have any other distinguishing features beyond matinee idol in the 1970s, a fact that has remained true of Philippine cinema until the most recent crop of male stars that embody a very different masculinity than that of Fernando Poe Jr, Joseph Estrada or Dolphy – a certain emotional vulnerability and lack of aggression in their images, as embodied by Aga Muhlach, Piolo Pascual and John Lloyd Cruz. At the time, such a vulnerability made them unsuitable for anything except the teenage angst and uncertainty they were called upon to play.

Cruz's membership of the middle class and markers of class such as his prominent family, education, English and fair skin meant that his ascent to stardom was a safe bet for Sampaguita and a smooth one. There is a certain inevitability to Cruz's stardom; in a way it feels like the fulfilling of destiny that the baby whose first role was the infant Messiah would grow up to be the prince of Philippine cinema. His stardom had the distance and extraordinary quality of the elite that differentiated him from the common folk, but it is precisely these things that made him most popular with the *bakya* crowd. Cruz performed for them the fantasy of the rich Prince Charming who would someday come and sweep their troubles away as easily as he swept them off their feet. At the same time, his youth lent him a quality of ordinariness – he was just like any other teenager regardless of social status or skin tone: obsessed with love, wanting freedom and exploring his identity.

But fans sometimes used his lineage against him, particularly when it involved the delicate matter of a love triangle between him and Edgar Mortiz for the affections of Aunor. After some time, Cruz's family drew the line and put a stop to the triangle, citing fan gossip and 'bashing' of their son and family. An article that interviews his parents and Aunor's parents quotes Cruz's mother as stating that fans gossiped about Cruz, the validity of her marriage with his father, and his grandfather's past negative press, asking God to forgive those who gossip about their family (Liza Jr 1969).

Much of Cruz's career and image has been irrevocably dominated by his love team with Nora Aunor. Despite his making a deliberate attempt to star in films with other female stars at the time, none of them had the same appeal as the Guy and Pip love team. The tandem loomed large in every interview he ever gave, and still attracts questions to this day. Beyond his teenage career, Cruz's popularity waned where Aunor's grew. Rumours that he was resentful of her popularity were regularly discussed in gossip columns and perpetuated by fans. For her part, Aunor was involved as a producer in several of his subsequent films in the later 1970s and 1980s (Aunor 2016). They also participated in concerts together in several countries when the opportunity arose. After his teenage fame, Cruz's career entered a slower period punctuated by occasional reunion love team films with Aunor, the most recent one a made-for-television film in 2014. The star image of Tirso Cruz III was bound up with his youth and courtship of Nora Aunor. He was the teenage singing star that did not transition as successfully as she did, and as such the very things that made him suited for stardom – his youth and musical abilities – were less relevant as he grew older and Philippine cinema moved beyond the demand for teenage jukebox musical films. He remained in the background until the 1990s and his age once more earned him a new place in Philippine cinema – that of respected character actor, specialising in paternal roles that relied on his maturity and the painstakingly learned dramatic performance skills the intervening years had brought.

Edgar Mortiz

Defined in opposition

Edgar Mortiz shares several aspects of his fame with Nora Aunor and differs in others. Firstly, he more closely physically resembles her than the pantheon of white stars he joined. Mortiz has a darker complexion and resembled much more closely the common man than his rival Tirso Cruz III. With his rounded face and features, he also more closely hewed to native features than the typically Spanish *mestizo* look favoured by Philippine cinema. Unlike the tall and thin Cruz, Mortiz possessed a bulkier build though almost the same height. In an article about matinee idols of the 1970s, another star of the era, Walter Navarro, describes Mortiz as 'constantly plagued by weight problem [*sic*]' (2017). Round cheeks, plump lips, a rounded nose and large eyes completed the picture along with thick, shiny hair that framed his face and swept across his forehead, characterised by the long sideburns of the 1970s. The full effect was an air of youth and innocence with hair carefully parted and a sweet smile.

Mortiz also shared Aunor's immediate pathway to fame, becoming the champion of the televised singing contest *Tawag ng Tanghalan* (Call of the Stage) aged just twelve years old and retaining his status as champion for fourteen weeks (Dasmarinas 1970: 40). Where they would diverge, however, was in how they reached the competition. With Aunor, there were stories of hastily altered dresses and a compelling background of poverty; with Mortiz, there was a mother who had pushed him to sing at the age of eight on the popular 1960s children's television show *Eskwelahang Munti*, where he received his training and was pointed in the direction of *Tawag ng Tanghalan* by a trainer who recognised his talent.

While Aunor and Mortiz shared their origins in television and song, they came from different class backgrounds and had different levels of access to the world of entertainment. Thus, Mortiz's start in show business was that of a child star rather than a fairy-tale fight against the odds. From his victory on *Tawag*, Mortiz began to work on various television shows where he was initially paired with Aunor, presumably by studio executives who saw their similarities in terms of musical performance and physical appearance. The pairing was not to be, and Aunor moved on to Cruz while Mortiz moved on to Santos.

Figure 3.5 Mortiz in his childhood television career. Left: *Eskwelahang Munti*. Right: *Tawag ng Tanghalan*

During this time, Mortiz also came under the purview of Wilear's Record, managed by the American William Leary, and under the training of Danny Subido, two important figures in his life who would also be responsible for shaping the career of his love team partner, Vilma Santos. With them he released records and received vocal training, earning the headline 'Edgar Mortiz 1970's Most Promising Recording Star' in the popular *Kislap* magazine (Tan n.d.). Mortiz was in his third year of high school at Far Eastern University when he was signed by Tagalog Ilang-Ilang Productions, the studio that would manage his teenage career and pair him with Santos at the age of fifteen (Dasmarinas 1970).

A modern masculinity

Mortiz was a different type of leading man from his peers, particularly Cruz, his closest rival. Lacking the confident manner of Cruz, Mortiz instead modelled a gentler masculinity, emphasising good manners, emotions and an air of genuineness that gives the impression of being a well-brought-up young man. Unfailingly polite in interviews, Mortiz did, however, made declarations of his true feelings, being far more open and direct about his love for Santos than she ever was (as was perhaps customary for the era). His openness and gentleness meant that the two offered very different kinds of masculine stardom, with Cruz embodying the more outgoing and assertive alpha male while Mortiz tended towards the agreeable buddy that gets along with everyone.

Despite also being a recording artist like Cruz, even Mortiz's musical performances differed. Where Cruz tended to sing covers of upbeat English pop songs like his partner Aunor, Mortiz often sang Tagalog songs in his films along with the obligatory English covers. The studio cultivated the image of the devoted balladeer for Mortiz, culminating in his singing the melancholy song 'Alaala' (Remember) while gently strumming the guitar in *Remembrance* (dir. Emmanuel H. Borlaza 1972) while his brother (Jay Ilagan) woos Santos. His voice was smooth and well suited to the love songs he sang, which tended to be in the minor key with hints of sadness about them. He is perhaps best known for the song 'My Pledge of Love', the main song from the 1970 film of the same title with Santos. The song won him Best Single of the Year at the 2nd Awit (Song) Awards in 1970, and put him in company with Aunor and Cruz, who also won individually in other categories (Salazar 1970). *My Pledge of Love* was also the title of his album released in 1969 and followed up with an album in Tagalog (a genre commonly known as Original Pilipino Music, or OPM, but which includes songs in English recorded by Filipino artistes) which, in keeping with the air of melancholy in his voice and persona, was chiefly concerned with memories of a love gone wrong and other songs about true love. He also tended towards full-voiced songs like 'People', the song from another album by the same name that he made. Among the love songs and songs of loss were sprinkled songs of faith, such as 'Walk With Faith in Your Heart' and 'Hear My Plea (O Lord)', which neatly bring together the separate aspects of his star image: the devoted loving youth with a pure and pious heart, a man of the people as it were, singing in their language and their love songs.

A Valentine's Day profile best demonstrates the image the studio was trying to cultivate for Mortiz. It consists of a three-page spread featuring pictures with Santos, including a medium shot of the pair cuddling puppies and smiling at the camera (Trinidad 1971). No attempt is made to make Mortiz look sexually attractive; instead he is pictured with the sweet, the cuddly and the young. The blurb at the top of the feature is provocative: 'Edgar dedicates the month of the heart to the three important women in his life – the women of his heart, life and soul. But why three and not one?' (ibid.). While indicating that three women will

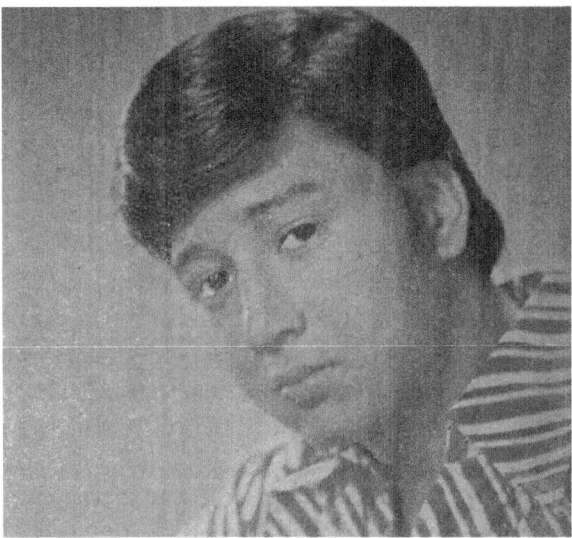

Figure 3.6 A typical image of Mortiz that emphasises his clean-cut looks and gentle nature. Source: from the collection of Nestor de Guzman, scan of *Liwayway*, 3 August 1970

be his priority this Valentine's Day, the blurb already gives clues as to whom he is speaking of. The article continues, referring to the woman of his heart as Santos, the woman of his life as his mother, and the woman of his soul as Mother Mary. Valentine's Day to Mortiz is not just for the romantic, but also the maternal and the spiritual, tying into three matters held close to the heart of Filipinos. Not coincidentally, two of his three figures are maternal, indicating a pure love, not just *eros* but *philia* in the maternal and *agape* in the spiritual. Mortiz confesses that Valentine's Day is shared not just with a romantic partner (a common practice in the Philippines), but with friends and family, while noting that this year (1971) is the first time he has dedicated the day to 'someone I love' in the person of Santos.

Mortiz's gentle soul and goodness is emphasised in the article when he continues to reveal his routine for Valentine's Day: early morning mass followed by giving his mother a present, then his siblings, and finally even the maids that care for him in his parents' absence. As a final reveal of his sweet and bashful nature, Mortiz discloses that he has handmade a card with a heart-shaped ring on it at the base for Santos. The entire feature is calculated to lend an air of non-threatening goodness and innocent love to Mortiz, from puppies to his appreciation for his domestic help.

'Santa Mariang Birheng Ina ng Diyos' (Virgin Mary, Mother of God) is also invoked to confer purity to his love, while his words for his mother and siblings indicate that he is a filial child who is mindful of his responsibilities towards the family.

In another article, Mortiz is described as 'very fond of his Mama, who acts as chaperone, adviser, confidante and manager where his entertainment transactions are concerned' (Dasmarinas 1970). Not content with merely discussing his mother, the article also includes a mention of his grandmother: 'On rare occasions, he also finds time to visit his grandma in the province' (ibid.). Mortiz's association with the maternal and feminine is strong through the persons of his mother and Mother Mary, both of whom are invoked regularly in his press. In *Tatlong Mukha ni Rosa Vilma* (Three Faces of Rosa Vilma) (dir. Romy Suzara 1972), he lives with his blind single mother, whom he cares for and tends to lovingly. In *Remembrance*, his father is killed, and it is his mother who is responsible for guiding him and primarily raising him in Manila. The absence of the maternal figure in *Edgar Loves Vilma* (dir. Leonardo L. Garcia 1970) sees him fall into vice under the care of an equally wayward father.

Mortiz spent most of his career as a young actor defined by his love team with Vilma Santos, whom he worked with regularly till 1975. In the absence of the love team, Mortiz also was unable to redefine himself to suit the more aggressive men of action and serious dramatic performers who would come to characterise the Second Golden Age of Philippine Cinema. Mortiz would ultimately find success again in his natural environment, as one of the male leads working with television studio ABS-CBN in the popular comedy and sketch show *Goin' Bananas*, which ran from 1986 to 1991 and also starred his old rival for Santos's affections in their love team films, Jay Ilagan. Mortiz is currently known as an experienced director of television variety shows such as *Goin' Bulilit* (2005–2019) and the *Banana Split* (2008) series, particularly those starring children, whom he helps train and develop into stars.

Conclusion

The four stars of the two love teams at the heart of this research embody the youth revolution of their generation, coming to the industry from various backgrounds and entrance points only to converge in the two most popular love teams of the 1970s. Each of these stars represents a different perspective on youth, some defined by narratives of conformity, while others bore a streak of rebellion. Aunor's difficult relationship with the studio demonstrates the lack of agency in both her professional and working lives, becoming the centre of a power struggle over control of her stardom (a subject to be discussed in greater detail in the next chapter). She represents the new stars and media of success in the television and radio studios, rising from obscurity to fame on the back of new media. Cruz and Santos represent a more well-established route to stardom in their careers, which began with the studios and remained compliant with establishment policies. Mortiz, on the other hand, treads a middle path, being a product of the televised singing contest but also being primed for stardom by his family, who ensured that he was immersed in the show business environment that led him to his big break.

The four stars employed a strategy of contrasts in differentiating themselves from their same-gender rivals. If Aunor sang, then Santos danced. If Cruz belted out rock numbers, then Mortiz sang soulful ballads. Where Aunor was a boisterous and tomboyish girl,[3] Santos was refined and poised. Where Cruz swaggered confidently, Mortiz charmed in a boy-next-door manner. Aunor was dark while Santos was fair, as were Mortiz and Cruz respectively. As a result, their distinct images complemented one another, providing a variety of teenage models of behaviour. Aunor was the suffering star of the masses, characterised by a Cinderella rags-to-riches narrative in which she transcended her poverty through her extraordinary talent. Santos was the sweet girl from the good family who took a level-headed approach to her stardom, characterised by her emphasis on the professional aspects of her career. Cruz was the scion of an entertainment dynasty, bearing a tinge of tradition through his modernising of the family business – singing and stage performance with matinee idol confidence. Mortiz was the devoted and earnest boy-next-door balladeer whom women of all ages trusted. The following chapter considers how these distinct images combined and interacted with their love team partner's image to create the unique joint love team images that characterised the Guy and Pip, and Vi and Bot tandems.

Notes

1. Aunor claims her mother fixed Our Lady of Sorrows in her mind when she was pregnant with Aunor (a Filipino custom called *paglilihi*) after following the statue

in a procession, captivated by her beautiful eyes. This anecdote not only ties Aunor to the Dolorosa, it calls attention to her famously expressive eyes (San Diego Jr 2017).
2. Filipino Academy of Movie Arts and Sciences (FAMAS) is the oldest existing film industry award-giving body in the Philippines.
3. 'Tomboyish' is not to be confused with the common Filipino use of the word 'tomboy', which refers to a lesbian.

Chapter 4

Reading the couple: joint star images

Introduction

In November 1971, Nora Aunor and Tirso Cruz III (affectionately known as Guy and Pip) were in their third year of screen partnership. Aged just eighteen years old at the time, the pair enjoyed unprecedented popularity in the Philippines, and were returning from a four-week-long shoot in Hawaii for their subsequent love team film, *My Blue Hawaii* (dir. Danny Holmsen and German Moreno 1972). Writing for *The Daily Mirror*, journalist Jose A. Quirino describes the scene unfolding on the airport tarmac:

> The Pan American World Airways Jumbo jet 747, which ferried the movie troupe from Honolulu to Manila, had to be surrounded by security guards as the welcoming crowd virtually became a mob in trying to reach Nora and her group. (Quirino 1971)

Quirino goes on to note that at least 10,000 fans were present to greet the pair, among them the mayor of Quezon City, Norberto S. Amoranto (Aunor's godfather, acquired after she became famous), while returning with the pair was former Commerce Secretary Ernesto Maceda (son-in-law of Doc Perez). Further evidence of the success of Guy and Pip ranges from filming overseas in a prime location to a private jet, large amounts of fans and the similarly heavy security to handle them, and the presence of political representatives. Indeed, Quirino's article recognises this, being titled 'Politicos Join Big Crowd to Welcome Back Tirso, Nora'. From the airport, the pair leaves in a private car escorted by security to Sampaguita studio, where they hold a press conference. Later that night, they are to be crowned the box-office champions at the Delta theatre.

This sort of encounter is far from being an exceptional event for Aunor and Cruz. In fact, it forms one of the tamer fan encounters that characterised their love team. In another instance, fans mobbed the VP Pictures studio on the morning of Aunor's birthday that same year:

> A car approached the gate and fans rushed towards the vehicle, screaming, shouting, cheering, pushing, crying, clapping, each one trying to talk to, shake hands with, touch or kiss the little movie star. So she could be seen by all, Nora was hoisted on the roof of the Sampaguita Pictures bus. Beside her was Pip (Tirso Cruz III) and the famous doll, their make-believe offspring, Maria Leonora Teresa. A fire-truck had to disperse the crowd. (Cordero-Fernando and Chaves 2001)

Their particular brand of hysteria was such that it spawned a doll child to ride with them on top of a bus, and the intervention of the fire department. Maria Leonora Teresa is very much part of the legend of Guy and Pip and will be discussed in Chapter 6.

At the same time, a second love team was just as famous and popular, drawing crowds of fans who were just as passionate about their favourite stars. Vilma Santos and Edgar Mortiz rose to prominence in 1970, making fifteen films together that year alone and going on to make further films together until their last tandem film in 1975 (Llanes 2008c). Inevitably, the two love teams would become rivals, inspiring a fierce loyalty in their fans. Butch Francisco, a member of the Manunuri ng Pelikulang Pilipino (the Filipino Film Critics) wrote about the rivalry between the two love teams:

> The Vilma–Edgar tandem developed its own following and was pitted against Nora and Tirso. The rivalry was so intense between the two love teams that during the staging of one Mr. & Miss RP Movies tilt (the forerunner of today's Box-Office Awards) at the Araneta Coliseum, Vilma was horrified to see fans hurling chairs and empty bottles at one another. At one premiere night, she was pricked with a pin by a fan, obviously from the rival camp. (Francisco 2017)

The pair worked exclusively with Tagalog Ilang-Ilang Productions, a studio owned by lawyer Espiridion Laxa, and recorded with William Leary, Santos's American manager. The Vi-Bot love team worked steadily and won various awards including Most Popular Movie, Radio and TV Love Team of 1971 bestowed by popular magazine publisher Liwayway Publishing Inc.

Stars are constructed images made up of visual, verbal and aural signs that can be found in their work in films and all kinds of media texts as well as aspects of their personal lives made publicly available (Dyer 1979).

This image is constructed by the star, the studios that employ them, and other professionals such as those who work on their physical appearance (for example, hair and make-up artists and stylists) and those who offer training to stars (including acting, singing and dialogue coaches). The star image can be discovered through examining filmic (their primary work – their performances on-screen) and extra-filmic material (interviews, photographs, endorsements, appearances across multiple media platforms and publicity).

This chapter examines the joint love team images of Nora Aunor and Tirso Cruz III, and Vilma Santos and Edgar Mortiz. It will explore how the studio created and initially utilised the love team, and the recurring collaborators that came to be associated with the love teams and the role they played in their success. It also considers alternatives or threats to the love teams, a concept that the studios try to present in a naturalised and inevitable manner but which may have been influenced by a variety of factors including the stars themselves, family members, rival studios and stars, and even the fans. The strategies of love teams in promoting a sense of authenticity for their joint images are discussed, including the question of whether the love was real or reel and how important this was to the love team, as well as the release of semi-biographical songs or songs that otherwise promote the idea that the love team shares a true love and is destined to be together. The joint image is also examined in the press coverage promoting the love teams and shaping the discourse of their partnerships, particularly in terms of endorsements and brand associations, nationally significant holidays and other cultural practices of the era.

Love team beginnings

This section explores the origins of each love team and their studios' early strategies in developing and promoting the stars in film and the media. The joint image of the stars is explored, considering how each star's image combines with their partner's image to form a new joint couple image. The relationship of the love team with the studio is also examined, particularly in terms of the competing interests of the studios and the stars, and the agency (or lack thereof) of stars in their working relationship with the studio. Another aspect of the studio's influence is in the recurring collaborators that play a role in the image of the love team in various ways, whether as mentors, rivals or members of love triangles.

Aunor and Cruz love team

The love team of Nora Aunor and Tirso Cruz III was the result of careful trial and error of multiple partners before hitting on the perfect combination. As Nora Aunor sought to gain roles on television and ultimately film, she was partnered with several young men to see which pairing had the best following. As she was primarily famous for her singing, many of her early appearances were on radio and television shows, where she would be paired with the up-and-coming young men of her age. Her most frequent partners included Edgar Mortiz (ultimately her rival, Vilma Santos's love team partner), Tirso Cruz III and Manny de León. Each star provided a different energy to the tandem.

She was first approached to star in a film for Sampaguita by the legendary star-maker, and himself a director and star of note, German Moreno. He was working at the behest of Doc Jose Perez, the then chairman and son-in-law of the founder of Sampaguita. Both men were to play an important role in the early days of the Aunor and Cruz love team. After signing Aunor to Sampaguita in 1967, Sampaguita went on to establish them in their tried and tested method of a slow build-up during which time Aunor would earn her star billing rather than achieving it instantly.

In a fan-authored biography written by journalist and friend of Aunor Baby K. Jimenez and based upon interviews with Aunor, a more detailed picture of the love team's start emerges. In this account, Aunor first met Cruz on 6 October 1967, around the same time she signed on with Alpha Records to produce her music (Jimenez 1983). Once she had signed on with Sampaguita for films, she began to think about having a love team: 'That time, too, Guy wondered: *uso na ang mga love teams. Sino kaya ang maging kaparehaniya? At sino ang babagay?*' (Love teams were the trend. Who would be her partner? And who was most suitable?) (ibid.: 41). As the account continues, the issue came up on national television during the *Oras ng Ligaya* show she guest-starred in on Tuesdays and Thursdays, when fans debated her two leading men: Tirso Cruz III and Edgar Mortiz. A third star was also in the mix: Eddie Peregrina, with whom she had *The Eddie-Nora Show* (ibid.). Ultimately, Jimenez identifies Aunor's uncle, Sergeant Aunor, as being the one with the final say, deeming Cruz to be the best choice. Aside from her uncle, Aunor's family were all invested to some degree or other and took sides in encouraging her to pursue a relationship with the different men.

Physically, the pair are a study in contrasts, with Aunor a petite 4 feet 11 inches while Cruz towered over her at 5 feet 8 inches tall (see Figure 4.1). In terms of skin tone, they are once again opposites, with Aunor's dusky *kayumanggi* skin contrasting with Cruz's much fairer *mestizo* tone. In terms of their singing voice, the pair complemented each other with her mature contralto and his pleasing pop tenor.

Their nicknames also look complementary together, each being three letters long and a single syllable, forming the pairing of Guy and Pip, the title of an eponymous song and film. Several of their early ensemble appearances included their first tandem film *D' Musical Teenage Idols!* and *Fiesta Extravaganza* (dir. Consuelo P. Osorio 1969). They were later cast in *The Young at Heart,* a double bill feature with the popular love team of the time, Ricky Belmonte and Rosemarie Sonora. They were the couple to beat, with their height, fair skin, and show business and *mestizo* pedigree. Sonora was the sister of the then Philippine Queen of Cinema,

Figure 4.1 Aunor and Cruz are a physically contrasting couple. Source: from the collection of Nestor de Guzman

Susan Roces, while Ricky Belmonte hailed from the showbiz Cruz clan and (in a typically Philippine showbiz twist) was Cruz's first cousin. But perhaps it is this slow build-up that Doc Perez had in mind that was the greatest threat to the Aunor–Cruz love team. Having cast the love team together and achieved early success with it, Sampaguita faced an unexpected challenge in its control over Aunor's star image. This uncertainty represented an unacceptable risk to its business interests and resulted in a legal battle with a rival studio, complete with a rival love team partner.

Star agency, fans and studio control

At this time, Aunor was in a non-exclusive contract with Sampaguita, and was able to make films with multiple studios in the late 1960s with ensemble casts that served as an extended screen test for screen couple chemistry. Perceiving a loophole in her contract, Artemio Marquez of Tower Productions signed Aunor up for several competing films with his studio. In fact, of the eighteen films that Aunor starred in during 1970, ten were with Manny de León at Tower Productions, some of which involved love triangles with either Mortiz or Cruz (Video 48 2008).

The explanation behind their frequent collaboration is due to a legal battle between the Sampaguita studio and Tower Productions (*The Philippine Daily Star* 1970). As Aunor was not exclusive to Sampaguita, she entered into a contemporaneous agreement with Tower Productions resulting in a lawsuit that took years to settle. The reason behind her rival love team with Cruz was that Tower Productions was at the time grooming de León to be the next big teenage star and hoped to achieve this by pairing him with Aunor, the most popular female teen star in the Philippines at the time. To ensure that this love team would not be derailed by fans of the Aunor–Cruz love team, Tower Productions placed Aunor under tight security to ensure that she would not see Cruz nor be seen together with him by fans of that love team (Llanes 2008a). The protracted legal battle plays a role in the path of Aunor and Cruz's love team in the early years.

The legal battle between Sampaguita and Tower Productions over the control of Aunor had multiple dimensions and implications. Firstly, there was the straightforward matter of each studio wanting to secure her exclusive labour. A second layer of complication lay in Aunor's family, which was also fighting for control over the star, with her mother accusing her aunt and uncle (who had been made her guardians) of exploiting her for profit and attempting to wrest control of her career from them (which led to the signing of the competing contract at Tower Productions) (Tolentino 1970). A third issue at hand was Aunor's romantic relationships with her leading men from either studio, Cruz and Manny de León. Studio and familial pressure was also brought to bear on the romantic relationship in order to gain the upper hand in her contractual battle. De León is said to have courted Aunor's family assiduously to win her love, and perhaps their support for the love team. A fourth dimension was the rival groups of fans who took sides and supported the love teams they preferred. All these elements would come together in the ultimate resolution of the complex relationship between Aunor and the studios.

Stars in love teams were routinely encouraged to make the reel relationship real in order to spice up the gossip columns and gain added publicity from the tandem. There was regular speculation about the extent of Aunor's relationships with her leading men. Journalist Nick Joaquin (de Manila 1977) reports that Edgar Mortiz was said to be her first love, while her relationship with Cruz may have shifted from a publicity move to a puppy-love affair. The same was said of Manny de León, but Joaquin writes that de León was more 'assertive' and 'brash' (ibid.: 12–13). Bearing in mind that de León was motivated by the threat of the Sampaguita pairing she had with Cruz, this relationship may also have been primarily cultivated by Tower Productions to keep a tighter grip on Aunor.

Another source, Butch Francisco writing on the website of the Manunuri ng Pelikulang Pilipino, states:

> Over at Tower Productions, she was given a new leading man – the dashing Manny de León, who lost no time winning her heart. Although she still cared very much for Tirso Cruz III, her first and true love, Nora decided to get into a romantic relationship with de León after she felt the pressure from family members who all favoured the new suitor... In Nora's case and by her own admission, it helps that she is in love with her co-star on the set. (Francisco 2017)

This confirms that Aunor was in a relationship with de León, and also explicitly states that she had romantic feelings for Cruz. It also raises the issue of her family's influence in her love team and off-screen romantic relationships. Joaquin also confirms in his account that her family played a role in these relationships, with her mother reportedly siding with de León while her sister preferred Cruz (de Manila 1977). In the same manner, the fans chose a team, with the Tirso fans purchasing the iconic Maria Leonora Teresa for their tandem – 'The Nora–Tirso camp bought that doll, Maria Leonora Teresa for Nora; when they felt that Nora had broken off with Tirso, they reclaimed the doll, handed it to Tirso' (ibid.: 13).[1]

Aunor has taken different approaches to acknowledging if her reel relationships ever turned real. In Joaquin's account, which states that she was seventeen years old at the time, she denies being in love with either partner. In Francisco's, she openly acknowledges that she had loved both Cruz and de León, and that it 'helps that she is in love with her co-star on the set'. In a personal interview in 2016, Aunor confirmed that her family preferred de León as he had courted her family better than Cruz had (Aunor 2016). The Manny de León affair was a tempestuous one, with his reported womanising ways and Aunor's temper. Francisco's (2017) account even claims that she shot a pistol at him that missed during a particularly heated argument. Francisco writes that finally de León ended things, saying that he only courted her because he was forced to (ibid.). Cruz and Sampaguita remained open to Aunor, with Cruz reiterating in multiple interviews that 'all she had to do was go back to the Sampaguita fold where three movies await us' (*Graphic* 1970). This coupled with the fact that Aunor had noticed that she was being overworked and exploited to produce multiple films without her knowledge led to 'The Great Escape', aided and abetted by her three mentors associated with Sampaguita and discussed in detail below.

The 5th Manila Film Festival formed a dramatic backdrop for the battle between Sampaguita and Tower Productions. At the time, Aunor was working for both studios, shooting *Darling* (dir. Artemio Marquez 1970) for Tower Productions on Mondays, Tuesdays and Wednesdays with Manny de León, and then shooting *The Young at Heart* for Sampaguita on Thursdays, Fridays and Saturdays with Tirso Cruz III (Evora 1970a), During this time, Cruz had fallen out of favour with Aunor and her family, and de León was often seen at Aunor's White Plains home in Quezon City. As a result, Aunor's seventeenth birthday was celebrated with Manny de León pictured at her side, first at the premiere of *Darling* and later at her birthday party at home, attended by busloads of fans as well as Aunor's celebrity friends (Ramos 1970a). Fans were divided into two camps, with a Nora–Tirso Fan Club against the Nora–Manny de León Fan Club. At her birthday party, the Cruz camp outnumbered the de León camp and in a sign of mute resistance, raised three fingers to make the Nora–Tirso signal, a popular sign of support for the love team possibly derived from the 'III' in Cruz's name (ibid.).

Later that year, the studios' official entries for the festival were *Nora in Wonderland* (dir. Artemio Marquez 1970) for Tower Productions and *The Young at Heart* for Sampaguita. The films went head to head at the Festival, with both studios guaranteed box-office success, but the real battle came during the Parade of Stars. The parade is a traditional feature of the Festival, with stars riding on a float that features the cast of the film. Aunor was in two films simultaneously, made by two different studios, and with two different leading men representing two of the most popular love teams in the Philippines. Choosing either float would undoubtedly be a political decision that the studios and fans would feel keenly. There was even talk that to avoid the choice entirely, Aunor should ride on her own float. In the end, Aunor chose de León, and rode on the *Nora in Wonderland* float (Evora 1970b). Not giving up without a fight, Cruz rode on *The Young at Heart* float with Maria Leonora Teresa held lovingly at his side, the symbol of his and Aunor's love, and a star in her own right.

Notably, the magazines with a teenage audience at the time often framed the coverage in terms of a romantic spat between Aunor and Cruz rather than a contractual dispute (a narrative that appeared more often in newspaper coverage instead). Figure 4.2 is typical of the magazine content during the time – eye-catching, sensational and deliberately provocative. Newspaper coverage was instead much more interested in the fact that Aunor was being sued for PHP750,000 (about US$127,120 then) for breach of contract, and instead framed the coverage around images and narratives that included Sampaguita head Doc Perez and his kind benevolence towards Aunor and Artemio Marquez (Tower Productions head, formerly of Sampaguita) in the past.

The phenomenon of Guy and Pip was carefully managed and supported by Sampaguita as well as the trio of entertainment figures that took them under their wing. German Moreno, Inday Badiday and Ike Lozada each played a vital role in the love team of Guy and Pip. In fact, German Moreno was the person who first approached Aunor to offer her a contract with Sampaguita which started her acting career. Over the years he appeared with the love team in multiple films, always playing variations of the same character: the bumbling, physically clumsy comic figure, often with a young boy (Romy Lapuz) as his foil, conspiring to push the two together. He also co-directed and wrote several of the love team films under Sampaguita Pictures. Aunor and Moreno hosted television shows together for years as well, cementing their relationship in the eyes of the public. Inday Badiday was a radio reporter and close friend of

Figure 4.2 Magazine article on the separation of Aunor and Cruz, dominated by the word 'TRIANGLE'. Source: from the collection of Nestor de Guzman

Aunor who frequently called fans to arms in support of their love team. Speaking of Badiday, Cruz said, 'She is the high priestess of Guy and Pip love team. She would devote time on her radio program for question and answer regarding our love team. She gives out the latest developments and knows the truth from the rumours' (Lo 2003). As well as acting as supporting cast in their films, Ike Lozada was a singer-songwriter whose songs added to the mythology of the couple. These three individuals and the fans would ultimately intervene in the battle between the studios and emerge victorious.

At the height of the lawsuit between Tower Productions and Sampaguita Pictures over Nora Aunor, Aunor wrote a letter to Badiday confiding in her that she missed Cruz. In response, Badiday called out 'Operation *Kumbento*' (Operation Convent) on air, and the Lucky 12, a group of the most devoted of Aunor's fans, engineered what they refer to as 'The Great Escape' (Llanes 2008a). On 1 May 1971, the Lucky 12 followed as Aunor got in a taxi and left her family and home in Pasig behind her, going straight to the Sampaguita compound where Moreno, Badiday, Lozada and Cruz were waiting for her and immediately began work on *Guy and Pip*. In a personal interview, Aunor recalls the horrified looks on her family's faces as she drove away but recognises that she was a determined person who valued love and following her heart, which favoured Cruz (Aunor 2016). The mayor of Quezon City, Norberto S. Amoranto, issued police security when two cars drove by the Sampaguita compound firing shots one night. The moment of triumph for fans came weeks later during Aunor's birthday when Guy and Pip, Maria Leonora Teresa and their trio of guardians were driven past a massive crowd of fans atop a large bus so they could be seen by all (Llanes 2008a). This celebrated footage later appeared as part of the narrative in *Guy and Pip* (discussed in the next chapter). When Aunor had her debut some time later,[2] Sampaguita threw a big party with the Perez family in attendance and – crucially – Aunor's aunt and uncle (Sergeant Aunor), the couple responsible for signing her contract with Sampaguita, present to represent her family.

The trio of Moreno, Badiday and Lozada would become narrators and presenters in an Aunor–Cruz film, *Memories of Our Love* (dir. Danny Holmsen 1975). The film is different than the love team's other films in terms of its format: it is structured as a documentary that recaps the triumphs and trials of the love team's career through the presenters and archival footage of the pair during publicity for their various films and celebrations, and is interspersed with scenes from their films, often featuring them singing. The total number of songs or musical snippets that the love team either performs or songs that feature the love team in the documentary is forty-two stretched over a run time of 1 hour 49 minutes. The film is introduced by the same man that plays the studio boss in *Young Love* (dir. Tony Cayado 1970), who addresses the audience and tells them that the film will trace the successful careers of Guy and Pip. The audience is then introduced to Moreno, Badiday and Lozada, who take turns reminiscing and telling their personal stories with a strong dose of comedy, which structures the film. The film itself begins by introducing Aunor and Cruz ('Every Cinderella must have her Prince Charming') and then looking at some of their early films and key performances together. It goes on to explore the tragedy of their separation during the legal dispute over Aunor's labour and celebrates the joyful reunion of the pair, even introducing Maria Leonora Teresa as the symbol of the love team. It also places emphasis on the international travel and shoots the love team went on, with segments on Hawaii, California and Japan. After *Guy and Pip*, the film focuses on the love team's transition to more dramatic roles, featuring extended scenes from several films. The film contains no footage of the love team shot specifically for the film but offers something new via its use of archival footage of the pair at public events. The film ends with the presenters noting that fans still hope that Guy and Pip will marry each other in real life and shows footage of their fantasy wedding sequence in *Guy and Pip* along with the song 'Together Again'. 'Together Again' is thus an important song for the love team, and perhaps their most iconic song, emerging years later in the repertoire of those that seek to invoke the legend of the love team in their own performances.

Aunor's star image of drama and suffering thus lent itself towards the joint image of their love team, which consisted of a series of victorious successes and agonising separations with fans watching anxiously as their love team triumphed and struggled. The love team is characterised by a series of dramatic ups and downs, sometimes featuring in magazines as being in love and at other times about to separate, with Maria Leonora Teresa being passed between them as their relationship waxes and wanes (Esteban 1970). Cruz, on the other hand, represented the establishment throughout, siding with Sampaguita and standing firm as an extension of the big studio and the old star system that Aunor is partially credited with helping dismantle through her rise to fame as a television star and the massive power of her superstardom post her love team career when she set up her own production company. The ultimate narrative represents the taming of Aunor's star image to the establishment's will. In the popular magazines of the time, this was equated with the romantic return of Aunor to Cruz, tying the romance and the success of the love team in this particular combination of stars firmly to the prevailing authority of the studio. The relationship between the stars and studio is portrayed as rightful and protected by the full force of the law and the influence of an industrial giant ensuring its investment was secure.

Santos and Mortiz love team

In what may have been a foreshadowing of the trajectory their career would take, the Vilma–Edgar tandem was launched in 1970 in *Young Love*, a joint film with Aunor and Cruz (see Figure 4.3). Santos and Mortiz played a secondary role in the film to the main love team partnership of Cruz and Aunor. In fact, there was no strong theme of romance in their

Figure 4.3 The poster for *Young Love*, featuring all four stars and the two love teams of this research. Source: from the collection of Nestor de Guzman

interactions, but rather they played supporting roles to the main couple, with Mortiz cast as the lower-class neighbourhood friend of Aunor from the countryside while Santos featured as the younger sister of the upper-class Cruz. Perhaps part of the reason they do not pursue a romance in the narrative is because Santos's character is younger than the other three characters, who are portrayed as peers. All the same, they partook in the highlights of the film, including travelling to Tagaytay for a picnic and frolicking among the trees. When Cruz goes to rescue Aunor during the film's climax, Mortiz replaces him onstage at a singing competition, performing a song that is met with enthusiastic applause. Primarily, the role of Mortiz and Santos is to support and defend Aunor and Cruz's fledgling romance in the face of challenges that include class and an overbearing parental figure.

The Santos–Mortiz love team took an approach of stability and even-temperedness in stark contrast to the dramatic highs and lows of the Aunor–Cruz tandem. Their interviews during the early 1970s revolved around several key talking points that included a focus on their career, family obligations and friendship. In several interviews, Santos emphasises their youth and the importance of their burgeoning career, leading interviewers away from the question of romance: 'Whatever destiny dictates for us in the name of love, then let it be for we know it's part of God's plan. For now, I should concentrate on my profession' (Liza Jr 1970c). Romance here is left up to the Almighty; in several interviews, Santos refers to 'God's will' and 'God's plan', while their parents speak of 'God's providence'. The importance of focusing on their career is underlined in multiple interviews as well, indicating that work is prioritised over romance, particularly in the case of Santos, who almost never deviates from this answer. The stability of the tandem soon earned them the title of 'Subok na Matibay, Subok na Matatag', the tagline of the popular Banco Filipino (Filipino Bank), which translates to 'Proven to be Stable, Proven to be Strong'.

The Santos–Mortiz tandem is similar to the Aunor–Cruz tandem in that they look physically contrasting. Santos is much smaller than Mortiz, standing at a petite 5 feet tall, dwarfed by Mortiz's bulkier figure. They also embody the contrast of the *kayumanggi–mestiza* look, but this time in reverse, with Santos's light skin and Chinese heritage *mestiza* looks combining with Mortiz's medium complexion. The pair share a certain roundness to their faces, making them look soft, innocent and sweet (see Figure 4.4).

Figure 4.4 Santos and Mortiz in *Edgar Loves Vilma*

Similar to the Aunor–Cruz tandem, the Santos–Mortiz tandem first met on music-based television variety show programmes where large ensemble casts of teenage stars were often cast together. In an interview in *Liwayway*, Santos recalls that the pair met on the Channel 7 show called *Eskwelahang Munti*. In a separate interview, Mortiz confirms this, and both mention that they were both shy and young, and so nothing of significance took place. This emphasises their similar personalities and also fixes their well-bred manners in the eyes of their fans. The interviews form part of a series featuring all four stars discussing their counterparts, with the provocative titles of 'Vilma Santos Talks . . . The Difference between Tirso and Edgar Mortiz' (Mendoza 1970) and 'Edgar Mortiz Talks . . . Who is Da Best between Nora and Vilma?' (Liza Jr 1970a). The interviews were calculated to attract the maximum readership and created a cross-readership from fans of both love teams. Mortiz's interview details their second meeting at Santos's house during a Christmas carolling session, expressing a wish that they would be matched in a film together, a wish that shortly came true. Because the interview directly pitted the love team partners against each other, both stars also shared their observations about the other love team's leading man and lady, with Santos remarking on the difference between Cruz and Mortiz's voice:

> Tirso and Edgar are very different when it comes to singing. Edgar's voice is more appropriate for sad songs or ballads. He sings with sincerity and soulful expressions – I can really feel the message of his song. For me, he really excels and is number one at this. Tirso? Well, his voice is more suited to pop music. He can also do ballads. But if you ask me about my personal feelings and observation, I prefer him singing pop music. (Mendoza 1970)

Santos consciously or unconsciously highlights a key difference between the two singing leading men in this manner. Cruz sings upbeat and even sometimes rock numbers in his films while Mortiz nearly always sings ballads – soulful songs of heartbreak and love that feature him roaming in a garden. In this manner, he is shot singing in a similar manner to Nora Aunor, and perhaps also reflects his beginnings in the singing contest that earned them fame. Santos goes on to say that Mortiz is the more serious of the two men, saying, 'Edgar is very attractive when the topic is about serious matters. His facial expressions always persuade me to just look at him because I can clearly see the sincerity of his feelings in every word he says.' This extends to his performance style, bringing a much more earnest and quiet touch to his delivery than Cruz, who is much more capable of bombast and intensity.

Mortiz meanwhile goes on to discuss his favourite aspect of Santos – her lips. This is an unexpectedly physical and sensuous attribute for Mortiz to pick up on and stands in sharp contrast to their otherwise completely innocent and mild interviews about their courtship and each other:

> Vilma also has beautiful lips. Don't get me wrong, okay? I mean, the most attractive feature of Vilma is her lips. Especially when she smiles. Ay! If you could only hear other guys say, 'Those kissable lips! Those irresistible lips of Vilma!' (Liza Jr 1970a)

The key strategy used to deflect from any lasciviousness on his own part is to quote the lustfulness of 'other guys' who admire her lips inappropriately. His own love is meant to be read as pure and respectful. In a separate interview, Mortiz confirms his affection for her lips, this time rendering the comments respectable by discussing her other features (some non-physical) as well:

> Her charm, and most of all, her affectionate nature. Vilma has all of these. Her beautiful lips that draws me into her love. She owns my heart. Her tantalizing eyes. Every time I look at her, I want to stop time for me to just look at her for a while. (Liza Jr 1970b)

In these interviews and real life, the spectre of the Aunor–Cruz love team hung over them. Both Mortiz and Santos are asked to give their thoughts on the two stars, with Santos praising Cruz's sense of humour and ability to sing pop songs, while Mortiz praises Aunor's 'speaking eyes' which irresistibly draw his gaze. When asked to name a negative aspect of both Santos and Aunor, his answer is revealing: Vilma laughs too easily, but Nora 'walks like a lesbian' and is 'moody'. He frames these as aspects of her image that can easily be improved upon to ensure that they do not affect their work, but they reveal an underlying bitterness towards Aunor that perhaps has its source in how they attained their stardom in show business. Sharing their origins in winning the same singing contest, *Tawag ng Tanghalan*, Mortiz and Aunor would seem to have been a much more suitable couple. Both stars resemble the masses rather than the luminous gods of the studio with their darker skin, rounded native features and shorter frames. Both are known for singing soulful ballads with plaintive expressions and minimal movement in their performance. And both began their career in an early love team triangle that comprised Aunor, Mortiz and Cruz, on radio, television and films appearing together in box-office successes such as *Oh, Delilah* and *Drakulita* (dir. Consuelo P. Osorio 1969).

These films were shot in the late 1960s before any of the stars had been exclusively contracted to specific studios and before their love teams became set in stone. With less concern about star images and creating a sustainable product for the long haul, these ensemble films were a testing ground of star couples in various combinations. In this early stage, Aunor with Mortiz was just as likely as Aunor and Cruz. The triangle ended abruptly because of intense fan speculation and 'bashing' that took place, resulting in the stars' families intervening. Cruz's mother complained that he was the target of fan displeasure, with fans apparently speculating about the character of his grandfather (the famous band leader and the first of the name Tirso Cruz, the source of the family's fame) and the status of Cruz's parents' marriage, ending by condemning the behaviour of the 'fans, viewers and bashers' of the triangle (Liza Jr 1969). Aunor's mother spoke out on the same issue, citing her husband's unwillingness to allow the tandem to continue. Her mother specifically goes on to deny that Aunor met Cruz secretly in a private room, an accusation made by fans that caused great distress to the family. As a result, speculation and articles were rife that Mortiz's hopes of partnering with Aunor as a love team were dashed, and instead he was paired with Santos, a less skilled singer but beloved child star. In this scenario, fans were able to directly influence the outcome of a potential love team through their negative interactions and behaviour, ultimately pushing the families of the young teens to withdraw them from the triangle to protect their good name.

Physically, Mortiz differed from Cruz's slim build, instead possessing a chubbier frame but almost a head taller than Santos. An article featuring the love team comments on the difference in their builds, noting that Mortiz's bigger frame dwarfs Santos's: 'It was Edgar Mortiz, with his height and size, who looked more like Vilma's bodyguard. If he were slim and shorter, he could pass for her shadow' (*Asia-Philippines Leader* 1971). The author continues to compare their physical features, describing Mortiz as baby-faced. Despite Santos's shorter stature and similarly youthful features, she is portrayed in the article as being the mature one, in no small part because she is a year older than him:

> Edgar Mortiz is, in fact, younger than Vilma Santos who, at 17, is no giggly teenager. She is a woman and she knows it. 'A LOT of people tell me that I am very mature for my age,' she says at the start of the interview. 'I feel it myself. I like to think that I have the mind of a 23-year old woman.' (Ibid., emphasis in original)

The framing of this article casts Santos as a mature woman in charge, relegating Mortiz to the role of immature bodyguard. It continues to feature Santos as the centre of the story, despite discussing their work together and physical closeness, ending with a provocative question. Santos states that she wants to last long in show business, and the final sentence of the article asks, 'Even without Edgar?', a hanging question left up to the imagination of the reader and never actually posed to Santos. Earlier in the same paragraph, the article notes that 'Love teams come and go', raising the possibility of Santos going on to have a solo career separate from Mortiz (ibid.). The focus on Santos is appropriate for a profile on the star, and arguably questions about her career beyond the love team are also fair game. But the overall tone appears to be one of introducing doubt about the suitability of the pair, from appearance to talent. Earlier in the piece, the author raises the question of their singing ability and whether their relationship is real:

> Whether their apparent fondness for each other is the real thing or just plain acting is hard to tell. When not holding hands, which they are most of the time, they have their arms around each other. 'I'm not really a singer,' Vilma admits, 'but Edgar is teaching me how to sing.' (Ibid.)

Santos in this instance turns their disparate singing abilities into a strength, raising it as a bonding point they use to draw them together in his singing lessons for her. The author, however, is also asking whether their love is real or performed for the sake of maintaining the love team, here speculating about it and stating that their physical touches are inconclusive as evidence. When the author goes a step further to question whether Santos ever gets tired of performing with Mortiz, the answer is emphatic: '"Of course not," she says petulantly' (ibid.). It is unusual for an interview in 1971 to have spent so much time picking apart the love team in the concluding paragraph, and Santos is vigorous in her rebuttal of it. This could be explained by the fact that the author was not writing for the popular teenage audience of the teen magazines, but for a non-entertainment magazine.

With such a safe and stable joint love team image, Santos and Mortiz gave the impression of being a natural and certain combination. The downside of this staid dependability was the risk of appearing boring, especially in the face of their dramatic competition in the Aunor–Cruz love team. How did the stars and studio manage this risk in their films and joint image?

Triangulating the couple

Mortiz and Santos is the love team that history remembers the best for the two stars, but they were by no means the only formulation that the studio attempted. Throughout their work together, there was a third star persistently linked to the pair, visible in three of the five films available of the tandem's work together. Jay Ilagan features in triangles in these films, in the first as Mortiz's on-screen sibling and in the second as his best friend and rival for Santos's affections, and in the third instance as a richer alternative to him in a plot that involves her having amnesia and meeting three separate men. Jay Ilagan was a second-generation film star, coming from parents who were famous in the 1940s and a family active in theatre and cinema, including among his relatives a grandfather, Hermogenes Ilagan, known as the father of the Filipino *sarsuwela* (and who wrote the *sarsuwela* that would be adapted into the first locally produced film,

Dalagang Bukid); Marcelino Ilagan, early theatre and film actor and performer of the lead role in *Dalagang Bukid*; and the celebrated director Gerry de León, his uncle. Ilagan began his career as a child star in his mother's film, subsequently becoming one of the most famous teenage stars in the 1970s. He was handsome, *mestizo*, easy-going and had grown up in the public eye, much like Santos. In fact, he was associated with her before Mortiz, and jokingly claimed to be wounded by the new triangle (Francisco 2017). Francisco writes that Mortiz was on the lookout for a new partner after his brief early partnership with Aunor dissolved and was recommended to work with Santos by Cornelia 'Angge' Lee, an actress, talent manager and casting director during the era.

Ilagan first appeared on-screen with Santos when they were both children in a film starring the popular Joseph Estrada before reuniting with her on radio in the late 1960s and starring in triangle films with Mortiz from 1971 onwards (after the Santos–Mortiz love team's uninterrupted first year of work together). The triangle films were a means of introducing more complex plots and character beats for the young stars, thus coming after the initial boy-meets-girl romances that characterised Santos and Mortiz's 1970 works. Santos would go on to star in a total of twelve films with Ilagan, who had a strong career as a dramatic performer beyond his teens, the pair starring in several critically acclaimed films after their transition into mature roles until his death in 1992, outlasting her partnership with Mortiz but never quite achieving the same devoted following (and real romance) as her love team with Mortiz. A 1971 *Teens Weekly* cover shows Mortiz and Ilagan flanking Santos as she sits in a chair with the headline 'Jay–Vilma–Edgar Love Triangle in Real Life?' The three stars appeared able to work together without major conflict despite Mortiz's admission of jealousy towards Ilagan, and the triangle was featured in promotions for their films including an advertisement on the poster for *Tatlong Mukha ni Rosa Vilma* that ran 'Vilma, Edgar and Jay will be at the lobby to greet their fans and give away photos and sign autographs.'

In *Remembrance*, the boys star as sibling rivals for Santos's affections. The roles play on the push and pull of jealousy and brotherly love, demonstrating a close relationship and good-natured rivalry that becomes serious when Ilagan, the older brother, is diagnosed with a life-threatening condition and taken into a 50–50 odds surgery to correct his congenital heart defect. The film takes an interesting and perhaps non-committal approach to resolving the rivalry: it ends with Ilagan's character cheerfully telling his younger brother that the competition for Santos's character will be on in earnest if he gets well, but if he dies, Mortiz is to take care of her in his place. The film's credits play as he is wheeled into the operating theatre, forever unresolved and ending with all characters having behaved nobly in the pursuit of love in the face of the sanctity of family ties.

This is reflective of the general tone of star images and their love team image. Unlike the drama of the Aunor–Cruz partnership discussed above, the Santos–Mortiz tandem thrived on a stolid temperament and a strong work ethic. Rather than emphasise the drama of separation, angst and heartbreak, the studio instead cultivated an air of friendly brotherly rivalry between Ilagan and Mortiz. Part of this was accomplished by allowing them to conclude the film without making an overt choice between the stars (*Remembrance*), or by initially both pursuing Santos and then separate women (*Leron-Leron Sinta*, dir. Emmanuel H. Borlaza 1972). Secondly, Santos only had a personal relationship with Mortiz and not her other love team partners. Thirdly, the films made did not threaten the business interests of the studios by involving stars belonging to rival companies as was the case of Cruz and Manny de León. Ilagan, Mortiz and Santos made their films with Tagalog Ilang-Ilang Productions and did not go through a separation or legal conflict with a rival studio. While magazines and interviews engaged in the standard speculation, as in the *Teens Weekly* cover mentioned above, the stars themselves and the studio maintained a friendly working relationship between the three stars.

The Santos–Mortiz love team could be considered to be the model love team of the era from the point of view of the studios. Compliant, professional, grateful and appealing, the pair came from strong families that encouraged such behaviour and fostered a positive working environment through their multi-generational collaboration with each other. All parties involved were keenly attuned to the opportunities and responsibilities of their roles and adhered to them. The love team could be viewed as being 'good' products of the studios that managed their career, with their phlegmatic cooperation ensuring that things progressed as planned in a dependable if less exciting manner. This also had the effect of differentiating the Aunor–Cruz and Santos–Mortiz love teams and ensuring that there was a broad range of love teams available to appeal to audiences. Taken in isolation, both represent extremes on the spectrum of drama and professionalism, but together, there is just enough in common and just enough difference to ensure that the two love teams complemented each other in terms of their images and appeals.

This chapter deals with the joint love team image of the love teams encountered in their films but also in extra-filmic materials. One of the primary extra-filmic products that the 1970s teenage love team was linked to was music – the means of discovery of two of the stars, and a featured talent of three of the four stars. The following section considers what kinds of songs love teams made, and how these songs impacted the joint images of the love team. The studio's role in leveraging the stars' musical careers to sell the love teams is also of interest along with the themes of their music and how were they integrated into their films.

Love team music

The music of the love teams was often closely related to their films, with both tandems releasing entire albums consisting of the various songs sung during their films, and with films named for the titles of the featured song. The nature of the songs of the jukebox musical are discussed in greater detail in the next chapter as unique features of the genre they worked in. This section is concerned with the original songs written for and about the love teams. There are two main strategies in these songs which bear the stars' names: firstly, that the individual stars sing songs about each other, and secondly, that a third party – a sort of personal love team bard – sings and records songs about the love team, adding to the mythology of the couple. The second approach is unique to the songs of Ike Lozada featuring the Aunor and Cruz love team and made possible by his close association with the tandem and the Sampaguita studio.

The first type of song is dedicated by one partner to the other and follows a fairly simple formula. In 'Then I Met You Edgar', Santos sings that he is the love that she was waiting for, enriching her previously boring existence and answering all her hopes and dreams about a future partner. She also references looking for a 'star' and explicitly names Mortiz as a star in the chorus. Mortiz is described as 'good and kind' in the song and follows the general pattern of his star image crafted by the studio of the era. Mortiz's song is simply titled 'Vilma' and paints a much more idealised portrait of Santos than her more practical ode to him. It references her youth, stating that she is 'only sweet sixteen', a lyric of particular interest as Mortiz was a year younger than her. In the song, the norm of the male partner being older than the female partner is implied through this phrase. It also refers to Santos's popular single titled 'Sixteen', which also features the same phrase in the chorus. The song goes on, and Mortiz likens Santos to the goddess of love and entreats her to be more than just friends because he is in love with her. The theme is carried across to the Aunor–Cruz love team, with Cruz pleading with Aunor to love him in a song titled 'Nora My Love'. Another key song of the tandem is of course Cruz's 'Maria Leonora Teresa', to be discussed in the next chapter.

The second form of love team song was the mythologising numbers of Ike Lozada. The role of Ike Lozada in the Aunor–Cruz love team was that of singer-songwriter, as well as supporting cast in their films. He wrote two songs in particular about the tandem – 'The Ballad of Nora and Tirso' and 'Guy and Pip'. In 'The Ballad', Lozada sings of the perfect love that Aunor and Cruz have for each other, and how he hopes to someday emulate it. The themes of love and marriage are scattered throughout the song, overtly in the verse, directly feeding fan narratives about their favourite tandem at the time. He also describes the fame of the tandem in his lyrics, encouraging the listener to think of them as the best and most loved tandem of their generation: 'They're such a perfect team adored by millions, They both create a scene wherever they may go.'

Lozada's agenda setting in the song paints their love as true, destined for the altar, and references their many enthusiastic fans. His song works to reinforce several 'truths' that fans accepted about their tandem at the time: that Guy and Pip were loving and kind, that their love was true and inevitable, that they and their love would never fade and, finally, it privileges his role in their creation.

In the song 'Guy and Pip', Lozada has a different purpose in mind, but also works to reinforce their love and inevitability. The song was written specifically to celebrate the reunion of the pair after their forced separation by the battle between Sampaguita and Tower Productions. It appears during the opening credits of the eponymous film, augmented by archival footage of Aunor's historic 1971 birthday party, with the credits declaring that the film also stars Lozada, Badiday, Moreno and Maria Leonora Teresa. Like 'The Ballad', the lyrics privilege Lozada's personal connection to the tandem, starting with the lyrics 'I know a story about a young girl and a boy', and then talking about the pair. The song begins by establishing Guy and Pip's love, and then continues to discuss their parting and reunion: 'One day they parted, and I thought that it was the end; Now I'm thanking the good Lord above they're together again!' By referring to Guy and Pip as only 'a young girl and a boy', Lozada makes the story general enough that it could be any girl and boy, only naming them in the chorus, which repeats their names four times. By the second verse, Lozada is talking specifically about Guy and Pip, and makes the reference to their eventual marriage: 'I pray that someday both their hearts will be tied into one.'

The song also functions to mythologise their tandem, their separation and eventual reunion, beginning with Lozada declaring, 'I know a story . . .' and ending with him declaring, 'That's the end of my story . . .'. It also adopts increasingly religious language towards the end: 'Let's sing together and rejoice this happy day . . .', exhorting listeners to forget the painful separation of the past as a happily ever after is at hand: 'That's the end of my story: they're together at last!' In this manner, the studio harnessed another means of marketing their stars through the popular music of the era. Not only did they employ the cross-media promotion that records and the radio allowed, they also utilised another recognisable employee who played a visible role in the love team and in the radio world to do so. The practice of writing songs around the names of their stars allowed them to remain current whether on film or over the airwaves. The songs also provided the studio with another means to craft the singer's star image as well as the star image of the star being sung about, shaping the teenage girls into young, desirable paragons of virtue being wooed by earnest, devoted and lovesick teenage boys. The narratives of the love team's joint image contained in the song indicates which elements the studio wished to foreground (the true love between the stars and the suggestions of forever) and those which it elided or diminished (Mortiz's age and the legal battle between Sampaguita and Tower Productions reduced to a lovers' 'parting').

Both love teams also produced 'destination' albums built around their Hawaiian feature films. Releasing albums that contained a film's musical numbers was a common means of cross-promotion employed by the studio. The Hawaiian albums of stars are of interest because they reflect a complex love affair with the island and what it signifies. While the obsession with Hawaii on film is not unique to the Philippines, the attraction also relies on the colonial ties between the United States of America and the Philippines. Hawaii is the state that Filipinos went to at the turn of the twentieth century to work as labourers on the sugarcane plantations, eventually resulting in a large migrant population that were exploited as being the cheapest form of labour available at the time (Teodoro Jr 1981). The travel film thus took on a larger significance of allowing Filipino stars to behave as symbolic tourists in a place of historical exploitation, a place that is also the home of Filipino expatriates and migrant workers (and thus, fans).

The choice of Hawaii also reflects a lingering colonial affection for America and the fantasies it offers. José Capino writes on this colonial legacy:

> In both the most extravagant and the most mundane of Filipino national daydreams, the American presence looms large .... American fantasies are transcultural imaginings defined by an American presence. The American landscape and its built environment – Central Park and the Golden Gate Bridge – furnish the setting for the triumphs and tragedies of Filipino nurses and migrant laborers. The stylistic and ideological features of Hollywood films that are present in Filipino movies constitute yet another example of such American fantasies. (Capino 2010: xix)

The love teams in this instance frolic through American landscapes, their leisure experiences of the islands an act of exploring the fantasy holiday location of Hawaii in the American empire on equal footing, and perhaps signalling their participation in global culture, or a cosmopolitanism acquired through their international travel and filmmaking (ibid.: xx).

Aunor made a solo album entitled *Blue Hawaii*, Cruz a solo album entitled *Hawaiian Souvenirs*, and Santos and Mortiz a joint album entitled *Aloha My Love*. All three albums have at their heart two basic assumptions: that Hawaii is exotic, and that Hawaii is linked inextricably with love. The tracks feature such titles as 'Aloha Oe', perhaps the most internationally recognisable Hawaiian song, a sprinkling of generic love songs and other markers of 'Hawaiianness' including references to the reef, paddles, sails, hulas and grass shacks in their titles. Some tie Hawaii overtly to love including 'The Hawaiian Wedding Song' and 'To You Sweetheart, Aloha'. Aunor's and Cruz's individual albums also take the unusual step of having both stars cover the same songs, but not as duets. This includes 'To You Sweetheart, Aloha', 'Beyond the Reef', 'Blue Hawaii' (referring to their 1972 film *My Blue Hawaii*) and 'Little Grass Shack'. These songs seem selected for containing the most stereotypical 'Hawaiianness' for a foreign audience as well as foregrounding the association between the two stars even through their solo projects. 'Beyond the Reef' is uniquely shared among all three albums, though the Santos–Mortiz album notably features more generic love songs than those that fetishise Hawaii.

The overall effect of this was to have all four stars and the two love teams remain competitive and offer roughly the same products of

'Hawaiianness' in 1972 in variations on the same theme. The title of Aunor and Cruz's *My Blue Hawaii* is also a direct reference to another popular musical film set in Hawaii: Elvis Presley's *Blue Hawaii* (dir. Norman Taurog 1961). Presley was another star closely associated with Hawaii and produced several albums and concerts there. In fact, Presley and Aunor share the song 'Blue Hawaii' in both films, which suggests that the studio was at least relying on the association between the two films in crafting Aunor's image that year. Hawaii brings to mind an air of leisure and sophistication and is perennially associated with the luxury once-in-a-lifetime dream honeymoon for lovers. The press was not blind to this association and speculated if Santos and Mortiz had got married off-screen as well as on-screen while shooting *Aloha My Love* (dir. Emmanuel H. Borlaza 1972), as discussed below (Juan 1972).

One of the main goals of the songs written about the love teams was to lend authenticity to the stars and their romance. Authenticity is an important aspect of stars that help create a sense of trust and relatability between stars and the audience. When applied to the film couple, authenticity becomes even more important in terms of how the couple positions their work and personal relationships. The following section discusses the love teams in terms of their authenticity, considering the importance of real relationships, how this affects the love team's performance and how the audience consumes the love team. The strategies of the love team in negotiating questions about their relationship from the press and their evolving relationships at different times of their career and love team is also of interest. The 'real' and 'reel' are terms that have been discussed at several points in this book, and this section considers the role of the fictional and the real in the love team image.

The distinction of authenticity

A common practice of studios with love teams is to build an aura of destiny and inevitability around the stars' partnership. To this end, love teams are encouraged to behave and speak in certain ways. This section documents the founding, challenges and general love team images that the studio built around the four teenage stars as well as how the relationship was discussed by the stars and written about in the press. The Guy and Pip tandem is used to explore the benefits of a love team cultivating a 'real' relationship, while the Vi and Bot tandem presents various styles of coverage and lines of questioning from the press about their relationship, revealing an evolving strategy over the course of the love team's time together. At times true love is paramount, while at others a sense of professionalism is privileged instead.

Love teams often provoke the question, 'Is it real or reel?' Studios often direct stars to blur the lines as much as possible to encourage this sort of speculation by fans for several reasons. The love team of Guy and Pip illustrates several of the benefits of being both an on- and off-screen couple. In a private interview with the author, Aunor stated that her relationship with Cruz was real and 'on and off for 12 years' (Aunor 2016). Because of the stormy nature of Aunor's life, this made for a lot of drama in the romance, even once the cameras stopped rolling. As discussed in the previous chapter, drama is a key factor of her image. Her highs and lows were taken by fans to be their own, and they rallied around her in good times and bad. Similarly, fans had a very real and serious emotional investment in the tandem. Their parting was a sorrow shared by thousands, and often involved fans intervening to try to save the relationship, congregating by the busload outside of Aunor's and Cruz's houses to anxiously look for any signs of discord or unity (Aunor 2016). All of this of course put pressure on two teenagers to satisfy the 'dictates' of the fans, sometimes to their own detriment (Aunor 2016). This was further complicated by Aunor's family taking sides against Cruz and for Manny de León, the partner she fled at Tower Productions.

There are several benefits of a real romance in love teams. Firstly, there is the emotional investment of fans in the tandem as being a real and tangible thing, discussed above. Secondly, the 'real' love of the pair had the effect of legitimising the films as being 'real' also and allowing fans to witness the private relationship of their love team made public. Dyer (2004) argues that it is the unrehearsed and natural moments that are perceived to be the 'realest' or most 'authentic' aspects of the stars. They also point to a revelation about the star – an uncovering of a truth that was previously hidden. Fans viewed a touch from Cruz's character as a touch from Cruz himself. The love in Aunor's character's eyes when gazing at Cruz's character was also read as her real love for him. Thus, their films can be read as a series of adventures for the young lovers to screen to their fans – an episodic telling of their love story. The slippages between the real and reel reinforced each other, becoming bound up in the overarching narrative of the love team as true and inevitable love.

Thirdly, and from an industrial standpoint, their real relationship helped to fill the periods between their films with a series of speculations, dramatic episodes, rescues and triumphs for fans that fantasy simply could not come close to replicating. The speculation and stories about Guy and Pip were a feature of entertainment media in the early 1970s, generating and feeding a multimedia and profitable micro-industry around the tandem alone. And finally, the real relationship of Guy and Pip fed into the fairy-tale nature of their partnership, with a bond so strong it transcended class, the trials and tribulations of the partnership, family disapproval and gossip to hopefully emerge someday as a happily ever after, immortalised in song and film. *Sinderella* meets her Prince Charming, and they live happily ever after. And even if they aren't together now, who is to say they won't be again someday? That is the hope that keeps the dream of Guy and Pip alive to the present.

In a similar vein, *Liwayway*'s coverage of the Santos–Mortiz tandem is geared towards encouraging speculation about 'forever' and 'marriage'. In one issue, it ran a headline 'Are Vilma and Edgar Headed for the Altar?' with an article that opens with a baiting sentence, 'Vilma and Edgar's wedding was held in Hawaii' (Juan 1972). The opening paragraph goes on to describe the on-set wedding they had for the taping of *Aloha My Love*, suggesting that during the taping 'their faces shone with total happiness and they were wondering when their own moment would come', and the paragraph ends with the question, 'When?' (ibid.). The same article features a fan quote that demonstrates the deep regard for the love team and how it ties back into the fans' aspirations and spiritual life: 'We pray for that [their wedding] because you know Vi is for Bobot and Bobot is for Vi only. They really are a perfect match' (ibid.). *Liwayway*'s coverage of the screen wedding concludes with observations of the stars in real life, stating that their families get along well:

> They look like one big happy family. That's why there really is a possibility they'll soon become real families through Vi and Bot, if and only if, the sweetness, caring and love they show to each other is real and not just in the films they make. (Ibid.)

The strategy of invoking the family to strengthen claims of real romance is a popular one with Philippine love teams and highlights the importance of not just the family unit but the goal of setting a new family up through marriage – a union of families. The tandem of Aunor and Cruz demonstrates a struggle between star, parents and studio for control over the underaged Aunor.

In contrast, the teens of the Santos–Mortiz love team had a different experience with their parents in moulding their star images. Santos's and Mortiz's parents took an active and united role in overseeing their careers, playing an alternate role of guiding, guarding, encouraging and advising their children to maintain a professional work ethic, prioritise their careers and treat each other respectfully. Interviews describe their mothers as working together during their shoots, even cooking to ensure that the families would have lunch while shooting on location (Santos 1971). Their parents also take on the role of hosts to the fans that come to their houses in Quezon City, ensuring that their needs are met and working as intermediaries between star and fan, sometimes providing a buffer to allow the teenage stars to sleep in a little after a shoot and keeping the assembled fans quiet until their rising (Juan 1971).

Popular coverage would often put the teenagers on the spot by asking the same question again and again: is it *really* love, or just pretend? In an early article that tries to pick apart the relationship, Santos is strident in her defence of the partnership. In more friendly coverage in *Liwayway*, Santos is careful to avoid committing fully to the relationship. Her discourse on the love team is built around the uncertainty of predicting the future in an article provocatively entitled "'If We're Not Really Destined for Each Other . . .' – Vilma Santos' (Ocarizawa 1971). In this article, she demurs, saying that it is hard to say if she and Mortiz are really destined for each other. Destiny plays a big role in her language, and she employs a much more philosophical approach to discussing their pairing:

> Why? We cannot dictate time. It's not always and all of the time that destiny goes along with what we want to happen. It depends on the situation. If we really are for one another, then it's also up to us to work on it. (Ibid.)

The practical language extends to her description of her relationship with Mortiz, when she says that she can only with real accuracy say that they are best friends, and that friendship is the beginning of love. She does not deny that he is courting her but explains that her affection for him is not just because of courtship but because they are best friends. The real/reel dichotomy is a commonly raised question in discussing love teams (and stars). In the search for authenticity, it becomes vital to uncover some hidden truth or shred of an essence that speaks to the real nature of the star. With relationships, particularly those that look compelling on-screen, the interest is doubled as though driven by the double stars that pose the question. In this article, Santos explains her 'sweetness' towards Mortiz as reflective of her care for him, saying, 'I'm a close friend of him, a sister sometimes and his good advisor' (ibid.). In a final bid to quell fan demands for their imminent marriage, Santos outright denies that she is currently in love with him:

> My heart doesn't long for Bobot right now. It's funny and weird but it's true. My heart now belongs to my movie career. I love my profession as well as Bot's career. I don't want to destroy this just because of issues of the heart. For now, I will concentrate more on my profession. No thoughts about marriage. (Ibid.)

But this coverage, dated November 1971, represents an about-face for the tandem. A May 1970 article featuring Mortiz, titled '"Why Do I Love Vilma Santos?" – Edgar Mortiz', takes a diametrically opposing position. Mortiz addresses questions that their relationship is a 'publicity gimmick' with a strong rebuttal, speaking in terms of love, jealousy and possessiveness. When asked if he has declared his true feelings to Santos yet, Mortiz answers in the negative but goes on to make a public declaration:

> You all know that I'm a shy man that is why even though I want to express my feelings towards her, I stop myself. I am worried and afraid of what she'll have to say. I don't want us to have a grudge towards one another. I don't want to lose one of my inspirations. But I know Vilma already knows my feelings towards her. So now I am declaring my feelings to Vilma in public. I really love you, Vilma. (Liza Jr 1970b)

Jealousy appears to be a feature of the love team, brought up in both articles. In this one, Mortiz acknowledges that he has a tendency towards jealous and over-protective behaviour, referring to an incident with fans 'bashing' Santos that she prevented him from intervening in. At the end of his declaration of love, Mortiz mentions his intense jealousy when Santos was matched up with Jay Ilagan in a solo project: 'I don't want Vilma with some other guy. I want her with me. One time, they matched her with Jay Ilagan. I felt so much jealousy then' (ibid.). In her own interview two years later in '"If We're Not Really Destined for Each Other . . ." – Vilma Santos', she brings up his possessiveness and jealousy as being two flaws in Mortiz that she dislikes and as the root of their misunderstandings

(Ocarizawa 1971). The change in the tone of the article and Santos's attitude towards the love team is summarised by the closing sentences:

> But if we're not really for each other in real life, maybe that's our luck. Maybe we're not really destined to be as one heart. I believe that love is a struggle, for that is part of our life. To suffer is to love. (Ibid.)

The shift in tone during the course of their love team is closely related to their age and popularity. Early on in the tandem, the pair encouraged the articles and passionately defended their pairing, real and reel. Team-ups with other stars were framed as sources of jealousy and anguish, and grand declarations of love made publicly. Two years on, cool logic was applied to the language of their partnership, with destiny and suffering leading the way. One year later, Santos would turn from making love team films to the next stage of her career, starring in roles that shifted her persona towards Darna, the Philippine *komiks* superhero in a suit that bared more flesh than her teenage career would allow her to. By then, Santos would be twenty, Mortiz would be nineteen, and their love team films would disappear to eventually give way to Santos's mature career that made her the face of several films of the Second Golden Age of Philippine Cinema.

Some would argue that in this love team Mortiz always loved more, and that Mortiz always stood to lose more. It is the case that Mortiz did not sustain much of a career post love team, gaining further weight and ageing out of his baby-faced looks, eventually turning to successful work behind the camera as a director on popular variety television with ABS-CBN. Perhaps the strength of his declarations could also be attributed to the norm of the male partner being the aggressor in romantic relationships in the Philippines, while the female partner is meant to be demure and pure. This was more in line with his earnest image as a balladeer and her mature image with eleven years in show business under her belt by the age of twenty.

The other main means of encountering the love teams outside their films and their music was in the press, particularly in the popular teenage magazines that they regularly featured in. Of interest are the attitudes of the Philippine press towards the love teams in the early 1970s and the difference between their coverage in entertainment magazines and the newspapers. The narratives that the press circulated about the love team in these publications formed one of the chief extra-filmic materials that shaped their star images through their coverage in various sections and formats.

In the press

In late 1969 and early 1970 when both love teams were in their early stages and worked within a series of ensemble cast performances and their first love team films, Philippine print media was split into two worlds. The first was the English language newspapers which prioritised hard news stories and entertainment stories from Hollywood, along with a smaller number of selected stories about local stars (usually mature and *mestizo*). The second was the teenage magazines written in Tagalog and aimed at an entirely different audience with a broad mixture of articles and comics series. An example of the former would be a newspaper such as *The Philippine Press*, while the latter included among others *Kislap Graphic* and *Liwayway*. It was among the latter that love teams and Philippine stars found their home.

A brief discussion of the differing content helps to contextualise the class-fragmented society that Guy and Pip were born of. A selection of articles from *The Philippines Free Press* at the time reveals daily articles about the Marcos presidency, international news, advertisements for industrial or farming machinery, a society section with glamourous pictures, and the entertainment section, which carried reviews and advertisements for films starring John Wayne, Vanessa Redgrave, Rita Hayworth, Gina Lollobrigida, Peter O'Toole, Mae West, Brigitte Bardot, Elizabeth Taylor, Mia Farrow and Raquel Welch. These stars have in common a mature or exotic image, performing either the sex symbol or the symbol of law and order, the mature establishment of civilised behaviour. Articles in the newspaper also point to a gap in the audience for Tagalog films among the upper class; for example, in one interview a young activist student dismisses Tagalog films as corny and only for his parents, with his preferred film of choice being similar to those starring Sidney Poitier (Reyes 1969).

Providing something of a middle ground in these papers were the more sophisticated local stars or the older, more established ones who sometimes appeared in the social section of the paper such as Pancho Magalona (screen idol of the 1940s). They proved unable to avoid young love teams entirely and *The Philippines Free Press* featured the love team of Hilda Koronel and Ed Finlan in its 14 February 1970 Valentine's Day special. It is worth noting, however, that Hilda Koronel was born Susan Reid, and between Finlan's and her exotic *mestizo* looks, they appealed to the upper-class audience that primarily read the paper. Appearing in the same publication on 31 January 1970 was the famous article by Jose F. Lacaba, 'Notes on Bakya: Being an Apologia of Sorts for Filipino Masscult', which opens with a quiz:

> LET'S BEGIN with a little quiz. Identify the following:
>
> a) 'Mardy'
> b) *Orasyon na naman*
> c) Nora Cabaltera Villamayor [Aunor's birth name]
> d) *Pilyo, nguni't* clean fun
> e) Ricky *Na*, Tirso *Pa*
>
> If you don't even get one answer right, you are, if not a foreigner, either a hopeless bourgeois or an incurable egghead. But if you guess . . . congratulations: you are a true connoisseur of *bakya* . . . . *bakya* now means anything that is cheap, gauche, naive, provincial, and terribly popular; and in this sense it is used more as an adjective than as a noun. (Ibid.)

In his article, Lacaba neatly describes the gulf between classes in their cultural consumption. If it is mass, it is 'cheap, gauche, naive, provincial, and terribly popular' – in short, Guy and Pip, and Vi and Bot on one hand, and Sidney Poitier and Vanessa Redgrave in English language films on the other.

From 1970 onwards, Aunor and Cruz dominated the pages of *Kislap Graphic* and *Liwayway*, sharing a monopoly of the cover with their rival tandem, Santos and Mortiz, or appearing solo on the cover with the certainty of a mention of their screen partner in the articles within. The headlines and images of the period formed much of the discourse framing the couple, with most themed around speculation about whether their partnership was real off camera, whether their real and reel relationships would last, whether they were iconic as a love team or whether they were fading already. In 1970, a pervasive theme was the rival love teams of Aunor and Cruz versus Aunor and de León. The press phrased this in such a manner that it became clear that the only threat to the popularity (and relationship) of Aunor and Cruz was the popularity (and relationship) of Aunor and de León. Headlines in *Liwayway* such as 'Tirso Cannot Defeat Manny?' (*Liwayway* 1970d) and 'What Chaos Will Result if Nora and Tirso Reconcile?' (*Liwayway* 1970e) pitted Aunor's leading men against each other regularly. Interviews featured speculation of whether de León caused the break-up of Aunor and Cruz, and quotes from de León stating that he believed Aunor and Cruz to be sweethearts in the movies only

(*Liwayway* 1970c). However, *Liwayway* was careful to also reinforce Cruz's status as Aunor's leading man by including them both in a supplementary issue for a contest sponsored by Tropicana to find 'The Most Popular Movie, Radio, TV Loveteam of 1970' (*Liwayway* 1970a). In the article, which called for votes, four main love teams were featured: Aunor and Cruz, Santos and Mortiz, Esperanza Fabon and Eddie Peregrina, and Hilda Koronel and Ed Finlan.

Liwayway also featured Aunor and Cruz (and teenage stars in general) as fashion models in its fashion section. The tandem modelled 1970s couture, either for Torino's fashion house in Quezon City (*Liwayway* 1970b) or the work of local designer Ernie Ma. Santiago (*Liwayway* 1970f), in a series of photos that showcased the bright colours, bold patterns, neckerchiefs, waistcoats, bell bottoms and short dresses of the era (see Figure 4.5). Love teams tended to be featured in the same collection, usually prominently pictured next to each other. In their films, Guy and Pip were also positioned as teenage icons of fashion, either appearing immaculately dressed or with

Figure 4.5 A typical example of a fashion layout from *Liwayway* featuring Aunor and Cruz. Source: from the collection of Nestor de Guzman

Aunor's character achieving the right dress through a shopping makeover once she was on her way to becoming famous (as seen in *Young Love*). Wearing the right kind of clothes for achieving the right public image featured as a plot point in *Young Love* and marks the turn of the character's fortune as well as her ability to match the snobbish girlfriend of Joey, who looks at her scornfully. Another fashion statement Aunor and Cruz made was during their visits to cold countries for shooting films.

The tandem was frequently featured in the studio happenings sections of teenage magazines, or sometimes with a full feature article dedicated to their off-screen exploits in or around their work environment. These photos included scenes of them facing a throng of fans at the premiere of their films or arriving at an event such as their coronation as Box Office King and Queen in 1971 (*Liwayway* 1971b). As the tandem grew more popular and well established, this included overseas shoots, among them the shooting of *My Blue Hawaii* and *A Gift of Love* (dir. Danny Holmsen and German Moreno 1972) in Hawaii and *Winter Holiday* (dir. Jose De Villa 1972) in Japan (see Figure 4.6). These tended to feature images that emphasised the exotic nature of their location, with pictures of Aunor in a kimono in Japan as well as pictures and scenes in the films of the pair bundled in various thick winter jackets and bobble hats in snow. These photos and scenes provided a glimpse of exotic and exciting foreign environments to the audience and showed the pair navigating these places together in a quintessentially Filipino style – the place was foreign, but the adventure shared with their favourite local icons. Trips abroad also conferred an increased intimacy and progress in the couple's relationship, and in an article written shortly after their return from Hong Kong, the tandem had to deny that they had got married there as rumours swirled (*Liwayway* 1972b).

Together, the love team were the endorsers of Philips transistor radios, appearing in a long-running print campaign in *Liwayway*. The advertisement featured the pair with their heads touching and a Philips radio, with print that read, 'Guy and Pip say: "Philips has a more natural sound"'. The advertisement relies on the musical talents of the tandem to lend weight to their endorsement of the radio's sound. The rest of the copy emphasises the radio's 'true to life', 'colourful' and 'unique' sound, words also associated with the love team's image. Aunor and Cruz were also endorsers of Coca-Cola (Coke) at the same time but appeared individually in print ads that ran in *Liwayway* among others. Coke leveraged their youthful and lively teenage personas to market the drink with the

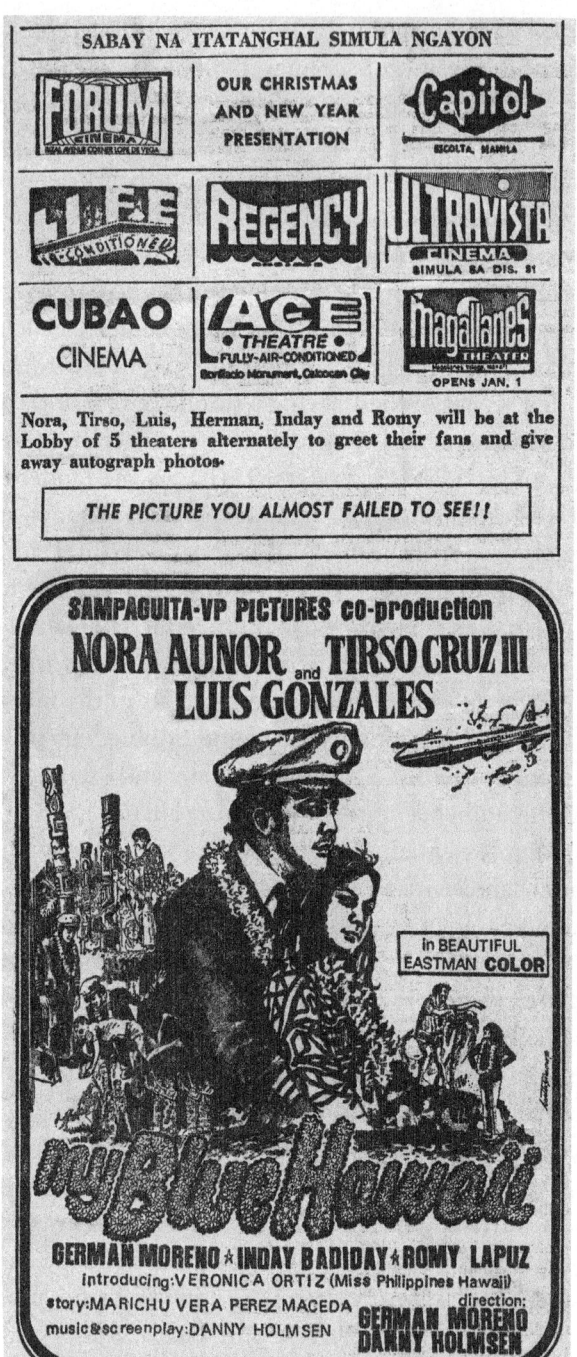

Figure 4.6 The poster for *My Blue Hawaii*, featuring garlands and carved wooden tiki. Source: from the collection of Nestor de Guzman

same characteristics – young, wholesome and fun. In *Young Love*, the characters of Aunor and Mortiz (whom alongside with Santos were also ambassadors for Coke) buy and hand out Coke bottles to their friends.

Liwayway often featured Aunor and Cruz around important Philippine calendar events, such as the Valentine's, Christmas and New Year's specials. These issues sought to allow fans an intimate glimpse of their stars during their favourite celebrations, especially Valentine's Day as a celebration of love, and Christmas and New Year's Day as the family-oriented time for giving and renewal. The Valentine's Day covers and articles include the 1971 issue which featured speculation about which of Aunor's leading men was her true Valentine – Cruz, de León or Victor Laurel (*Liwayway* 1971a). The magazine left the fans in no doubt about the answer though: later in the issue, a full-page colour poster titled 'Liwayway 1971 Valentine' featured Aunor and Cruz together. The following year featured the headline 'Guy is the Most Loved "Valentine" of Pip', with a picture of the pair and red roses on the cover. In the studio happenings section within, *Liwayway* printed pictures of them singing during a televised Valentine's special on KBS Channel 9.

Christmas specials tended to foreground their families and traditional elements of their images. The 1970 Christmas cover featured Cruz giving a present to Aunor, while the articles within leaned heavily on their individual families. Aunor's article revolved around her hope of having a family reunion for Christmas, while Cruz's article featured pictures of his role as the baby Jesus in the nativity film *Ang Pagsilang ng Mesiyas* and an interview with his parents about their son. The following year saw the pair on the cover again, this time foregrounding their musical talents and traditional values. Cruz plays a guitar while Aunor sings from a carol book, the pair standing in front of a traditional *bahay kubo* (wooden hut) with a bright *parol* (Christmas lantern) hanging prominently from the house. The hut and the *parol* are traditional elements of Philippine culture that serve to represent tradition and Christmas alongside the modern yet traditional teenage love team on the cover. New Year's covers tended to focus on framing the coming year around the love team, with the 3 January 1972 issue of *Liwayway* asking, 'Is 1972 Still the Year of the Nora–Tirso "Love Team"?' (1972a).

Another memorable cover featured Aunor and Cruz kneeling in prayer with Aunor holding a rosary as they pray before a stained-glass window depicting Jesus praying in the garden of Gethsemane in the final hours before his arrest and subsequent death, released in time to mark

Holy Week and Easter (*Liwayway* 1972c). The photo is sombre in tone, both heads bowed in prayer. The religious iconography and devotion are recurring elements of their joint image that appear in their films as well, discussed in detail later in this chapter. Care is taken to frame the two teenagers as upholding traditional Philippine values, such as Roman Catholicism, respect for elders, and modest and appropriate behaviour, a practice that is visible in all of their magazine covers. They are never shown kissing on the lips or in any explicit physical displays of affection beyond hand holding, leaning their heads together or a casual hug. Aunor in particular is carefully modest in her image, sometimes covering her head in a scarf or appearing with a veil covering her hair as she kneels in prayer on at least one other occasion than the 3 April cover (*Liwayway* 1972c).

The Santos–Mortiz tandem is the more elusive of the two love teams, dwarfed both historically by the coverage granted to the Aunor–Cruz love team as well as in the present reality of materials preserved in the National Archives of the Philippines. As such, a far more limited database on the tandem is present. The imbalance stretches over to their fans, with Vilmanians being much less inclined to share their thoughts on their favourite star as the Noranians during my fieldwork. Fans of the Santos–Mortiz love team have long felt that the press favours Aunor and Cruz, complaining to the writers of *Liwayway*, as featured in one article:

> We once went to ABS-CBN's cafeteria to talk to the director of one of the shows of Vilma and Edgar. Out of nowhere we were persecuted by one of Vi and Bot's fans.
> 'Why do you always have an interest in Nora and Tirso but not Vilma and Edgar?'
> 'But Vilma and Edgar are always in our magazine! And it is almost 2 pages or 3.'
> 'Definitely! But why not on the front page?'
> 'Oh! Even in calendars,' we answered while smiling. (Juan 1972)

Similarly, the availability of films featuring the pair is severely limited, possibly because while Sampaguita's collection was taken over by ABS-CBN, it is not clear what happened to the archives of TIIP. Video 48 is a video rental and DVD sales shop located in Manila. Despite consisting primarily of VHS tapes as well as personal recordings of televised films, Video 48's collection is possibly the best archive for older films outside of private collections, and many film directors, stars, critics and students visit the store to track down difficult to find films. Even in this collection, only five films featuring the tandem exist, a number which is particularly low taking into consideration the fact that the pair produced fifteen films together in 1970 alone.

Conclusion

Questions of agency, authenticity and passionate love are bound up inextricably in the love team of Aunor and Cruz. Caught between the corporate, personal and public natures of their image, the love team was constantly under pressure from various quarters to embody an authentic 'real' relationship that fed into the official narratives set out for the love team: love the 'right' boy and choose the 'right' love team partner (two widely differing concepts nonetheless bundled together due to the nature of their work), work with the 'right' studio and please the 'right' relatives. As a result, the push and pull between the corporate, personal and public led to a sense of unpredictability and drama in the joint couple image, bolstered by the strong personalities of the two stars involved.

On the other hand, the love team of Santos and Mortiz earned a reputation for steady and professional work, an ethic encouraged by the pair's middle-class parents and studio. A team born of less conflict, the pair prized their work and careers, embodying a different kind of romantic relationship. As they matured, their discourse also shifted further away from emphasising the romantic to longevity and professional development, highlighting the individual star, rather than the couple, closer to their eventual separation. Discussing a future without the love team was something that Santos was more comfortable with than Mortiz, indicating a possible imbalance in prioritising the love team and also ultimately symptomatic of the trajectory of their individual careers beyond the love team.

The following chapter is an in-depth examination of the genre of the teenage jukebox musical in the Philippines and its music and conventions. It will examine Aunor's other commonalities with Elvis Presley in terms of genre and star image and lay out the common aspects of the genre's *mise en scène*, particularly the settings of their films and where the teenage stars are encouraged to be and discouraged from being. The love teams' performances in two of their films will be examined along with the cinematographic strategies in filming the love team films set in the studio and how the studio is shot and portrayed in the teenage jukebox musical.

Notes

1. Accounts of Maria Leonora Teresa's purchase differ. Another interview with Cruz indicates that his mother purchased the doll for Aunor from a store in Carriedo Street (Ramos 1970b).
2. The debut is a traditional Filipino coming-of-age celebration which celebrates a young woman's eighteenth birthday.

Chapter 5

Filming the couple: the teenage jukebox musical genre

Introduction

The love team films of the 1970s in the Philippines are under-explored, and this includes their genre. Noted cultural academic and critic Bienvenido Lumbera (from whom I borrow the term 'jukebox musicals') wrote of the films of Aunor, Santos, Cruz and Mortiz, 'In the one genre that was specifically aimed at the young – the jukebox musical – flimsy narrative was employed for the sole purpose of stringing together musical numbers performed by teenage pop singers glamourized by television and the recording industry' (2011: 40).

His discussion of the genre is entirely couched in terms of a crisis: the quote comes from a section titled 'Rampant Commercialism and Artistic Decline (1960–1975)' in a chapter titled 'Problems in Philippine Film History'. Lumbera also highlights a key criticism against the genre that is often made, namely, that the musical numbers lack merit because they are not integrated, nor do they directly contribute to the plot and drive the narrative forward. The very definition of a jukebox musical lies in incorporating previously popular songs in a film, part of another criticism of unoriginality. Furthermore, Lumbera's quote appears to distinguish between stars produced by the cinema and those 'glamourized' by television and the recording industry. This is a reaction in some way to the new mode of star production in the Philippines that was moving from the cinema to the television, and particularly Aunor's and Mortiz's stardom, made possible by winning a talent contest rather than being selected from a chosen demographic by a studio head as was previously the route to achieving stardom.

Taken in its wider context, this quote reflects a particularly turbulent time in Philippine cinema history, with the large studios on the verge of shutting down, popular stars freelancing and starting their own production companies, the rise of the more political *bomba* (soft porn films) cinema, and coming immediately before the celebrated Second Golden

Age of Philippine Cinema, a period much better explored academically in its auteur films and social commentary plots. Certainly, teenagers singing love songs to each other while their peers are arrested on the streets makes for a startling contrast in an era with increasing authoritarianism. But this also comes on the heels of a global youth revolution that arrived belatedly in the Philippine national consciousness in the late 1960s and turned teenagers for the first time into a socially cohesive group and a consumer market, and it builds on similar successes internationally such as Elvis Presley in the 1950s (whose generic similarity to Aunor is discussed below) and the Beatles in the 1960s. In the following chapter, the ideological implications of the youth and authoritarianism are a key focus. To critics of the period, the teenage jukebox musical seemed little more than a spectacle designed to distract the masses from important national issues.

This chapter first examines the Philippine teenage jukebox musical genre as largely consisting of unintegrated numbers that consist of covers of popular songs, or films where the songs do not drive the plot forward, nor do they necessarily relate to the plot at all. Instead, they form brief musical interludes that allow the star to showcase their musical talent in the film. The teenage jukebox musical functions as a sort of star vehicle film, showcasing the era's stars in their element and embracing their origins in the television variety shows that were popular at the time. It then considers the generic conventions of the film, focusing particularly on the setting aspect of the genre's *mise en scène*. The films privilege certain settings, one of which is the studio, or the genesis of stars and love teams. The studio films come with their particular plotlines and cinematographic techniques which represent the studio and the audience in particular ways. The performance styles of the two love teams as well as how the love team is filmed play a key role in distinguishing the genre and vice versa. The chapter concludes by exploring the teenage jukebox musical in two films: *Guy and Pip*, a semi-biographical film set in the studio starring Aunor and Cruz, and *Edgar Loves Vilma*, a narrative-driven film that stars Santos and Mortiz.

What is the teenage jukebox musical?

Despite the popularity of the teenage love team films in the Philippines, no academic writing has explored them in detail. Thus far

I have referred to them as teenage 'jukebox musicals', a name taken from a scathing description by Lumbera of them in a single sentence about 1970s Philippine cinema. His attitude towards them is exemplary of the general scholarly tone discussing the films of the era and indeed a more generalised denigration of the jukebox musical genre in scholarly writing on both theatre and film, which favoured instead the more traditional 'integrated' musicals that merge original songs with the narrative (Taylor 2016: 151), or 'book' musicals, based on literature, and those written expressly for plays (Knapp et al. 2013: 248). The difference between these various kinds of musicals is the subject of a chapter titled 'Class and Culture' in Raymond Knapp, Mitchell Morris and Stacy Wolf's edited volume *The Oxford Handbook of the American Musical*, and neatly demonstrates the relationship between class and culture: 'high culture' comes from literature or playwrights, while 'low culture' is embedded in the very definition of the jukebox musical as 'a production in which there is no original musical score, and which uses existing well-known music' (ibid.: 1277). Lack of originality and the appeal to audiences' pre-existing popular culture favourites are deemed to be markers of low culture and considered a purely profit-based formula. I distinguish them from other jukebox musicals as uniquely featuring teenage and young adult performers and thematically featuring plots that concern themselves with the youth, thus calling them 'teenage jukebox musicals' – the primary form of musical in the Philippines during the era. It is also equally telling that three of the four sources I discuss in this chapter examine the jukebox musical in theatre rather than in film, while the main writing about the jukebox musical film is the eponymously titled chapter in a book titled *Rock 'N' Film: Cinema's Dance with Popular Music* by David E. James (2015).

The jukebox musicals discussed by James are remarkably similar in some respects to the 1970s Philippine jukebox musical, particularly what he calls the 'subgenre of musician biopics' that focus on a musician's 'rise to stardom' and involve a parallel love interest subordinate to the music plot (ibid.: 44). Where they fundamentally diverge is in the importance granted to the romance, which is foregrounded in the love team film in an industry built around film couples. Other forms of the popular jukebox musical during this era in the Philippines carried strong elements of either melodrama or comedy, often driven by conflict between the expectations of parents and teenage interests.

While both love teams performed in both kinds of films, they are perhaps more strongly associated with different types. Aunor and Cruz in particular performed in three semi-biographical jukebox musicals that dealt directly with the industry and mechanics of their fame, while the rest of their work as well as the work of Santos and Mortiz relied more on melodrama or comedy.

In discussing the jukebox musical, James highlights several key features in addition to musician biopics, including foregrounding the industrial apparatuses of music such as radio and television programmes, concerts and theatrical revues (ibid.: 44), how the narrative resolves the threat of teenage delinquency in conflicts between other bad teenagers and parents (ibid.: 45–47), and how the jukebox musical moves from integrated and unintegrated modes of singing within the musician biopic, swinging from performing onstage as part of televised shows to narratively integrated love songs sung directly to the star's love interest (ibid.: 48). One key way in which the Philippine love team teenage jukebox musical departs from the type highlighted by James is in the centrality of the couple. James writes that the romance (and usually the woman) is subordinated to the male star's biographical success in the narratives of the rock 'n' roll films discussed in his work. The love team film is about the film couple first and foremost, followed in significance by the music and finally the plot. Perhaps unusually, the stronger star of both love teams is its woman, and their real-life success far outstripped that of their male counterparts. In fact, the story being retold in the teenage jukebox musicals biopics of Aunor and Cruz is Aunor's success and rise to fame and her subsequent partnership with Cruz.

One of the concerns in academic writing on the musical is whether the numbers of the musical are integrated or not. When discussing a musical, one of the things that come to mind is how the numbers are tied to the plot, and how the number advances the understanding of the audience in terms of characters and their internal emotions. These internal emotions are often left unsaid in other genres; in musicals, they are the subject of extravagant and intricate numbers. Musicals generate moments of spectacle precisely through their numbers, and thus, the question of the number's relationship to the narrative is crucial to understanding the musical; however, the jukebox musical has a different relationship to its numbers, so how does the jukebox musical combine plot and numbers?

The importance of being integrated

The teenage jukebox musical is not a musical in which the musical numbers are all necessarily integrated. John Mueller describes the integrated musical as a musical in which song, dance and story are artfully blended to produce a combined effect (1984: 28). Mueller further elaborates six subtypes of musical numbers and how they fit into the categories of integrated to unintegrated. Singing in the Philippine teenage jukebox musical is paramount; dancing does not feature as commonly and is usually minimal. In the sample of films watched, there are no elaborately staged numbers that feature spectacular choreography or large ensemble numbers. Songs are usually smaller and more intimate – a solo, duet or two couples singing together. This is because spectacle in the teenage jukebox musical is primarily derived from the main star or film couple singing. When the film is set in and around the studio, it often involves colourful and elaborate sets themed around the songs. Film titles were frequently taken from song titles or from lyrics within the songs performed in the film. Costumes are era and colour specific and often tied into sponsorship by fashion brands for which the stars appeared in magazines, matching or accentuating some motif in the sets.

In *Guy and Pip* for example, Aunor and Cruz sing on a brightly coloured set that prominently features the letters 'A', 'B' and 'C' as they perform 'Alphabet Song (A You're Adorable)'. Later in the film they have an elaborate on-set wedding, with a large pair of white wedding bells that release white doves from within them (see Figure 5.1). In *The Young at Heart*, Aunor is introduced singing 'Moonlight Becomes You', the song with which she won the real-life competition *Tawag ng Tanghalan*, while standing on a raised platform shaped like a star and surrounded by smaller scattered stars and with a crescent moon backdrop. Where the film is set outside the studio, the most commonly featured spaces are domestic and outdoors in nature. The setting of teenage jukebox musical films is explored in greater detail below.

In general, the jukebox musical tends to feature three types of integrated and unintegrated numbers. The first of these are numbers whose existence is relevant to the plot but whose content is not (ibid.: 29). This refers specifically to musicals that feature show business as a plot concern within the film with main cast members performing within a show (ibid.). These may be considered an unintegrated musical, but since performing and putting on a show is one of the key concerns of the plot, the

Figure 5.1 A poster for *Guy and Pip*, featuring illustrations of the 'Alphabet Song' and the fantasy wedding scene of the pair. Source: from the collection of Nestor de Guzman

performances may be seen as fulfilling the narrative's goals and therefore become important to the plot and integrated within it through the sub-type of the studio or bio-musical (discussed below). The second type of common jukebox musical number is that which enriches the plot but does not advance it (ibid.). These numbers establish the emotional state and build understanding of the character, though they can be removed from the plot without a loss in logic (ibid.). The majority of love team film songs fall into this category as numbers in these films often serve to allow the love team to romp through a picturesque landscape of popular holiday destinations or otherwise sing of their emotions after some event – be it love, heartbreak, sorrow or triumph. Instances of these numbers include Vilma's character of the same name crying while looking at her love letters after being parted from Edgar's character, singing the main title of the eponymous *Love Letters* (dir. Abraham Cruz 1970); and Aunor and Cruz running amongst coconut trees in Tagaytay (a popular daytrip destination from Manila) to express their joyful and exuberant love in *Young Love*. A third kind of number commonly seen in the love team teenage jukebox musical is those that advance the plot but not by their content (ibid.). The example that Mueller uses in this scenario is perfectly applicable to the studio-based jukebox musical and relates to auditions or a big performance where the stakes are high, but the exact content of the performance is irrelevant except that it achieves the plot's goal of being very good or very bad (ibid.: 29–30). Cruz's character of the same name in *Young Love* has exactly such a number during the first performance on the television contest show where they meet. Aunor's number adds more meaning to the narrative as she performs 'Moonlight Becomes You', a song that has particular significance to her own fame and victory in a real-life contest.

But was the Philippine jukebox musical unprecedented, and is the question of integration particularly relevant to love team films at all? Where the star is the centre of the spectacle and the source of pleasure in the film, integration becomes less important and secondary to the star and their particular brand of the musical. Another star with some similarities to Aunor in particular and the teenage jukebox musical in general is Elvis Presley and his films of the 1950s.

The unusual musicals of Aunor and Presley

Discussing the films of Elvis Presley, Rick Altman asks, 'When is a musical not a musical?' (1989: 92). This points to one of the difficulties in categorising both Presley's films and the early films of the Aunor–Cruz love team. Aunor in particular shares several aspects of Presley's early stardom, as discussed in Julie Lobalzo Wright's *Crossover Stardom: Popular Male Music Stars in American Cinema* (2018). Working on a similar theme to James's work on the rock 'n' roll jukebox musical, Wright's chapter on Presley discusses the unusual relationship with the musical genre that his films had especially during his early career, when the songs featured had little to do with the plot. This centred instead on Presley's rags-to-riches narrative, finding success by becoming a rock 'n' roll star who was appealing to adolescent audiences and simultaneously non-threatening to the adult audience through his films' support of American patriarchal society. Presley's stardom was transgressive in certain ways, particularly in what were perceived to be overtly sexual performances with an unrestrained physical exuberance that often required strategic camera angles to tame his vigorous physical gyrations, and his role in bringing to the mainstream what was considered African American music through the safe and acceptable medium of his whiteness (ibid.: 49).

Wright (ibid.: 49) quotes the work of Simon Frith (2002: 279), stating that Presley's film stardom was an extension of the popular television variety shows where he first achieved his musical stardom in the 1950s, when the music industry realised that television could be a vital component of star-making. This was tied to the emergence of the teen consumer as an important demographic group in America, which provided a boost to its emerging consumer-based economy. As a result, studios began to produce cheap films designed to appeal to teenagers that included rock 'n' roll. Studios also realised that they had an inbuilt advantage of having a star that could make a film and publicise it through a soundtrack, with an image that could be circulated in various media, simultaneously promoting both films and music. Wright notes that for a period of three years, Presley virtually abandoned his music career to sell soundtracks of his films instead as a marketing strategy (2018: 49). In an earlier chapter on Bing Crosby, Wright argues that Crosby's films were not so much musicals as they were films that incorporated his vocal performances. Wright extends this argument to Presley, whose musical numbers in his early film roles functioned as moments for the star to 'do his thing', referring to Dyer's explanation of star vehicles, and blur the lines between Presley and the character he portrays (ibid.: 57).

Similarly, the earliest Aunor–Cruz love team films were not strictly musicals by Altman's standards, and yet contained more musical performances than scenes of dialogue. The songs in their early films were not much integrated with the narrative of the film, nor did they serve to drive the plot or characterisation forward. Instead, the films were semi-biographical (certainly in the case of Aunor) and strung together ten or more songs with brief lines of dialogue to form a rudimentary plot that focused on Aunor's rags-to-riches narrative and her fame earned through winning a singing competition. To this extent, the films and her journey to becoming a star are a site of deliberate slippage between fiction and fact and the films offer a certain authenticity through the conceit of the retelling of her real-life television triumph.

As discussed in previous chapters, Aunor's stardom is transgressive in that she did not fit any of the established prerequisites for stardom, be it physically, in terms of class or in her performance of being the star Nora Aunor. But to make up for the transgressiveness of her intrusion into what was previously the realm of the very fair, the beautiful and the upper class, Aunor's roles and films conformed to societal norms of respect, filial piety, Catholicism and nobility of character. In contrast, Cruz was afforded more latitude due to his membership of the accepted identities of class, ethnicity and appearance. This meant that his roles were less constrained by societal expectations, allowing him to play a rebel of sorts against his parents, affluence and expectations – a poor little rich boy with a good heart hidden beneath frustration, ultimately made tame and respectable by the steadying influence that Aunor provides (this will be discussed in greater detail in the next chapter on ideology).

Teenage jukebox musical cinematography

Much like Presley's, Aunor's film stardom was launched as a result of her popular appearances on television variety shows in the late 1960s. During this time, she was paired with multiple suitable teenage boys, but her pairing with Tirso Cruz III was the most popular, in part because he shared a musical talent that provided good chemistry and synergy between the two. Their early success in television carried over into their early film roles, filmed with aesthetics much closer to the television variety show than feature films. The first aspect of this was the setting of their films, revolving around television studios and sets. The sets play a core role in the films' aesthetics, often with Aunor and Cruz wandering around the sets wistfully singing a song. When they were not filmed on an indoor set, they were often filmed on the Sampaguita studio lot, a location so famous as the setting for many other films that it was familiar to the regular 1970s filmgoer. During this time, Aunor and Cruz almost exclusively recorded, released and promoted soundtrack albums that worked to simultaneously promote their musical and film careers. They also continued to maintain their presence on television throughout.

Aunor's first roles and the way she was filmed owe much to her early television and radio stardom. Several early films are little more than a series of songs sung by Aunor and Cruz on a studio set and filmed to appear as though they are performing before a live audience, sometimes featuring the audience as part of the proceedings. This technique brings Aunor closer to fans through the act of putting her singing performances on the big screen. Fans are able to imagine themselves as being part of that live audience, watching their idol sing in person at a big studio in Manila, no matter where they actually live. As part of this technique, Aunor and Cruz are filmed during their songs using camera techniques often employed in live television shows. These include the use of a crane to provide a swooping view of the star from above, various cameras dotted strategically throughout the set, and the use of camera angles that include part of the audience or stage personnel (such as hosts and producers) in the frame. Sets also play a key feature in this technique, with elaborate themed sets that sometimes change midway through a song. Vibrant colours and pastels; balloons and letters from the alphabet; indoor and outdoor sets – each set plays a part in constructing the backdrop of their love songs. Their early love team films feel like big screen adaptations of a variety show, taking the television spectacle to the cinema.

The camera also fixes them at the centre of attention, allowing the audience to look closely at the star in both close-ups and long shots, both within the narrative through the studio set filming technique and as a deliberate cinematographic choice of framing of the film. The close-ups provide the chance to be closer to the star than possible during a real-life performance, larger than life on the silver screen, and for fans to experience their star's gaze directly upon them in a very personal way as they sing. The long shots, on the other hand, encourage the audience to imagine themselves among the live audience in the studio, in the star's presence and in the company of like-minded fans, mirroring the experience of watching the film in a cinema filled with fans. These films can be read as the enshrining of Aunor's talent and discovery – with each set and song a devotion to her initial stardom and massive following that ensued. This reinforces the notion that these early films were star vehicles that allowed them to showcase their unique talents. The use of close-ups, shots of the audience and high angle shots that encompass most of the studio are uniquely cinematic techniques, while shots from the perspective of spectators at the show actively mimic the perspective of a live studio audience, making the experience of watching the jukebox musical biopic the best of both worlds.

An example of the kind of cinematography employed in these films is in *The Young at Heart* in which Aunor and Cruz play a modified fictionalised version of themselves, retaining their real names. The integral nature of music and stage performances to their love team image is always foregrounded, with the film beginning and ending with song performances and more songs spread evenly throughout the plot. In the film, Aunor wins a singing contest and goes on tour with her uncle (and manager), played by German Moreno. The film opens with what is very much a star entrance – an audience applauds, and Aunor is shown head bowed and shot from above with a crane, standing on a star-shaped platform at centre stage with a crescent moon hung as the backdrop. The song begins, and she looks up, singing directly to the camera, gazing at the viewers. She wears a short frilly dress with a ribbon in her hair, and sings seriously, with no hint of a smile, the song that made her famous when she won *Tawag ng Tanghalan* – 'Moonlight Becomes You'. The narrative is so bent on ensuring that the audience has no difficulty conflating the star persona of Aunor with the character in the film that her name is retained as well as the use of her first hit song. The set literally features Aunor as a star among other smaller scattered stars, with camera angles deliberately framing shots around them.

The songs featured are also rarely original, nor are they always relevant to the plot or characterisation. Rather, they are covers of popular contemporary American standards, rendered by the local superstar. Some parties have been critical of Aunor's tendency to sing mostly English covers rather than Original Pilipino Music (OPM) that might have been expected from a star that was perceived to be so completely Filipino and local in her background and image (discussed in greater detail in the next chapter). This could be something of an indigenising strategy in the use of the local star to render a song by the former colonial power. It demonstrates both the continuing grip of American culture on the Philippines and the attempt to localise these songs.

James writes about combining the integrated and unintegrated modes of the musical via the studio performance and the teenage romance of the narrative. The example given is a teenage male singer who has won a singing contest at the studio and performs a song onstage, simultaneously dedicating it to his love interest, combining his professional and personal lives, or the folk and industrial forms of musical production (James 2015: 48). It is of interest that when stars play characters who are performers in their films, there is an extra level of analysis involved in the couple. Already at play are Aunor and Cruz, the star, celebrity and screen couple in their love team film. Within the film, they play performers who are lovers, creating yet another star, celebrity and screen couple. The lines are often deliberately blurred by retaining their real names and nicknames for their characters, which encourages the audience to read the two levels of performance as being one and the same. Cruz's and Aunor's characters sing to each other both in their exploits offstage in the film (the folk musical production) and onstage (their industrial performances for the studio audience). By the end of the narrative, they combine the two, singing together onstage to each other, bringing the folk to the industrial. This joining of folk and industrial musical productions also reflects the binary between real and reel, and authentic and constructed reflected in their stardom and joint image.

Also of interest in the distinction between folk and industrial performances are the locations and audiences of their performances. In *The Young at Heart*, Aunor and Mortiz are from a lower-class neighbourhood outside of the city. Aunor is introduced singing a song requested by her friends, which she sings as she walks among tables of mahjong players at a roadside restaurant. The audience for this performance is her peers – playmates and neighbours who are dressed to reflect their humble means. The film represents her transition away from this folk entertainment outdoors by a roadside to her ultimate destiny of industrial performances, glittering atop a star onstage before a new audience – the live audience of the studio as well as the televised audience indicated by the presence of cameras.

The new audience is composed of city dwellers of the middle class, well dressed and unlike Aunor's peers in the countryside. The shift from folk to industrial is marked by locations, audiences and the technologies of her stardom, visible markers of her rise to fame. Once in the city, Aunor no longer performs impromptu numbers for her friends but rather songs onstage as well as unintegrated solo or duet songs that reflect her emotional state.

The setting of the numbers in the teenage jukebox musical has been shown to have an influence on the musical in terms of performance – whether it is folk (singing in a casual setting) or industrial (a professional performance, singing as work). What else can be learned from examining the love team in its various settings, and how do the couple and the setting influence each other?

Setting the couple

There is something of a recurring *mise en scène* for love teams, as teenage jukebox musicals tend to be set in several key locations. The first section below deals with the studio, or the place of birth and work of the love team showcased within their films and is followed by an analysis of other recurring spaces in the teenage jukebox musical. The real and imaginary spaces inhabited by the love team in their films reflect the image of the society that studios were intent on (re)producing. The genre prioritises the role of the family and good, clean, youthful play, visible in their settings, which primarily consist of two recurring spaces – the domestic space and open nature spaces – along with others in different films, such as places of work, like the studio or school, and houses of worship. Forbidden spaces also play an important role in the love team film, and chiefly consist of the bedroom, bars and clubs, or any other place that represents vice and unacceptable behaviour.

The studio is a key location in the genre of the jukebox musical. It is simultaneously a glimpse into the workings of the entertainment industry, the place of work of the stars, and an aspirational stage that offers the chance of success and liberty. The studio is the setting for the love teams' coupledom on multiple occasions in their early films, a site of slippage where the fantasy of fame became real for Aunor and Mortiz, and that fame was then mythologised and retold in fantasy in several films (such as *The Young at Heart* and *Young Love*). In the studio film setting, the audience is offered a chance to see the stars at work. In the case of Aunor, it is also the site of her liberation and ascent to superstardom. The television studio set is the site of the contest that she won and became famous through, an apt source of fame for a star of the masses. Aunor also represented an unlikely star in that she did not fit the mould of what stars in Philippine cinema traditionally looked like (discussed in Chapter 3).

The entertainment industry forms such a large part of jukebox musicals that the role of key personnel in the construction of stars, films and music is foregrounded in the form of the studio boss and the radio personalities associated with the love team's fame. In these films, they become celebrities in their own right, particularly the associated talent and radio stars such as German Moreno, Ike Lozada and Inday Badiday, a key trio that supported the Aunor–Cruz love team. As discussed in the previous chapter, Lozada wrote and sang songs about the love team including the eponymous 'Guy and Pip'. Moreno is credited as the go-between that recruited Aunor to Sampaguita, and Badiday was crucial in keeping the love team present on the airwaves daily for their fans. The casting of famous entertainment personalities in the film served the dual purpose of elevating their own celebrity while also bringing an element of realism to the film. Badiday and Lozada were familiar voices on the radio, while Moreno was active in the film industry, producing, directing and starring in films as well as recruiting talent on behalf of the studios he was associated with (see Figure 5.2).

The studio boss has traditionally been a position of respect and associated fame in the Philippines, including Doc Perez of Sampaguita (discussed earlier with regards to Aunor's recruitment and early film stardom), Dr Ciriaco Santiago of Premiere Productions and Doña Sisang of LVN Pictures. All these figures maintained a vital if off-screen presence in the day-to-day running of their studios, but never offered themselves as stars. The studio heads of the jukebox musical films of Aunor's and Cruz's early career were perhaps based on Perez, and as such treated as figures of kindly paternal virtue. In these films, the studio boss often stood in for parental figures, sometimes portraying the only good adult authority figure in the film. Studio heads guided the new stars, offering advice, monetary support and the democratic liberation from servitude through talent, a means of escaping the confines of class hierarchy not previously available on-screen, through the person of Aunor, an example of the noble poor – respectful, compliant and submissive.

The domestic space or the house is the natural domain of family life and represents both a comforting familiarity as well as the authority of the parents. In this setting, love teams are required to be submissive and filial, uphold family honour and sometimes work in service of the family. In happier family settings, the house represents family and the expectations, pleasures, trials and duties that come with it. This is often signified through the expectations to study hard, get a job and help the family.

Figure 5.2 The poster for *The Young at Heart*, featuring the names of Moreno, Lozada and Badiday. Source: from the collection of Nestor de Guzman

Younger siblings may also act as an added responsibility, or perhaps indicate an absent parent, placing the teenager in a role of additional responsibility. As teenagers, love teams occupy a liminal space somewhere between their parents and their younger siblings – neither fully adult nor child. The crucial late teen years represent the embarking on adult life, a stage of life that sometimes rejects the authority that parents represent in favour of their own choices while being cognisant of certain expectations, which the films often reinforce. At the upper-class end of the scale these expectations include honouring the family name, acceptable behaviour and marrying well. Expected patterns of behaviour among the lower class include helping to provide for and better the circumstances of the family.

Trappings of class are most easily and quickly signified through the domestic space, often with contrasting houses for the two love team stars, such as an upper-class house and a humble abode. Another way class changes how the domestic space is experienced is in whether the house represents a home or a place of employment. For Aunor, the house is oftentimes a place of exploitation and labour. Being made to live in someone else's domestic space comes with rigid rules of conduct. The house then becomes less a symbol of comfort and protection than a prison that restricts and oppresses. These oppressive domestic spaces feature in *Young Love*, where Aunor lives with an abusive guardian who exploits her for labour, and in *My Little Brown Girl* (dir. Danny Holmsen 1972), where Aunor plays the titular lead who is employed in the house of Cruz's abusive mother. Gender also plays into the ways the domestic space is experienced, with male stars lounging around the house while female stars are expected to perform domestic tasks.

The spaces within the house also take on different meanings and rules, with the bedroom being the most private and solemn space. In films of the love team, the bedroom tends to be the setting for negative experiences, including heartbreak, sickness, internal conflict and crime. In several tandem films, the teen stars withdraw to the privacy of their rooms to mourn the end of a relationship. In the bedroom, they cry, remember happier times, sing of their heartbreak and hold mementoes of their ill-fated love. The bedroom is also where the girls become inconsolably ill, often with concerned parents and doctors tending to them there. In *The Young at Heart*, Aunor's character is confined to her bed and visited by the doctor until her parents reunite as a family at her bedside. In *Edgar Loves Vilma*, Santos's character's mother lies ill and inconsolable after the disappearance of Santos, only to recover when she returns. Notably in *My Little Brown Girl*, it is Cruz who is confined to bed after an overdose of drugs, which his *yaya* (nanny) and Aunor rescue him from by taking him to the countryside. This also represents one use of the bedroom as the scene of a crime, repeated later in the same film when Cruz finds Aunor screaming and clutching a bloody knife over his mother's corpse (see Figure 5.3). In *Love Letters*, Santos's and Mortiz's characters run into legal trouble when he sneaks into her room in the middle of the night to retrieve their love letters. A courtroom drama ensues about the propriety of his presence there. Earlier in the same film, Santos clutches the same letters in her bedroom and sings and cries as she has a flashback of their happier times.

Keeping the bedroom largely off-limits or with a negative association in teenage jukebox musical films emphasises a chaste courtship. It also signals strongly that the bedroom is the most private sanctuary, a place only for the individual and the family. And even when those are present, the bedroom tends to be a place of misery and repairing wounds inflicted by the world. Love team partners are almost never left alone

Figure 5.3 The poster for *My Little Brown Girl* shows Aunor imprisoned and crouched over a corpse. Source: from the collection of Nestor de Guzman

in the bedroom with a notable exception in *Guy and Pip*, when Maria Leonora Teresa (representing the innocence of a child) chaperones them. The bedroom features then as almost a taboo space – sacred and off limits, sometimes a place of mourning and heartbreak. The areas of the house that the love team are encouraged to be in represent community, labour and family, while the private and personal spaces are out of bounds, and often off-screen. Even in this scenario, he enters to coax Aunor out of a lover's tiff with the support (and initial presence) of her grandmother and younger brother. The strongest condemnation of the breach of privacy is in *Love Letters*, where a full court case ensues and Mortiz is only saved by the intervention of the mayor in his favour – a clear social indictment of the impropriety of being together in an intimate space played out in film.

Because the house represents parental authority, it is also a place of some restrictions. In many love team films, there are scenes that celebrate the more open spaces of the garden, or park. Wide open spaces allow for exuberant play and freedom to explore identity that the house discourages. But it is also noteworthy that these spaces are still curated in some way – love teams wander around their gardens, public gardens and public paths. Even in freedom, there is some structure in the paths and uses of the space permitted – these are public spaces which inhibit impropriety. They are carefully manicured and mapped out, leaving clear paths and permissible behaviours while discouraging wandering off the path and hiding in enclosed spaces, as in *Always in My Heart* (dir. Mar S. Torres 1971), where the roses of a public park become associated with their love and St Teresa, subverting the traditionally more mature romantic symbolism of the flower for the purity of a saint known as Little Flower of Jesus and the sanctity of the church they celebrate their love in. The church represents the purity of the love team's relationship, and also confers authenticity to it: their love has divine blessing and their sincere commitment, signified in their prayer together in the church. Love team films do not typically show locations such as the wild tangle of the jungle; the love that these spaces promote is open, without darkness or secrets, and follows socially mandated paths well trodden by others.

The public park is the setting for many of the young lovers' rendezvous in *Love Letters* and is a space that is comforting and special to Edgar and Vilma, a site they return to in times of trouble to reaffirm their love, and where they go to wait for each other. It is simultaneously the location of their happiest times as a couple as well as the site where the narrative sets their heartbreak when only one teenager is there waiting or searching for the other in tears. By contrast, the house in *Love Letters* is a forbidding prison in which Vilma is incarcerated while Edgar and his friends camp outside for several days in an impromptu demonstration to appeal to her parents after their relationship is forbidden, and before he sneaks into her room in search of their love letters and is taken to court by her parents.

Among the spaces forbidden to the love team are clubs and bars, presented as darkened dens of sin. Smoke and strobe lighting cuts through the darkness that permeates clubs and bars peopled with scantily clad women and lascivious men. Care is taken to avoid making these spaces seem desirable; in fact, they are made to look as dingy and as uninviting as possible. In *Edgar Loves Vilma*, Edgar's and Vilma's single parents meet at a nightclub where Vilma's mother Lisa sings. Edgar's father Armando falls for Lisa but is forbidden by his snobbish mother to pursue her as she is a club performer. The narrative redeems Lisa by making it clear that she is only performing because the family is in dire financial straits after the loss of her husband. The nightclub in this film is a temporary indignity, with both the woman saved and the woman saving Armando from his habit of frequenting the nightclub, and it is replaced with sunny, wholesome scenes of the blended family visiting Manila zoo. The narrative sometimes distinguishes between classier nightclubs and sleazy ones. In *Tatlong Mukha ni Rosa Vilma*, Mortiz's character works dressed in a suit in a brightly lit establishment where upper-class members dine, depicted as earning an honest wage through his singing. The difference between Lisa's work at the nightclub and Edgardo's work boils down to both gender and class: while the narrative ensures that Edgardo is seen as earning a living, it also gives the impression that Lisa is desperate and selling herself short, flirting with customers to ensure job security.

The cityscape sometimes takes on negative connotations, being too loud, too hectic and too crowded, with a darkness that the countryside does not possess. While the countryside is soaked in warm sunshine and soothing green, the city is a procession of opulent houses or confining buildings. This features in the film *My Little Brown Girl*, where Cruz's character falls prey to the darkened nightclub he performs in with his band. His character becomes a drug addict, a fate tied to his identity as a city dweller and frequenter of 'bad' places. To rescue him, he is taken to the countryside where he can heal and be out in the open rather than the darkened, crowded interiors of the city. It often recurs with the characters of both Cruz and Mortiz: when separated from the pure and true guidance of their leading ladies' characters, both turn to alcohol and nightclubs for consolation (as Mortiz does in *Remembrance*). The promotion of the countryside as healing and enriching also reflects the distancing of the university-educated youth from the troublesome Manila, epicentre of dissent and youthful rebellion. Pushing the narrative away to the countryside represents moving into a neutral, apolitical safe space that instead fetishises the ideologies of rural life and the noble work of the simple peasantry.

The university is one real-life youth space of the era that remains pointedly off-screen except in brief transitional scenes. In the teenage jukebox musical, the university is more of a lifestyle statement than a place of learning – characters are shown lingering outside briefly between classes or heading to or from classes. Studying is never prioritised in love team narratives; in fact, the love team are more likely to be working than studying. Aunor is working in four of the seven narratives discussed in detail in this work, twice as domestic labour (and forced to labour in the family home in at least one other film) and twice in a studio. The narrative is more concerned with the romance, and the university in the romance forms a backdrop rather than a feature of the films in contrast to the care and detail devoted to the home space. Santos plays a college student in *Love Letters* and *Edgar Loves Vilma*, shown either arriving for or departing from her classes. In *Love Letters*, a study group is briefly shown in a café where the college students discuss the relationships of classmates during their meeting. In *Edgar Loves Vilma*, a jealous boyfriend manhandles Vilma and provokes conflict with Edgar outside class. Edgar also notes Vilma's absence from class and surmises that something is wrong with her when she runs away from home in the film. Santos plays a secondary school student in *Tatlong Mukha ni Rosa Vilma*, an identity that is significant only insofar as she appears in school uniform while talking to her father in one scene. This is in keeping with the era's difficult relationship with the urban educated middle-class university students that formed a key part of the resistance against Marcos's rule of the Philippines.

The genre of the teenage jukebox musical is built around specific codes and conventions, among which are the musical numbers, the *mise en scène* and cinematographic techniques that it utilises, and its stars. The performances of the stars in the jukebox musical form a key aspect of the genre, combining music with film and requiring a specific set of skills to do this. What are the key aspects of the love team's performance in the films, and how does the love team utilise their bodies and voices to achieve this?

How does the studio utilise biographical details and real events in their films and integrate these different levels of performance?

Performance in the teenage jukebox musical

Guy and Pip (1971)

Aunor and Cruz have very distinct performance styles in the musical numbers of their studio films which form a key aspect of their star images. These films prioritise the musical numbers set primarily in the studio, though they also feature musical numbers shot on location. Analysis of the stars' performances in *Guy and Pip* can best be undertaken from two angles: the love team performance in the musical numbers, and their performance of the narrative. Each has a distinct style, and operates almost completely independently of the other, resulting in two very different performance styles: that of the pop star performing to a live audience, and that of the film star performing a (semi)fictional narrative for the camera. This is characteristic of their musical performances in films and the particular plot of the film, which features the pair in semi-biographical roles as stars in the process of making a film. The narrative has them sing unintegrated numbers for the most part, but they are also explicitly filmed in the process of making a new film, thus they perform the performance of performing in a film within a film.

The film retains their real names and opens with real footage from Aunor's birthday celebrations after her triumphant return from Tower Productions, framing the film as a homecoming celebration and one of the ways the audience is encouraged to blur the boundaries between the real and the fictional (see Figure 5.4). The plot is built around the separation of the Aunor–Cruz love team and their romantic relationships with the children of the studio owner, featuring fans picketing outside the studio to have the love team reunited in yet another reference to the off-screen separation of the love team in the legal battle over Aunor and her rival romantic relationship with Manny de León. There is no integration between the numbers and the plot; in fact, this film is the most extreme example of the love team's unintegrated numbers. The film has multiple numbers back to back with no explanation given for their presence, nor is any attempt made to segue from plot to number. The numbers almost seem to exist in a separate fictional

Figure 5.4 A poster for *Guy and Pip*, featuring the crowds at Aunor's birthday party, included prominently in the film. Source: from the collection of Nestor de Guzman

world within the film, making no reference to each other but serving as something akin to music videos for covers of popular contemporary American songs by local stars. Cuts to and between numbers as well as cuts between the numbers and the plot are arbitrary, and truly put the jukebox in the musical.

A recurring feature of Aunor's musical numbers in *Guy and Pip* is that of stillness. The camera frames her in a series of long and medium shots on colourful pastel sets, either standing in one spot for the entirety of a song as in 'Love Story (Where Do I Begin?)', or walking slowly in a small area around the set as in 'The Song of My Life'. In both songs, she does not dance or sway, but rather stands still, though she occasionally lifts her hands to emphasise particular lyrics. Her eyebrows raise, her forehead wrinkles and occasionally her head tilts as she conveys the emotion of her song, particularly when framed in a medium close-up. Plaintive eyes, a serious expression and her steady gaze accompany these performances as she looks directly into the camera and the eyes of her audience, singing directly to them in a very personal way. In being frozen as though in a frame in 'Love Story', and in her stillness in other songs, Aunor conveys the impression of a passive and poised stillness – as though she is frozen in time and place for her fans. This is a different energy from the usual fast pace of musicals, creating instead a reflective mood and one that invites the audience to pause and match the star's pace.

Cruz's performance is much more dynamic, if a little disconnected from the audience. His numbers in the film are upbeat and shot on vivid sets. This allows him some freedom to dance, which he does by bopping on the spot, snapping his fingers and raising his arms as though jogging occasionally. During one song, a close-up of his white shoes shuffling in place creates a sense of movement. His songs allow him to walk about the set a little, but, much like Aunor's, these movements are slow, unhurried and give the impression of being unchoreographed and the natural instinct of a spontaneous and slightly self-conscious dancer. Unlike Aunor, Cruz does not look directly at the camera very often, and when he does, it is always swift as though accidental. Where Aunor is allowed to gaze at her fans and connect to them personally, Cruz more often sings to a point just to the side of the camera, looking sheepish when he is caught looking directly at it. When Aunor sings, she sings to the audience, inviting a connection. When Cruz sings, he either sings to her while looking at her, or off camera to some distant point. Visually, these performance cues can be read to suggest that she acts as his musical and performance anchor and that he is incomplete in her absence from the frame, leaving him nothing to connect with.

When performing in duets, the pair spend a lot of time holding hands and touching their foreheads together. While they do look at each other, it is sometimes bashful and awkward, betraying a certain self-consciousness that makes them prone to breaking into fits of laughter and looking away hastily. These bursts of emotion are left intact in the film, inviting the audience to look on them in a moment of authenticity – being their real selves with the awkwardness of teenagers being instructed to gaze lovingly at each other while a camera crew records them. When they are able to control their reactions, they gaze intently into each other's eyes as they do in their reunion song 'Together Again', sitting on a park bench and walking sedately down the stairs in an indoor set that brings the outdoors inside.

Even in their duet performances, Aunor looks at the camera while Cruz looks away, as though she is aware of the audience looking at them and invites them to do so while Cruz remains unaware of their presence (discussed in detail in the next chapter). A close-up of the pair leaning their foreheads together demonstrates this dynamic as they perform 'Ikaw' (You), the only Tagalog song in the film, dressed in provincial clothes, the traditional butterfly sleeves of Aunor's *terno* visible in the frame. Aunor's glance in this shot is a little mischievous and shy, betraying her awkwardness at the intimacy of the pose while gazing at the camera. Pip is performing the traditional *harana*, or serenade to win Guy's affection. The traditional aspects of the scene are emphasised by the wooden hut and the *parol* (Christmas lanterns) that adorn it.

In the pair's duets, Aunor dances more freely as in the upbeat song 'Together' that features the pair on a set decorated with Chinese lanterns in varying shades of red. The two stars stand next to each other, snapping their fingers and swaying to the beat and occasionally exchanging radiant smiles. They are often shot sitting or facing in the same direction to create a sense of harmony throughout the film's musical numbers. In Cruz's number 'Maria Leonora Teresa', the pair are linked together through holding the doll's hands as they walk through the Sampaguita gardens, playing make-believe with the doll. The doll is key in this scene, as are the lyrics of the song which tell of both Cruz's and its heartbreak ('forsaken doll') when Aunor leaves them. This moment in the film marks the reunion of the tandem after Cruz was left to ride on the float with only the doll during the 5th Manila Film Festival. Later in the film, the couple have a disagreement and are separated, each filmed during songs of heartbreak in their respective bedrooms, with Aunor walking through her bedroom and turning down three different framed photographs of Cruz while he restlessly paces and leaves his room for the open night air on the balcony.

Outside of the musical numbers, the pair employ an exaggerated style to suit the comedic tone of the film. Aunor expresses her annoyance at Cruz by pouting, turning her back on him and crossing her arms in one scene, and in another playfully kicks and punches her character's younger brother in a mock fight, demonstrating a physical exuberance that sets her apart from her peers in terms of being less ladylike than her rivals, including Santos. Cruz exaggerates his discomfort for full comic effect when he is physically cornered by the bold daughter of the studio owner. She touches his thigh and chest, causing him to sink back into his chair, and slide away when perched on a desk to avoid her amorous hands. His speech becomes awkward, his hands gently remove her hands from his body, and his movements become jerky and clumsy while she becomes more aggressive.

In contrast to the aggressive pursuit staged by the studio owner's daughter, the love team go to a church to make their true feelings known to each other, with Pip saying, 'I think I know a place where we can really prove to each other what we mean', followed by a montage of the pair at church. They kneel at the altar in prayer, make the sign of the cross and then run out of the church hand-in-hand. The playfulness and innocence that the montage contains is one of the key aspects of their love team performance, featuring scenes of them running, jumping, tumbling and rolling together in slow motion on the church grounds, with Cruz finally lifting Aunor into his arms and spinning with her in front of a grotto for the Virgin Mary.

Edgar Loves Vilma (1970)

In *Edgar Loves Vilma*, Santos and Mortiz play characters that retain their real names in the film and fall in love with each other. The narrative also has their single parents fall in love with each other, uniting their two families. Unlike *Guy and Pip*, this film is not set in or around the studio and features fewer musical numbers and more plot. As a result, the musical numbers that are performed in the film are either specifically required by the narrative, such as the individual songs that Santos and Mortiz perform while at a party, or songs that exist to allow the characters to express their emotions, such as the two songs Mortiz sings in his garden when he first falls in love with Vilma, and then when his heart is broken when she ends their relationship. The film opens with Mortiz's song 'Edgar Loves Vilma' playing over the opening credits, which contain shots of nature, a non-diegetic song that sets the tone for the film. The choice of this song means that the film opens by encouraging the audience to blur the boundaries between the characters, Edgar and Vilma, and the stars, Mortiz and Santos. The film closes with a sixth upbeat song sung by Santos that serves to unite all the main characters in a happy ending.

In the narrative, Vilma and her younger brother live with their single mother, Lisa, who sings at a nightclub to support their middle-class family. The film opens with Vilma's disappointment with Lisa's work at the nightclub, which frequently sees her return late and drunk, sitting with her shoulders slumped, head drooping and eyes downcast. Santos furrows her eyebrows in concern and speaks gently and respectfully, sounding anxious about the welfare of Lisa. However, Lisa becomes enraged when she sees that Vilma has been looking at a picture of her father, whom Lisa refuses to speak of. Vilma is horrified and shocked when Lisa tears the photograph to pieces, gasping and crying as she asks her mother, in a voice that grows increasingly loud and distraught, why Lisa is angry with her father. A medium shot frames her face as tears glitter in her eyes and she tries to blink them away, even as her voice becomes choked with emotion. It is only then that she shows anger at Lisa's drunkenness, her head snapping round sharply as she speaks through clenched teeth. Lisa slaps her then, and Santos brings her hand to her cheek before running away. She goes into her garden, where she stands dejectedly with her head bowed, her hands pressed against her abdomen while her fingers fidget with her nightgown. Their interactions get more emotionally charged throughout the film, with Santos raising her voice in anger and hurt on several occasions.

Mortiz plays against type early in the film, playing a teenage boy that lacks supervision and discipline from his father, Armando, who instead frequents the nightclub where he meets Lisa. Edgar is introduced in the film lounging lazily by the telephone – leaning back against the sofa with his ankle propped against his opposite knee. He interacts roughly with his younger sister, first threatening her with a finger in her face, and then leaning forward and planting his arm forcefully on the sofa, making himself broader and assertive. His sister does not show any fear of him, suggesting that his bark is worse than his bite. In another scene with his father, Edgar is caught reading a *Playboy* magazine. Edgar is startled when his father returns home unexpectedly, and hastily attempts to hide the magazine, his eyes wide with guilt and mouth slackened in shock. He rises quickly, and shoves a hand into his hair awkwardly, kissing his father immediately and speaking to him in an overly polite tone. He is sheepish when he is caught by his father, smiling uneasily while his hand returns to his hair. Throughout the film, and especially after he meets Vilma, Edgar becomes a kinder and better person, eventually softening into the gentle and sweet boy of his star image.

Vilma and Edgar meet at a dance party, with Edgar commenting that she has a good voice as she sings into a microphone, his eyes fixed on her. Vilma dances a little on the spot, swaying and moving her head to emphasise lyrics and smiling as she sings (see Figure 5.5, left). Her performance of the song is a little more energetic than Aunor's, perhaps a strategy to distract from a weaker singing voice. When it is Edgar's turn to sing, he looks directly at Vilma and winks, which she returns, hugging her younger brother (who is there as chaperone). Edgar's performance is confident, as is the wink he sends her, an unusually overt expression of interest between strangers present at the party as the dates of other people in a Philippine teenage jukebox musical film. Edgar's musical performance is upbeat and energetic. While he does not move from the spot, he bounces and taps his feet to the beat. He continues to look at her occasionally in the song, smiling and being smiled at in return (see Figure 5.5, right).

His vigorous movements are especially evident in a medium close-up that shows his head bobbing in the frame. As the song progresses, he

Figure 5.5 Left: Santos tilts her head and smiles as she sings. Right: Mortiz looks off-screen at Santos and smiles at her in *Edgar Loves Vilma*

twists the microphone and flaps his arms rhythmically during a musical interlude. Again, the dancing in the jukebox musical appears to be spontaneous and unchoreographed, the natural impulses of the star in an authentic moment.

There is no duet between the two in the film; however, there is an extended dance scene that has them dance together for a full 3 minutes 20 seconds. In this sequence, it becomes clear that Santos is the more competent dancer of the two, varying her moves more than he does. The pair face each other and stay largely stationary, with Santos turning around several times in the song (see Figure 5.6). Their dancing corresponds to the general look and feel of all the dancing described in the two films discussed here – snapping fingers, shuffling feet, the jogger arms and the body bopping. Santos varies this by adding a rhythmic tilting and shaking of her head and her occasional spins. The camera remains stationary for the entire 3 minutes, with the shifting of position coming from their respective dates, who dance with each other and attempt to discomfort Vilma and Edgar by cutting between them and taking up positions on either side of them.

Figure 5.6 Vilma and Edgar dance surrounded by young people and their respective dates (behind and right of Edgar) in *Edgar Loves Vilma*

A second date sees the two families visit Manila zoo together, an opportunity for wholesome fun outdoors. Edgar and Vilma walk hand in hand, running excitedly and pointing out the various animals to each other in a music montage. Edgar's hand is always touching Vilma's, whether holding her hand or her arm as he guides her into place. This is mirrored to an extent by their parents, who also hold and swing their joined hands, walking jauntily amidst the group. After the zoo, both couples sit on the grass near Manila Bay, yachts bobbing on the sea in the background. Edgar tries to put a hand on Vilma's shoulder, but she gently shifts away, smiling shyly.

The couple's only point of conflict comes when Vilma runs away from home, driven out by a drunken Lisa who is heartbroken after Edgar's grandmother demands that she leave Armando. Edgar searches for Vilma and begs her to return home, where her mother is ill and confined to bed. The conflict is shot with Vilma turning her back on a seated Edgar, blocking him out as tears run down her face. This marks a direct contrast to the scene in which they sit side by side on the grass after their date at the zoo, or next to each other on a bench with their knees touching to signify their harmonious relationship. Harmony is later restored to the couple as they stand facing each other closely in between classes after resolving their differences.

Edgar's two numbers in the film take place in the garden, where he escapes to from the house to process his feelings through song. In the garden, he can be his most unfiltered self, walking and singing first in a speculative and romantic mood, and later in heartbreak. In the first number, he is watched secretly by his younger siblings, a reminder that he is still in the domestic space and cannot fully escape it. Edgar walks slowly through the garden in both songs, the first a romantic scene set at night. As he walks, he pauses to examine flowers reflected in his lyrics – 'roses for lovers', leaning forward with an elbow against his knee. In contrast, the second number is about heartbreak and is shot during the day, featuring a series of medium shots that emphasise his sad expression, shot from a low angle. He ends the song in despair, his head slumping forward to rest against his chest and his eyes closing with the final note as his hands hang helplessly under the weight of his heartbreak.

The two love team performances analysed in *Guy and Pip* and *Edgar Loves Vilma* are exemplary of the love teams' filmography. The love team of Aunor and Cruz is strongly associated with the studio and the production of singing teenage stars. They also share a unique love team performance style in terms of their musical performances, with Aunor seemingly aware of the camera and audience and willing to interact with them directly, while Cruz instead interacts with Aunor, or the thought of Aunor when she is not present on-screen. Their films make the most of the indoor studio sets in their pastel colours and gardens tamed and brought indoors. Innocent play and running through gardens also mark several of their films, a recurring theme of freedom that allows the love team to be themselves away from their place of work (the studio, and sometimes the house for Aunor) and their family homes. Santos and Mortiz tend to sing individually, and their films focus more on the narrative, playing to Santos's strengths in acting and dancing. Their numbers are more likely to flow directly from the plot, rather than existing in an isolated fictional world within the film.

Conclusion

The jukebox musical's unique ability to offer music and romance built around its teenage love teams formed a key part of its attraction immediately before Martial Law and during its early years. The genre distinguished itself by offering colourful images and gentler emotions in an industry that consisted of martial arts or action films, pornographic films and local versions of popular imports of Hollywood films. In that crowded field of violence, sex and Hollywood, the innocent romance of the jukebox musical offered the respite of the universally relatable young love plot replete with a blend of traditional and modern values and popular love songs – that other national pastime of the Philippines. This chapter has explored how the love team is filmed in the teenage jukebox musical, from its genre to its cinematographic techniques, recurring settings, and the love team's performance. Each of these aspects contributes to the instantly recognisable format of these films and they are as much shaped by the love team as they shape the love team in return.

The following chapter will examine the ideological dimension of the love team, uncovering intended and unintended meanings in their images and films. The role of the family as a key institution in transmitting hierarchies of power and submission at the national level will be explored. Heteronormative society encourages the idea that the natural progression for individuals (and thus stars) is to become a couple (the prerequisite for the family unit). Becoming the couple is at the heart of the 1970s Philippine teenage jukebox musical, a lesson taught through the real and reel lives of the stars and the genre, and it forms the subject of the next chapter's analysis.

Chapter 6

Becoming the couple

Introduction

Philippine love teams in the 1970s stood at the juncture of change. As teenagers, they represented a new kind of star: youths, taking the place of more mature and glamorous idols of the past. Inherent in this change was the tension between modernity and tradition, a tension that overflowed into various aspects of society including authority, family and youth culture. From these stemmed further conflicts and evolutions of identity as varied as language, ethnicity, class and religion. At the heart of these issues was a constant negotiation about what Philippine culture itself was. At times, there was a tendency to blame the youth, represented in the love team, for everything perceived by some parties to be undesirable about contemporary Philippine culture in the 1970s. This chapter will explore how the joint star images of the two love teams of this research interacted with 1970s Philippine culture, considering all the questions of identity raised above and how they negotiated them in tandem.

It will first examine teenagers and tradition through a contemporary sociological source, Belen T.G. Medina's *The Filipino Family* (2001), which identifies key ways in which youth alternately compromise with and adhere to traditional values, and explores how the love team builds on this in their joint images and films. Next, it will consider the role of another traditional institution, Catholicism, in the love team image and its films, particularly in terms of courtship and their extra-filmic image. It uncovers discourses on gender and its intersection with class in the love team with far-reaching implications that include questions of colonial influence and anxieties over linguistic and cultural purity. The anxieties over language and youth were representative of the authoritarian era, with local cultures and traditions privileged by some over Western culture. The chapter explores how authoritarian values were naturalised through the family unit, the hierarchy into which individuals are born and which they then recreate when they become a couple. It also considers how Marcos positioned himself and his family as the head of the nation through a popular teenage magazine of the era, and then investigates the role of the love team in perpetuating narratives of family in their image and films.

Modern teenagers and traditional culture

Teenage jukebox musicals deal with the tensions of youth facing courtship, love and tradition. We see couples playing out different anxieties of courtship in their films with different levels of agency and external pressures. Freedom, individuality and authenticity in the notion of 'true love' take centre stage as the teenagers work out their place in society and the relationships they have with each other and their families. A key function of these films is to reinforce Philippine society's values of heterosexuality, monogamy and marriage. At stake are the individual's struggle for independence and freedom versus the traditional ways of the older generation that seek to impose limits and appropriate life choices on their young.

Sociologist Belen T.G. Medina's *The Filipino Family* identifies several of the points of struggle between youth and their elders that are commonly found in the genre of the teenage jukebox musical. The first is the tension between traditional notions of courtship and marriage and modern freedom. Traditionally, Filipino families view marriage as not just the union between two individuals but also the union of families (Medina 2001: 79). When matters of inheritance, family honour and status are involved, families have traditionally sought to control marriages as a strategic means of improving or at the very least preserving family status. The altered cultural environment of the young post 1950s undermined the system of family control and presented new freedom and agency to youth (ibid.: 81). In the era of modernisation, urbanisation and industrialisation, youth in the 1960s sought more personal independence and freedom, extending this to their choice of courtship and selection of partners (ibid.).

The changing of the guard from the system of family control to the emergence of youth as the masters of their own fate is a crucial element of the teenage jukebox musical. Aunor and Cruz escape the tender tyranny of their guardians through the various means available to them. With Aunor, it is often the case that her raw talent allows her to rise above an oppressive guardian. Issues of class are also at play when it comes to Aunor's ability to gain freedom: what keeps her tied to an abusive parent figure is her poverty or state of being an orphan in the first place. With the fame and money gained through her talent, Aunor is able to escape her oppressive guardians and poverty simultaneously, as she does in *Young Love*. Cruz's oppression tends to be tied to his status as a member of the middle to upper class in their films together. Cruz suffers the unique burden of privilege: having to live up to the expectations of his parents to marry a certain girl and live in a certain way. His poor-little-rich-boy troubles often see him either leaving his home to escape his parents (as in *The Young at Heart*) or tricking them outright into letting him have his way (as he tricks his grandmother in *Young Love* into allowing him to stay in the Philippines).

Other traditional values explored in the teenage musical include courtship practices. As their main audience were teenagers themselves, the films sought to portray images of acceptable courtship. In some instances, this involved teaching lessons about promiscuous behaviour through a male or female star that would be chided by their partner, as takes place in the Rosemarie and Ricky love team in *The Young at Heart* when Rosemarie insists, 'No touch!' when Ricky attempts to kiss her on the lips. Predatory or sexually aggressive partners sometimes also appear, with Cruz being pursued by the daughter of the studio head in *Guy and Pip*, whose hands boldly roam his body at any given chance. Cruz's reaction to this is one of extreme discomfort, catching at her hands and shifting uneasily away. The Aunor–Cruz and Santos–Mortiz tandems are nearly always held up as an example of good courtship behaviour. Their dates are always full of exuberant games, such as chasing each other or teasing each other like children. They hold hands cautiously and never straight away, but after some on-screen dates have passed and they have grown comfortable with each other. It is always late in the course of the film and after some time has passed in their courtship when they progress to a gentle peck on the cheek or the forehead, more reverent than sensual.

Traditional cultural practices also make their way into these films. The Filipino *harana* or serenade where a young suitor sings outside a girl's house, perhaps with a guitar and the help of some of his friends (ibid.: 80), is modernised in the teenage musical genre, or sometimes included unchanged. In *Guy and Pip*, Pip stands outside the set of a traditional wooden house in his *barong* and sings in Tagalog to Guy in her *terno* (traditional attire for men and women) in a nostalgic tribute to the lost art of traditional wooing in the film they are shooting within the film. In *Leron-Leron Sinta*, Mortiz's character sings outside Santos's character's window in an attempt to win her favour. The practice of the suitor wooing the entire family (ibid.) is also celebrated in *Guy and Pip* when Pip ensures that he treats Guy's grandmother and brother with respect and affection, winning them over to his side. Cruz also often brings gifts when he visits Aunor, whether boxed flowers or the doll Maria Leonora Teresa in multiple films. The traditional practice of chaperoned dates is also portrayed in their films, whether it is with a younger sibling (as was custom, ibid.) as seen in *The Young at Heart* and *Guy and Pip* or in dating in pairs as in *Young Love* and *Love Letters*, a more modern solution to courtship that forms a compromise with tradition.

Modern courtship includes being able to select a partner without parental interference. Cruz in particular struggles against this in *Young Love* and *The Young at Heart*, with his parents insisting that he marry more suitably. *Edgar Loves Vilma* demonstrates that this pressure is not just limited to the youth but exists for all parent–child relationships through Edgar's grandmother, who forbids her adult son Armando from marrying a lowly nightclub singer. *Always in My Heart* introduces such a conflict for Aunor's character Teresita, whose mother insists that she marry advantageously to better the family's circumstances. She is conflicted about this, torn between Cruz's character Artur and her mother's recommended candidate for marriage, her fiancé David. In this scenario, it is eventually her grandmother who encourages her to follow her heart and champions Artur's cause. Despite yearning for freedom, the teenage couples that the two love teams portray almost never turn away from their legitimate parental figures completely, usually pleading with them to understand as in *Young Love* and *The Young at Heart*, and eventually winning them over to their side. This matches with Medina's finding that while freedom and independence are what youth want, they still value parental approval as important or necessary (ibid.: 93).

The concept of romantic love is foregrounded in the films of both love teams with 'true love' being a vital aspect of their on- and off-screen images. Romantic love in Medina's text belongs to a Western conception of love that has replaced the traditional Filipino mate selection (ibid.: 107). Where once the emphasis of partner selection was placed on practical considerations such as socio-economic compatibility, and the ability to nurture and provide, youths now place a great deal of value on 'physical attraction and intense emotional interaction between "true lovers"' (ibid.). According to Medina, this is reinforced by yet another Western idea introduced primarily by mass media: that marriage exists primarily for the personal happiness of husband and wife (ibid.). Extra-filmic discourse on both love teams embodies this off-screen in their real-life relationship that fans single out as being the best because it is 'real', 'not fake like the other love teams' and 'authentic'.

The love teams of 1970s Philippine cinema were thus modern in nature, but also able to navigate questions of tradition and modernity skilfully with respect, never pushing the boundaries too far and always making an attempt to compromise. Another aspect of traditional Philippine culture is Catholicism, a key part of an individual's life, and the means by which the individual officially becomes the couple and, subsequently, the family. Catholicism thus influences the individual and joint images of the love team, and the next section considers how Catholic values and practices are transmitted through the love team's films and images, and the role the Church plays in structuring the teenage love team's trajectory and narratives in their films and in society.

Catholicism and the love team

The ultimate celebration of true love in the majority Catholic Philippines is matrimony. The love team works in every film to reinforce the norm of heterosexual coupledom and marriage. Some films convey this overtly, such as the wedding scene that ends *Guy and Pip* as well as the white dress and suit they wear in the film. In *Always in My Heart* and *Guy and Pip*, the religious aspect of the teenage relationship is foregrounded, with the pair professing their love in a church. The church is depicted as the place where their true intentions and feelings can be known, and the symbol of the sacrament of matrimony. The scene in which the pair kneel at the altar in *Guy and Pip* is an example of the importance the teenage couple place on attaining divine benediction for their relationship. In the same film, they run together in the church grounds before a statue of the Virgin Mary in a grotto, signifying the purity and innocence of their love. In *Always in My Heart*, Teresita requests the guidance of God and St Teresa to help her decide between her true love or marrying out of filial piety to her mother. The church is the setting for the climax of the film, where Artur begs the paralysed Teresita before God and St Teresa to walk if she still loves him. The ending of the film is presented as a miracle as she rises from her wheelchair and walks, and the church bells are heard ringing, yet another symbol of matrimony. The tandem thus also works to preserve the place of the Church in society, grounding their relationship in Catholic imagery and demonstrating a faith that is central to their characters' lives.

Guy and Pip features a fantasy wedding that marries the two stars after the resolution of the real-life drama of the legal tussle between Sampaguita and Tower Productions – a fitting ending to the drama of being separated from each other during the course of the film. Santos and Mortiz's *Love Letters* concludes with a friend being married and the pair singing lovingly as they gaze at each other in the choir loft, the narrative unable to join them after featuring a court case about trespassing and improper behaviour (albeit for innocent reasons) between the two. *And God Smiled at Me* (dir. Danny Holmsen and Mar S. Torres 1972) features an impoverished illegitimate Celina (Aunor) and blind Carding (Cruz) mistreated by her father's rich wife. Celina prays and begs for God's help, culminating in a scene in which the voice of God addresses her in church as she kneels and prays, leading her to sing in joy. The narrative presents this as a miraculous event as previously she sang badly until approaching the altar on her knees all the way down the aisle in the church. She is delivered by her beautiful singing voice when her talent is subsequently discovered at church by a wealthy parishioner, who adopts Celina and pays for surgery that Carding requires to see. The operation is initially unsuccessful until Celina returns to church to pray once more for Carding's sight. In the hospital, Carding looks up to see a dazzling image of Jesus on the cross, his sight miraculously restored.

And God Smiled at Me posits faith repeatedly as the cure to all ills, be it an oppressive figure of authority, poverty or literal blindness, first giving Celina a new parental figure from the church who loves her and is financially able to support her. It then rewards Celina's faith with a second miracle – Carding's sight. It is also unique among the films analysed because it prioritises a direct relationship with male divinity in the figure of Jesus rather than the more commonly featured Mother Mary in the majority of the films. The maternal Marian figure features much more commonly in love team films as a nurturing and tender presence, perhaps absent in this film due to the death of Celina's mother and her subsequent reliance on her father (who fails her and her mother through his infidelity that rendered her illegitimate, and his subsequent death that leaves Celina at the mercy of his enraged widow). The film thus reconciles Celina's relationship with the divine Paternal figure when she seeks help, soothing the failure of her biological father and providing a new mother figure in the form of her rich patroness at the church.

The close association to Catholicism also exists in love team extra-filmic images, with stars posing in magazines for covers associated with Holy Week and Christmas and making religious figures central in their lives, such as in Mortiz's devotion to Mary in a Valentine's Day profile, combining divine and romantic love in his interview. Aunor goes so far as to mention her mother's devotion to Mater Dolorosa (Our Lady of Sorrows) in influencing her life (San Diego Jr 2017). Images of Aunor such as that shown in Figure 6.1 are common, reflecting the traditional and respectful attire of the churchgoer but also invoking an association to Marian imagery. The image is particularly solemn and was the *Liwayway* cover for All Saints Day 1970, a feast celebrated in November.

Santos and Mortiz were also sent to *Santakrusan*, religious festivals dedicated to Mary during the month of May in which young men and women appear in a processional pageant dressed up as various biblical and Marian characters, which have become a popular event for celebrities to appear at (Morota 1971a).

The Church acts in the love team film as yet another form of authority: heavenly authority that can confer divine approval of the relationship and also shape patterns of behaviour. But it also performs another key function in teaching submission: in passively accepting suffering like the *babaeng martir*, or 'female martyr' (referring to a common female archetype in Philippine culture, particularly associated with Aunor (Tadiar 2002: 705)), blind, enduring faith is rewarded with miraculous salvation. Aside from family and work, Catholicism features as a force that regulates real and on-screen lives with stars and characters turning to the Church for guidance and blessings on important occasions and in their day-to-day lives. Figures like St Teresa, Mother Mary and Christ stand in as extra parental figures, the latter two referred to as 'Mama Mary' and 'Papa Jesus' in films. Religion is normalised in their daily lives, sometimes consisting of as little as a cross hanging on the wall or being as central as the figure of St Teresa in *Always in My Heart*, with the opening and closing shot of the film focusing on the saint and the recurring motif of red roses in the film, which is explicitly associated with St Teresa. Religious figures and the grounds of the church inspire purity in the love team's courtship and relationship, leading to innocent and respectful play in its grounds as in *Guy and Pip*, discussed in the previous chapter. Catholicism thus teaches gender-specific lessons, encouraging female sacrifice as an act of devotion and faith.

Figure 6.1 Aunor on the cover of *Liwayway* for All Saints Day, 1970. Source: from the collection of Nestor de Guzman

The *babaeng martir* or taming the teenage male

Aunor's characters often espouse a respect for superiors and eventually lead co-stars and supporting cast towards a better relationship with their parents and society. In *Guy and Pip*, both the studio boss's children and Cruz's character descend into vices such as promiscuous behaviour, drinking and smoking. Cruz plays a co-star of Aunor as they work for a studio boss to make a film. When the studio management and the owner's daughter (whom he is in a relationship with) conspire to keep him apart from Aunor, Cruz falls into a depression, smoking and singing brokenheartedly about his loss. Aunor serves as a steadying influence in the case of her co-star, reforming him and repairing his relationship with his mother, while the offspring of the studio boss serve as a cautionary tale for the audience. The pattern is also seen in *The Young at Heart*, in which Aunor is a role model for good behaviour while her female co-star demonstrates the tragedy in being isolated from her parents, who are desperately searching for her after she ran away from home after a misunderstanding.

Santos and Mortiz's film *Tatlong Mukha ni Rosa Vilma* is built entirely around Santos's good influence on her men. The film centres around an upper-class, privately educated Santos who lives with her adoring lawyer father. She suffers severe headaches and runs away from the house while driven mad by pain. The film has Santos meeting and reforming no fewer than three suitors: the spoiled, upper-class Jimmy (Ilagan), who has turned his back on his parents; a poor, unemployed drunkard named Ziggy and his young sister from the countryside; and a middle-class, teenage nightclub performer named Edgardo (Mortiz). Vilma is revealed to have amnesia as a result of her mysterious headaches and is taken in by each of the three youths in turn. First, she is taken in by Jimmy, who knocks her down with his car as she runs from her father's house. Naming her Rose, he takes her back to his house and out shopping for clothes. She is perplexed by his lifestyle, which appears to involve tinkering with his beloved sports car during the day and drinking at night. Learning that his parents have not seen him in a while, she pushes him to go visit them, which he does, speaking to them in English. Wishing to introduce her to them, he returns to invite her in from his car in the garden only to find her missing.

Her upper-class background is central to her subsequent reformation of Ziggy, who is inspired by her goodness to clean up his act and earn an honest living away from the bad influence of his drinking buddies. His sister Ligaya (Joy) finds and names the lost and confused girl Pilar, or 'pillar', referring to the Virgin Mary María del Pilar. In their humble wooden hut, she is the pillar she is named for, teaching Ligaya to read in English. Both Pilar and Ligaya are named for virtuous behaviour – strong support and bringer of happiness. These names bear out the roles they perform for Ziggy, with Ligaya caring for him by cooking the meals and keeping the hut tidy, while Pilar gives him support. While staying with them, Pilar changes from the expensive fashionable clothes of Jimmy's house to the simple house coat of the humble country girl. She runs away from the hut one night when attacked by a group of Ziggy's drunken friends and is found by Edgardo, who names her Helen. She discovers that he is a talented singer who is trapped singing in seedy bars, in one of which he gets into a fight with a rowdy patron. He takes her home to his blind mother, and Helen now slots into a middle-class existence, watering plants and dusting furniture. The full extent of her intervention in Edgardo's life comes towards the end of the film, but unfortunately the copy of the film procured for this research is incomplete, thus leaving the final message the studio was pushing with regards to class and her ultimate suitor unknown. The last scene of the incomplete copy of the film shows her father mediating when a fight breaks out between all three suitors who are anxiously pacing in a waiting room as she undergoes an operation to relieve her headaches. The men sit as in a tableau, accompanied by a nun who recites the rosary unstintingly, even as Vilma goes into cardiac arrest. The narrative shows some hint of prioritising Edgardo's suit, having him sing and dedicate a song to her while waiting, titled 'Ikaw ang Aking Anghel Ko Rosa Vilma' (You Are My Angel Rosa Vilma).

In this narrative, Santos is a pliable vessel of virtue and redemption or a *tabula rasa*, moulded in turn by each man and his circumstances, dispensing class-specific panaceas and transcending class with good values and a family-driven mindset. Each man names her and brings into being what he needs from her, with the notable exception of Pilar, a name given by a female child named Joy. Perhaps uncoincidentally, this is also her only name that does not have connotations of beauty and elegance. As Pilar she is sturdy and practical. As Helen she is a beautiful muse for the lost artist Edgardo and his blind mother. To Jimmy she is Rose, a name that brings to mind images of the delicate, romantic and sophisticated flower. Jimmy is also the man who comes closest to her actual name, perhaps suggesting that the person who shares her class identity is also the person who has the best understanding of her, or at any rate is the one who changes her identity the least. Her identity and class are bound up inextricably in the film, which takes the audience on a journey through three classes and the ideal female behaviour to be emulated in each. This behaviour is patterned on the image of an upper-class *mestiza* girl educating the lower class through Ligaya and Ziggy, inspiring the middle class through her beauty with Edgardo, and instilling a sense of purpose and filial piety in the spoilt, rich Jimmy.

This Catholic-inspired spirit of female self-sacrifice is one means by which women are recruited to serve and save men, binding women into submissive service. But what happens when a female star is unruly, or carries within her image a subversive potential, an ability to destabilise the establishment? What happens when a truly powerful figure of identification inspires an unprecedented following among the most marginalised and ignored class of people in the Philippines? These are questions that the establishment of the film industry and President Ferdinand Marcos found themselves contemplating in the face of Aunor's superstardom, some of the answers to which lay in the love team.

Taming Aunor through authority

Nora Aunor was an unlikely and unprecedented Filipino star, attaining fame through the merit of her vocal talent at the age of fourteen despite being among the poor of the Philippines, a demographic that was not represented in leading roles in cinema at the time. Rafael characterises the Philippines during this period as shifting away from a long-held system of patronage towards an expanding capitalist market, with a breakdown in the patron–client ties of Philippine society (2000: 139–141). The resultant lingering longing for hierarchy (ibid.: 140) continued to bind the elite and the dependent poor in a relationship that Aunor's films depicted as a benign hierarchy of mutual benefit, and one that Marcos would exploit to his advantage. In theory, Aunor represented a dangerous cross-section of dissent found in the First Quarter Storm – the poor masses (farmers and labourers) and the youth (student revolutionaries), whom she could mobilise in large numbers. Knowing this, Marcos sought the support of Aunor in 1971, his wife Imelda offering Aunor the chance to live at Malacañang Palace and study with their children (Lim 2012: 196–197). Aware of the dangers of overt support, Aunor declined, saying that it would be 'tricky' to accept (Lim 2012: 197). Ultimately, the student protestors and Aunor did not intersect; while Aunor appealed to the youth, it was a specific youth – the lower class of which she was a member, and not the urban, educated, middle-class youth revolutionaries of Manila's universities.

Through her work in love team films, Aunor's potentially subversive star image was tempered into a safe expression of the freedoms permitted by authorities during this period. These popular films mirrored official policy governing film production during the era and became a means of promoting desirable behaviour and values that simultaneously inhibited dissent, walking a tightrope between relatability and compliance. Aunor's love team films demonstrate how hierarchies of power and submission were reinforced through her persona and films, particularly those of family, employment and social class as they pertained to the youth and the lower class, encouraging a form of noble suffering and the general acceptance of one's fate.

Several of Aunor's early films follow a narrative in which the character succeeds against the odds, with themes of escaping poverty through hard work, being a dutiful and filial child, piety, being respectful to superiors and being of noble character in the face of hardship. In *The Young at Heart* and *Young Love*, Aunor's role is that of the semi-biographical talent contestant on a television show, while in *Guy and Pip*, she is a singer and actress shooting a film on a studio set. In *Young Love*, Aunor is a poor orphan whose salvation comes from the noble studio boss who imparts advice and grooms her for success. In contrast, her character's trials stem from the guardian figure in her life who, through jealousy and malice, does everything in her power to prevent Aunor's character from achieving success and liberty. The guardian beats, berates and even imprisons Aunor to prevent her from attending the final life-changing competition. In this scenario, there are two forms of authority: good authority in the form of the studio boss who is nurturing and transformative, and bad authority in the form of the tyrannical guardian, a caricature of evil. In the absence of biological parents, the studio boss is a calm, kind man who takes on the role of parent and offers opportunities and liberty, recommending and advancing cash for the purchase of a new wardrobe to suit her needs for the contest.

In *Guy and Pip*, other rival superiors in terms of class – the studio boss's children – conspire to keep her apart from her true love and co-star because of jealousy and romantic rivalry. In *And God Smiled at Me*, good and bad authority (and parental) figures go head to head against each other. Celina (Aunor) is an illegitimate child from Davao who has to live with her father and his enraged wife and two legitimate daughters in the city after her biological mother's death. Celina's father also dies, resulting in his wife mistreating her badly, slapping her and forcing food from the floor into her mouth. The widow is stereotypically evil, and Celina only escapes when she is found by a woman who is the exact opposite of the widow – a rich, kind and childless parishioner who hears her singing at church. While the widow is a cruel figure of authority, the narrative is careful to include a benevolent figure of authority as well.

Thus, class plays a role in the obstacles that Aunor's characters face, with clear distinctions being made between good authority and bad. The distinction between the two is admittedly a smokescreen for the ultimate message it contains: respect authority. Even in the cruellest taunt from her guardian, Aunor's character remains respectful and filial, accepting suffering at the hands of her superiors as her fate. 'Authority is oppressive' is a potentially subversive message, but it is negated by the existence of 'good' superiors. This converts the message instead to 'There are noble superiors and wicked superiors, but if you are of noble character, you will be saved.' Aunor's films are also about the tension between youth and their more immediate authority, parents. Parents are not always uncomplicatedly good characters in the narrative, and sometimes serve as the catalyst for a teenage character's search for a nurturing parental or authority figure. This can come in the form of a benevolent employer or some other noble benefactor that acts in the teenager's best interests, replicating the old system of patronage in Philippine society. Aunor's characters chiefly battle poverty, class inequality and abuse, but in all those scenarios, she remains passive, patient and accepting of her fate. This patient suffering, dubbed 'sufferance' by Flores (2001), characterises much of Aunor's work and persona.

The theme of suffering is a key feature of Philippine popular art forms, and is one of Tiongson's 'four values in Filipino drama and film', *mabuti ang inaapi* (the oppressed are virtuous), enthroning suffering and submissiveness, a trope born of the Spanish and American colonial regimes and replicated in contemporary cinema (2008: 272). Tiongson (a leading scholar and critic of Philippine arts and culture that includes film, theatre and literature) notes that Aunor followed in a tradition of suffering heroines (ibid.: 273). This echoes the Catholic belief that suffering on earth is rewarded in heaven, so one should persist even in an untenable situation because of the reward in eternal life. In this manner, Aunor serves more as a passive example of virtue reinforcing authority and the accepted norms and values of the era. In her youthful quest for identity formation, Aunor's characters and indeed her star persona repeatedly behave respectfully, submissively and in an exemplary manner. Freedom is encouraged, though within accepted parameters, a powerlessness that also mirrors Aunor's own position as an actress at this time during her legal battle against Sampaguita and her parents' control over her romantic and professional relationships.

Passivity is a trait that the studio attempts to pin on Aunor repeatedly, through her submission to authority in films and her work as a star with the studio, as well as Catholic narratives of submission and faith in her films. While Aunor would notably upend this dynamic in *Himala* (see Tadiar 2002; Lim 2004), even in her early love team films her stardom shows signs of resisting these narratives of submission, particularly in her performance. The previous chapter discusses Aunor's habit of looking directly at the camera in her semi-biographical studio films, unblinking and with a steady resolve. This is not a trait that is shared by Cruz, Santos or Mortiz, and marks her out as unique among them. The power dynamics of a young woman gazing directly at the camera when the same privilege or opportunity is not shared by her male co-star is undeniably skewed towards Aunor. When the audience looks at Aunor, Aunor looks back – unflinching and revelling in her power. This steady gaze (though not typically aimed at the audience for the rest of her career) would go on to become one of the hallmarks of Aunor's performance style post jukebox musical, looking with silent and expressive eyes rather than the more emotionally explicit and verbal performances of her peers. This small act of looking steadily at the viewer as she sings with confidence subverts the passivity that the studios and authority figures enforced. And Cruz, uncomfortable in the scrutiny, blinks and looks away.

Suffering, submissiveness and *mestizaje* were not the only colonial legacies that Aunor's star image struggled with. The other legacy of the extended colonisation of the Philippines by the Spanish and Americans was in their languages, which left their mark on the new national language that was introduced in the 1950s. Nationalists of the era were particularly defensive of the new national language, seen to be an important step away from the past colonial masters and a means of unifying a nation of diverse languages. The influence of the love teams on the language of the 1970s and vice versa through their films and star personas is of interest in the next section along with the impact that language and the accompanying implications of speaking and singing in popular culture had on the love teams. What assumptions are made about stars, songs and films based on the languages associated with their stardom, and were these standards applied evenly to all four stars of the love teams in this research?

'Neo-colonial' love teams: intersections of language and class

Academic Luis V. Teodoro Jr considered the role of the stars and films of the genre in terms of what he called a 'neo-colonial cultural offensive' (1970). Teodoro Jr was referring to the Philippine films of the 5th Manila Film Festival (which he was critical of) and their role in promoting English and neo-colonial values and culture over local ones. He criticised both the new darker stars of the era (writing that it is assumed that such stars are a sign of decolonisation) and the popular films with English titles, English songs and English words slipped into the script:

> Pilipino movies have ... become ... less of a vehicle for the language itself. This extends to the increasing use of English, apparently meant to suggest that the film is 'literate', the degree of this literacy dependent upon the amount of English dialogue it contains ... This development [corrupted Pilipino] is ignored by the view that the change in standards of measuring beauty among movie stars, both male and female, is a sign that there has taken place a subtle but profound decolonization in the attitudes of Filipino moviegoers. (Ibid.: 31)

The anxiety around language and nationalist sentiment had its roots in the history of languages in the Philippines. Spanish was the exclusive province of the elite and educated *mestizos* while English was the more democratic language, taught to the general public during thirty-five years of US education policy (Thompson 2003: 27). Outside of Spanish and English, Filipinos were linguistically segregated as they spoke 156 languages and as many as 500 community dialects (ibid.: 28). By the time of Independence in 1935, the official languages of the Constitution were English and Spanish with a provision for an indigenous national language, which President Quezon would announce as Tagalog in 1937 (ibid.). The cinema played a key role in popularising and teaching Tagalog, with early stars of Philippine cinema having to quickly learn the language when talkies and the policy changed their industry. Tagalog (also the name of an ethnic group and their language) would later come to be known as 'Pilipino' in the 1950s, and 'Filipino' in the late 1970s in an attempt to give the language a more national identity. 'Tagalog', 'Pilipino' and 'Filipino' are colloquially still used almost interchangeably to refer to the language, with ideological implications inherent in the choice of name used. Taglish first emerged in the 1960s and is the creation of educated

Filipinos (ibid.: 40), with its use partially facilitated by a bilingual education policy of English and Filipino passed in 1974 (ibid.: 39–40). Thompson writes that 'Taglish spread rapidly from the classroom to the general populace through radio and television in much the same way that Tagalog had spread earlier' (ibid.: 41).

The use of English as a spoken marker of class and sophistication has been discussed already in this book when examining issues of the urban educated preferring foreign films, and in examining Cruz's image. Teodoro Jr singles out Aunor as being representative of leading this shift, saying:

> the stars that the public now worships are the epitome of the Filipino who has arrived in the neo-colonial setting: full of English slang and belting out American pop songs. Their colour and their appearance emphasize their being of this race, but language that they speak and the songs that they sing reveal them to be the quintessence of what the colonial Filipino would like to be. (Ibid.: 42)

Teodoro Jr emphasises that the stars of the era (teenagers) particularly represent the neo-colonial in terms of language and the songs they reproduce in their films. The 5th Manila Film Festival that prompted Teodoro Jr's article only had nine Pilipino titles out of twenty-five films, while the rest featured English titles (thirteen), a mixture (one) or even Spanish titles (two) (ibid.).

Writing in 2000, Rafael offered a much more positive outlook on the emergence of this mixture of languages, or 'Taglish' as it has come to be known, describing the panic surrounding it as 'symptomatic of larger nationalist anxieties about the ability to shape the terrain of a national-popular culture and the language appropriate to it' (171). In referring to the writing of nationalist historian and Tagalog writer Teodoro Agoncillo, who considered Taglish a 'bastard language', Rafael then linked this nationalist anxiety to an attempt to regulate the use of Taglish, which ultimately resulted in the birth of another concept discussed in this research: *bakya*: 'In the late 1960s and early 1970s, nationalist attempts to contain the effects of Taglish were reflected in the urban, middle-class discourse regarding the lower classes. A new term emerged to designate this heterogenous population: the *bakya* crowd' (ibid.). Yet again, the class anxieties of the 1970s arrive at the juncture of *bakya*, or tackiness. It is also no coincidence that the period of concern Rafael highlights also marks the rise of the teenage jukebox genre and the teenage stars who were a key factor in popularising Taglish in the first instance through their creation of popular culture products. Rafael goes on to defend the use of Taglish, writing that it later became a language of dissent, one that allowed the speaker to slip between languages and create new constellations of meaning in the hands of a popular cartoonist between 1983 and 1986 (ibid.: 176–179). Rafael also includes a hierarchy of audiences that may be perceived in the industry:

> The hierarchy of viewership is aligned with a linguistic hierarchy as well. 'A' and 'B' audiences watch movies in English, thereby signifying their proximity to outside sources of knowledge and the larger networks of power to which they are attached ... Their access to English is an indication of their place on the social map as part of, yet apart from 'A', a hierarchy of languages. By contrast, 'C' and 'D' audiences gravitate towards movies in Taglish, the lingua franca of Filipino movies ... More important in setting Filipino movies apart from other films is the use of Taglish ... Taglish has the effect of maintaining viewers within the borders of the existing social imaginary. (Ibid.: 182)

As Rafael discusses it, Taglish worked to maintain established class lines. This can be seen in the love team films of the era, which used English in order either to distinguish the main characters as urban and cool (the 'literacy' which Teodoro Jr referred to), or to confer a villainous slant on an overbearing or outrightly abusive upper-class character. Sometimes particularly cruel figures of authority adopt Spanish words into their vocabulary, a key indicator of old money and privilege. Spanish is the title of the oppressive *Remembrance* character Don Gregorio, owner of a hacienda, which calls to mind the old patron–client ties of Philippine society. Don Gregorio is a throwback to this era, while his sons represent the new Philippine society through their urban capitalist lifestyle that has sports cars instead of their father's horses, and a city mansion instead of a sprawling hacienda. The servants of the Manila house are largely invisible in the film, while the many labourers and farmers of the hacienda are conspicuously apparent. The new system of capitalism is signified as triumphant in the film through the death of the patron Don, slain by an oppressed peasant who is sentenced to life in prison for his defiance of rightful (albeit tyrannical) authority. The struggle between proponents of pure Tagalog and Taglish can also be viewed as a struggle between the old and the young over the control of language and culture, with the teenagers representing a shift away from the purity advocated by the academics and nationalists, here reflected in the Taglish of the boys in contrast to the

Tagalog and (worse yet) Spanish words and implications of the hacienda in their father's title.

Taglish and English are strongly associated with the well-educated, upper-class Rosa Vilma in her interactions with the three male characters of different classes in *Tatlong Mukha ni Rosa Vilma*. With rich Jimmy she speaks Taglish, comfortable in the slang together, while with poor Ligaya she teaches English, the product of her privileged education. With Edgardo and his mother she speaks Tagalog, suggesting that Filipino is the neutral language of the middle class while the poor should acquire English to better themselves. In *Edgar Loves Vilma*, the pushy rival for Edgar's love is a teenage girl who speaks mostly in English, while Edgar and Vilma themselves speak Tagalog or Taglish. The narrative uses the languages in order to subtly promote one suitor and discredit the other through a discourse of which girl is more Filipino in her speech. In *Love Letters*, a girl is accused of having 'colonial mentality' when she takes the position of dating an American in a debate between the differences in dating a Filipino and an American; in the question of life partners, the films take the side of the native rather than the colonial (even though the native boy in question was raised in America). One may acquire the polish of the colonisers, or even resemble them, but one must also be unquestionably Filipino.

Aunor had a particularly interesting relationship with Taglish. While her films often used Taglish, it frequently appeared as shorthand for class when it was used by her superiors against her, or in films where she is comfortably middle class and uses it herself. Lim writes of the *colegiala*, or the elite Catholic college girl (relevant also to the discussion of Santos above) in her analysis of the films of Sharon Cuneta in the 1980s, comparing her stardom and its strategic appropriation of Aunor's trajectory in a 2015 article that also raises the 1970 move of Aunor to attract urban *mestiza colegiala* fans, in part demonstrated through her use of Taglish. Where Aunor interacted the most with English was in her songs, which were initially primarily in English. A popular magazine related her unwillingness to sing in Tagalog and expressed shock when she indicated that she preferred English songs during a live radio performance:

> When Nora arrived, the emcee asked her to sing a Tagalog song but Nora said that she didn't know any Tagalog songs, only English. (WHAT?) 'Even in Bicolano, the language of your home province, I'm sure you know one,' the emcee insisted. 'I don't know any, and I'm not used to speaking their language,' Nora answered. Because the emcee was so shocked by Nora's answers, he just let her sing

> an English song. Some days later, the issue of Nora and Tagalog songs or native Filipino songs spread and was discussed by many people. How could it be? She is known as a top recording star and is admired by children, youths and even elders. And this is the calibre of her singing? What a shock! Pure Filipino but doesn't know at least one Tagalog song? What an obvious insult! (Morota 1971b)

The article goes on to state that the studio recognised that Aunor needed to sing in Tagalog for the good of her star image, and a month later she did so, ultimately even recording an album of Filipino songs. The language used is strong, and outrightly berates and shames Aunor for her use of English and betrayal of the 'Filipinoness' she supposedly represents.

Aunor's singing in English may have been a deliberate strategy to lend her star image some of the 'literacy' that Teodoro Jr speaks of. Thompson, quoting Gonzalez (1982), notes that 'Filipinos learned English during the Marcos era because they aspired to the riches and grandeur of the elite', noting that power and privileges were conferred through English (2003: 211). In an environment where she was an obvious outsider, English may have been the means of conforming to the norm and attempting to acquire the sophistication associated with the English language as well as borrowing glamour from popular English stars and songs. Notably, Santos was not held to the same standard despite releasing primarily English songs herself. Cruz's discography also consisted of many English covers as well as even some Spanish songs, and of the four stars, Mortiz sang in Tagalog the most. At the intersection of class and language, Aunor was condemned both for not being sophisticated enough (*bakya*) and for attempting to gain sophistication through English music.

Alex B. Brillantes (1987) and Albert F. Celoza (1997) describe Marcos's rule as an authoritarian regime. One of the key ways Marcos was able to retain power was through the propagation of authoritarian values. Authoritarianism in political psychology is 'about the psychological profile of people characterized by a desire for order and hierarchy and a fear of outsiders' (Glasius 2018: 515). Extrapolating from this definition, authoritarian values are those values that promote order, hierarchy and a fear of outsiders. This section on language and the neo-colonial influence of love teams in 'corrupting' Tagalog through English and Taglish perfectly demonstrates some of the anxieties that nationalists and those that psychology would profile as authoritarians (as opposed to libertarians) had with regards to foreign influences on local culture. And the first hierarchy that individuals are born into is the hierarchy of the family. How did

Marcos use hierarchies of power and the family to govern the nation and how did he encourage the internalisation of authoritarian values through the family?

Authoritarian hierarchies of power and the family

In the run-up to Martial Law, Marcos was working on several fronts to use the institution of the family to invoke submission and institute a nationwide hierarchy of behaviour that placed him at the apex of power (discussed in Chapter 2). To this end, he relied on melodramatic codes found in *sarsuwelas* and films, particularly in the person of his wife, Imelda, who was able to position herself as a melodramatic victim-heroine in the Marcos romance (Espiritu 2017: 75). These hierarchies of power are embedded casually in the love team film and images in the form of lessons such as respect for parents, respect for employers, and respect for superiors (whether in terms of class, age or power) and are discussed in this book in the relationship stars had with their studios and the compliance and family atmosphere present there; the regulations of the film industry in 1972 shortly after Martial Law but already present within internal studio policy prior to the era; and within the films themselves, discussed in this chapter and earlier in Chapter 2.

A *Kislap* article in 1968 painted the Marcos family as a typical family, with a headline that ran 'The President and the First Lady as Parents – an Ordinary Mommy and Daddy' (Esguerra 1968). It features a posed portrait of the family, referring to them as the 'First Family of the Philippines', in a nod to the phrase used to refer to the US presidential families. Two other pictures include a picture of the children with their mother on an official national campaign to plant vegetables, captioned 'One of the First Lady's projects is setting an example as the Mother of the nation by planting a variety of vegetables. She demonstrates that a mother can contribute widely to the country', as well as a picture of the children with the family's pet dogs. Throughout the article there are references to the celebrity family of President John F. Kennedy, with Marcos declaring a reluctance to have his children in the public eye like the Kennedys did with their children as well as Imelda stating her priority of being wife first and then mother, the opposite of what Jacqueline Kennedy said (ibid.: 5–6). To Imelda, the father is the pillar of the household and thus her priority. The article states that 'President Marcos is not just the Father of the Nation.

Even if he has a lot of problems that weigh heavily on him, he still finds time for his children', and it includes a quote, emphasising Marcos's good parenting, from an unnamed Australian ambassador, who is said to have told Marcos, 'It is commendable to witness the great President of a nation still able to fulfil his duties as a father' (ibid.: 5).

Several agendas are present in the article. Firstly, it sets up the Marcos family as the First Family, comparable to the US presidential family. Secondly, it associates the family with the most glamourous and popular political dynasty of America, the Kennedys. Along with this come the attendant associations of class, celebrity and affection that the American public had for the Kennedys. Imelda reinforces the primacy of the patriarch of the family and nation, comparing the head of the family (and state) to the pillar of the national household that requires the full support and obedience of the family. The First Lady is also established as the Mother of the nation, imparting lessons to her Children (both literal and metaphorical) of obedience and contributing to the Nation's development. It also works to soften the image of Marcos, painting him as an ordinary family man, with their family just like any other in the Philippines.

Shortly after declaring Martial Law, Marcos commissioned veteran psychological warfare specialist Jose Ma. Crisol, in tandem with the Army's Office of Civil Relations, to create a master plan for social reform titled 'Towards the Restructuring of Filipino Values'. This recommended that Marcos exploit the Filipino family paradigm to structure his New Society:

> What is recommended therefore is an expansion of the family to a larger group – the country. We should treat the country as our very own family, where the President of the Republic is the father and all the citizens as our brothers. From this new value we develop a strong sense of oneness, loyalty to the country, and a feeling of nationalism. Because all Filipinos are brothers, we become just and sincere. (Quoted in McCoy 2009: 16)

The 1968 *Kislap* article demonstrates that Marcos was already using the ideology of the family to shape Philippine society in his paternal image. The subsequent report issued in the 1970s only emphasises the importance of Marcos's appropriation of the family, and the role it would play in his New Society.

The New Society was a direct response to the tumult of the preceding two years and sought to address the 'Sick Society' Marcos perceived in the Philippines. The official slogan of the New Society movement was 'Sa ikauunlad ng bayan, disiplina ang kailangan' (For the nation to progress, there must be discipline). Among the values he pushed for were 'the primacy of personal connections, the importance of maintaining in-group harmony and coherence', and a spirit of self-sacrifice (Dolan 1993: 52–53). These are key themes of popular cinema during the time and can be seen in the love team films discussed in this chapter. Indeed, Aunor's characters in particular invariably prioritise close relationships and maintain a good connection with peers, while a strong self-sacrificing nature preserves these ties despite great personal cost and suffering.

If the family was seen as a vital means of teaching submission and respect for hierarchies of power, how did the love teams of this research address the family in their joint images and films? Love teams are first and foremost multimedia narratives of becoming the couple, and from there, forming the basis of becoming the family. The following section explores how love teams invoke the family in different ways, including their real lives and prioritising of family ties, the narratives of their films which teach lessons of reconciliation and filial piety, and the family-like unit that Aunor and Cruz formed with their doll daughter, Maria Leonora Teresa. It also becomes evident that the couple and the family unit can be used to suppress elements of subversion in a threatening star image, as the establishment did with Aunor's through narratives of 'marrying' into the establishment rather than posing a threat to it as an individual. Santos and Mortiz make unthreatening films that represent and reiterate the establishment stand on personhood, coupledom and family.

Becoming the family

Philippine love teams are appealing to audiences in part because they perform the ideological function of becoming the couple, and because their fundamental function is to become the couple (or give the impression or hope of becoming a couple) in a multimedia process that covers all aspects of their images: the personal (the celebrity couple), the professional (the star couple) and the fictional (the screen couple). The love team produces texts about becoming the couple in their films as well as in their extra-filmic body of work, including interviews, images and public appearances. As soon as they are launched in their first appearance together, they are always in the process of becoming the couple, whether in the public eye, in the narrative of their films or in the duets they sing. An entire industry is built around the existence of the couple, in print, photography, radio, television and film, each building on the other to produce the complete physical and joint star image of the couple as well as ideological messages and signals around what it means to be a couple of their era and society. A tried and tested path to stardom lies in combining two stars to make a couple, a strategy that is echoed in societal cues and discourse surrounding coupledom.

The heterosexual married couple is described by the state as the foundation of the family in the majority Catholic Philippines (Office of the President of the Philippines 1987). The strong kinship and familial ties in the Philippines mean that narratives about becoming a couple often lead to becoming a family, whether the foundation of a new nuclear family, inclusion into the extended family or the joining of families. Questions of courtship in teenage love team films involve the family as a matter of course and feature frequently in the narratives, while the absence of family is cause for sympathy and a source of tragedy. The family is the first and primary hierarchy of power and authority individuals are born into, and it continues to shape the trajectory of the individual and their relative positions within that hierarchy during the course of their life and the film narrative. The family represents authority in its first and most enduring form, laying out a hierarchy of patriarchal power that plays out in different ways in the love team and its films. The sanctity of marriage and family in the Philippines is enshrined by the Catholic Church, which exhorts certain behaviours and mores that in turn shape the couple in terms of courtship, marriage and family, not least through the Holy Family, the exemplary nuclear family of Catholicism. At the heart of the teenage jukebox musical is the struggle between traditional values and modern practices, and the wants of the individual and the family.

The love team and film couple work to naturalise the idea of coupledom in popular culture. Themes of courtship, suitability, love and the negotiation of a romantic relationship run through both their on- and off-screen lives. Their work can be said to be the act of becoming the couple, played out across a variety of texts, be it magazine articles, interviews, film roles, pictorials, or simply the act of being with each other in public – always a couple, or in various stages of portraying a couple. The phrase 'becoming the couple' is appropriate here because their film roles are precisely about the process of becoming the couple that their fans know them to be on-screen. Films therefore act as extended scenarios in which the pair come together again and again, perhaps with a different challenge or meet cute each time, all with the ultimate goal of achieving a long-term, committed relationship. Sometimes this culminates in an on-screen wedding, while at other times a happily ever after is implied.

The role of 'fantasy' is forefront in the star image of Nora Aunor. Her very stardom is the dream of the masses made flesh, a narrative of rising from poverty and misery to become extraordinary. One way this fantasy plays out in her love team is by the inevitable comparison of Aunor's image to Cinderella, and in casting Tirso Cruz III – a man who has a Roman numeral suffix in his name – as her Prince Charming. The irony in the fantasy, of course, is that the very fantasy of waiting for her prince to come (perhaps her own fantasy, but also one prescribed by the fans, as Aunor recounts in Chapter 4) removes significant power and agency from her. The reliance on a rich man as saviour to a poor woman plays to a specific fantasy: hypergamy, or the act of marrying 'up'. The following section explores the class and power imbalance inherent in the Cinderella–Prince Charming dynamic between Aunor and Cruz, and how it manifested itself in their films and joint love team image, demonstrating how fantasy can be restricting when used to suppress a threatening force.

Cinderella–Prince Charming

Aunor's subversive star image contained a dangerous potential that would form a threat to Marcos and the studio (as it would function when she was an individual star later in her career), and a prediction that came true when she was poached by rival studio Tower Productions. One key means of taming Aunor's potentially subversive image was through the joining of her image to a much safer one such as Cruz's. Cruz's image (as discussed in Chapter 3) was a much more typical star image of the era. His famous *mestizo* musical family origins and proximity to star-makers and the studio ensured his early fame, his first role as the Messiah cementing his role as the fortunate son. Their love team films together cast Cruz as Aunor's Prince Charming, sweeping her off her feet with the promise of a better life. Their joint image was characterised by this 'opposites attract' dynamic, from their socio-economic backgrounds to their physical features. As a couple, Cruz and Aunor embody the binary opposition of rich versus poor, with Aunor's poor background meeting its saviour in Cruz's upper-class background in both fantasy and reality. And the Cinderella–Prince Charming dynamic played itself out in their film roles as well.

Aunor plays a poor teenager living in miserable conditions in *Young Love* and *My Little Brown Girl*. In both films, Cruz plays a bored, rebellious rich boy trying to escape the expectations of his parents to marry well and behave a certain way. In *Always in My Heart*, Aunor plays an impoverished teenage girl of noble birth living in the countryside whose single mother is struggling to get her married to a rich family in Manila, while Cruz plays a well-to-do teenager from the same area. In all three films, marriage to a rich man would immediately improve her circumstances, particularly in *My Little Brown Girl*, where the mother of Henry (Cruz's character) is enraged when he announces his desire to marry Marita (Aunor's character), a maid from the countryside working in their Manila house. In *Always in My Heart*, it is Aunor's character's mother who turns out to be a snob when it comes to her daughter's marriage; only the very elite from Manila will be considered. In *Young Love*, Aunor is an orphan living with a cruel guardian who mistreats her and actively blocks her from achieving success through competing in a singing competition. In sharp contrast, Cruz plays a rich teenage boy who is attempting to escape from his grandmother's attempts to send him to Australia to study. Their motivations for joining the singing contest are very different, with Aunor dreaming of a better life without abuse while Cruz is avoiding family expectations. In both *My Little Brown Girl* and *Young Love*, Aunor is rescued from a life of misery, labouring under unjust figures of authority and oppression, and is buoyed by her romance with Cruz and the freedom he represents.

Cruz often plays poor-little-rich-boy roles where he escapes from his family's expectations of him with regards to marriage, education and employment. In *The Young at Heart* and *Always in My Heart*, he flees his home to avoid his parents' matchmaking, choosing to be with Aunor instead. In *My Little Brown Girl*, his mother threatens to disown him when he announces that he wants to marry their maid. Within their love team, a fantasy of hypergamy is playing out. An issue that constantly recurs in Aunor and Cruz's love team is that of class. The tandem represents the ideal union of two different worlds: the upper-class, *mestizo*, unreachable prince of the traditional screen and the poor, dark *Sinderella* from the masses. Specifically, the pair subvert homogamy, the practice of a person selecting a partner who has similar characteristics to themselves (Medina 2001: 108). Homogamy can extend to religion, as demonstrated by the shared Catholic values in the love team's films, but in this case also to their social class. The pressure to marry within the same class is especially strong in the upper strata, where issues of inheritance and lineage come into play. Cruz and Aunor represent a very specific kind of interclass marriage where the man marries down (hypogamy) and the woman marries up (hypergamy), a direction of social mobility consistent with male-dominated societies (ibid.: 109). Through this union, the problem of poverty in Aunor's life is solved by the affluence in Cruz's life, both on-screen and off, in a national fantasy played out in their films and in the pages of magazines for the consumption of fans.

Notably, Aunor is 'rescued' by Cruz in their purely fictional films, driven by original narratives written by the studio, rather than in their semi-biographical films, in which the studio is unable to fully bury Aunor's subversive climb from poverty on her own merits of talent and hard work. In the semi-biographical films, Aunor is either independent (*The Young at Heart* and *Guy and Pip*) or on the verge of breaking free from oppressive authority by herself, though *Young Love* features Nora being physically saved by Tirso, who fights the boyfriend of Nora's abusive guardian and breaks her out of her house where she has been locked up.

Maria Leonora Teresa and the family

Maria Leonora Teresa (MLT) is the name given to the doll presented to Aunor by Cruz. The doll quickly became a feature of the love team, appearing in their films, becoming the subject of a song written by Cruz, and even releasing her own album with her voice provided by Cruz and Aunor (Aunor 2016). MLT was often dressed in clothes and complementary jewellery made lovingly by fans. Imbued with life from the devotion of the love team's fans, MLT soon developed a star image and fame that contemporary human stars would envy. Wilfredo Pascual's essay 'Devotion' gives a vivid picture of her own stardom:

> Christened by the fans as Maria Leonora Teresa, people wrote to the doll and sent her handmade cards. And as if that breathed life to the doll, Maria Leonora Teresa wrote back and eased the people's worries. They pierced her ear and made her wore [sic] earrings. They lavished her with jewelries [sic] and expensive clothes. And when the death toll of the deadly typhoons rose, the most photographed doll in Philippine history went to church and wept. In the editorials she wrote for magazines, the doll inspired the Noranians to mobilize truckloads of fans to help the victims by donating food and clothes, to preach the doll's message of love and charity. (Pascual 2005: 308)

MLT served several functions in the love team. Firstly, she was a visual barometer of the state of the relationship between Aunor and Cruz. This could be indicated by factors such as whose custody she was in (with fans ferrying her between Aunor and Cruz during times of discord) and how she was dressed (sometimes wearing dark clothes, which indicated a stormy patch in their relationship) (Francisco 2004) Aunor and Cruz would reinforce the image of the family, referring to each other as 'Mommy' and 'Daddy'. MLT also appeared in their films, memorably serving as an intermediary during an argument between the young couple, solved when Aunor lifts her dress to reveal the words 'I'm Sorry' printed on her slip by Cruz in *Guy and Pip*.

This corresponds with the main function that MLT served in the love team of Aunor and Cruz: the glue that joins them as a 'family', the child that cements the union and the fruit of their love. Aunor and Cruz never married each other, but in the 1970s, they performed the role of the family, complete with a doll child onto which fans projected their desire to see the pair as a family. This instant and pure family is not without its familiar inspirations and mimics the Holy Family to an extent – a pure and chaste marriage to raise a child immaculately conceived and without the taint of earthly desires. MLT represents that purity and destiny of the love team, a child without the associated act of creating life. A child brought to life by the love that fans had for the love team. A child bearing the markers of her parents' stardom in her name: Maria, the Catholic practice of dedicating a girl child to Mary, Leonora, containing Aunor's given name, and Teresa, bearing the 'T' and sounding as similar to 'Tirso' as possible while remaining feminine (see Figure 6.2). The doll is always known by her full, formal name – no nicknames for her despite becoming famous in an industry full of stars with nicknames, perhaps precisely because her name and identity are encoded with the names and identities of her 'parents' and to abbreviate or change this would be to misidentify the 'child' of Aunor and Cruz.

Her other function in the tandem included the role traditionally assigned to younger siblings in courtship: to stand as a chaperone and ensure proper behaviour through her innocent presence. As discussed in the previous chapter, MLT also stood in to signify the presence of Aunor when Aunor rejected Cruz to be with Manny de León during the Manila Film Festival at the height of the conflict between Sampaguita and Tower Productions, mimicking the tumult of a custody battle between separated

Figure 6.2 Maria Leonora Teresa with Cruz. Source: from the collection of Nestor de Guzman

parents (Evora 1970b). Cruz released a popular song in 1971 entitled 'Maria Leonora Teresa', written by Ike Lozada, about the doll's heartbreak due to the separation of her parents and Aunor finding a new love and returning the doll to Cruz during the Sampaguita–Tower Productions legal battle. This song was featured in *Guy and Pip* in a scene with the pair walking with the doll through a garden. The incorporation of Maria Leonora Teresa into Aunor and Cruz's films is another form of slippage. The doll signified their relationship as a family in both filmic and extra-filmic appearances, conferring a sense of permanence to their relationship that their youth prevented from being reality in a marriage. Thus, the doll has the distinction of existing in the real and reel lives of the love team, blurring the lines between fact and fiction in her appearances with Aunor and Cruz.

Santos and Mortiz lacked a child, though at least one source refers to a puppy, 'Honey', given to Santos by Mortiz as a present and a symbol of their love (Llanes 2008c). Without the benefits of having a doll child, how did Santos and Mortiz reinforce narratives of family in their image and films? If Aunor and Cruz's relationship was a fantasy of the masses, the love team of Santos and Mortiz often portrayed middle- to upper-class fantasies of sedate family life, facing problems generally more representative of those classes.

Joining families together

The Santos–Mortiz love team also performs becoming the couple through their extra-filmic emphasis on family. The pair worked together harmoniously in part due to supportive families that encouraged and shaped the steady and professional nature of their love team. This narrative of joining families is supported by magazine articles at the time that suggested that their families were already joined together and merely waiting for the formality of a wedding between the pair (Juan 1972). This tactic of coupledom relies on the suggestion that the pair are so inevitable and so favoured because they are practically already a family. The love team portrays an alternate model of permissible teenage behaviour of the era. Unfailingly compliant and polite, they are the 'good' teenagers – filial, respectful and submissive to authority. Their interviews demonstrate a respect for their parents and the studio, moving systematically through the career course plotted for them by their handlers. Through Santos's long-standing stardom stemming from her child star days in Sampaguita and Mortiz's middle-class background, the pair are establishment figures that rock no boats and threaten no one, offering a steady alternative to the stormy love team of Aunor and Cruz.

The love team of Santos and Mortiz have a joint image of harmony and unity, with journalists often commenting on the visible accord between the families of Santos and Mortiz, discussed in Chapter 4. This is also visible in *Edgar Loves Vilma*, where Mortiz plays a rich boy who lacks a firm guiding influence in his home, which consists of his grandmother, rich father Armando who smokes, drinks and is often away from home, and a younger brother. Armando and Edgar have a dysfunctional relationship, demonstrated by a scene in which he chuckles when he finds Edgar looking at a *Playboy* magazine, only commenting that his son is growing up. Armando meets Lisa, Vilma's mother, at a seedy nightclub, unaware that Edgar and Vilma are classmates. The film throws the four together, resulting in joint dates such as a family trip to Manila zoo as both generations fall in love. This is complicated by Edgar's disapproving grandmother, who forbids Armando from marrying a lowly nightclub singer.

In Vilma's house, it is revealed that her mother is only performing at nightclubs because she is struggling to maintain the family's middle-class lifestyle without her husband. This is resolved when Vilma runs away and Lisa falls sick and is confined to bed, resulting in Armando and Edgar disobeying their matriarch to save their women.

The narrative here clearly frames Lisa and Vilma's plight as an indignity that is suffered due to difficult finances rather than a deliberate choice, ensuring that the nightclub does not reflect badly on Lisa's character, but rather portrays her as a working single mother struggling to keep the family afloat. Armando is prone to vice, but promptly gives them up when he falls in love with Lisa, also proof that it is not a moral defect in him but rather caused by the absence of the love of a good woman. Vilma is a loving and good child throughout, though conflicted by the toll that the nightclub takes on her mother in the headaches and hangovers she suffers. Edgar immediately reforms himself upon the entrance of Vilma into his life. The zoo outing signifies that the family is complete and happy, enjoying wholesome activities together in contrast to the smoky, dark nightclub in which the parents are introduced. Vilma is the moral centre of the film, desperate to get her mother away from the nightclub and the occupational hazards that come with it, and is a good influence on Edgar. It is Vilma's disappearance that ultimately drives all the characters to overcome the various obstacles that keep them from being together in order to ensure her safety when it is revealed that she has been kidnapped at gunpoint by a romantic rival and classmate, Oscar.

The film works as a multi-generational romance, bent on knitting two broken families together to form a new whole. Each member of the family has a positive effect on the other: the women reform the men, the men lend respectability to and rescue the women from dangerous situations, while the children gain the benefit of having both a paternal and maternal influence in their lives. The narrative portrays both families as missing some key element that is solved by the joining of the parents in a relationship and mirrored by the teenagers. In times of crisis, the family unit is shown to triumph, while individuals are isolated and ill equipped to navigate the challenges of life. The obstacle of class is surmounted by the circumstances that lead the woman to desperate measures, and they are given the protection of the affluent through Armando.

Conclusion

In the run-up to Martial Law in the Philippines, Marcos faced increasing resistance from the middle-class, educated youth of the capital and labourers via the First Quarter Storm in the 1970s. As a result, he sought to suppress dissent in those demographics, and targeted the youth with, amongst other things, a film industry that would replicate the values of authoritarianism via regulating film policy. Marcos also recognised the power inherent in Aunor's star image and attempted to cultivate it, while the studio, her love team partner, doll 'daughter' and the genre worked to neutralise her subversive potential in narratives of love, matrimony and sufferance. Examination of love team films of the era demonstrates the relationship between the popular and authority during a time when the President claimed to be acting in the interest of the working class but, in fact, used popular media to keep the masses under control. This and previous chapters have demonstrated how the popular self-regulates via the studios and a hierarchy that ultimately resembles a familial structure, in which elders and superiors set and police acceptable behaviour. In effect, the state was taking the place of parents, a tactic visible in Marcos's public performance of his family as assuming parental roles for the nation.

This was intentionally and unintentionally mirrored in the family-centric narratives of the teenage jukebox musical films of the love teams in the 1970s. Despite being teenagers, the stars primarily worked to naturalise the state of being a couple both in their star images and in their films. The act of becoming the couple is played out in a variety of texts associated with the love team from duets to endorsements that work towards binding individuals into a couple. The end destination for the couple is matrimony and the family, a fantasy played out in film narratives that join the love team eternally before God and the audience. The family is invoked either by narratives of joining families or by the creation of a chaste family complete with a child of the tandem in the stardom of Maria Leonora Teresa. The couple and the family cast individuals into their appropriate places in hierarchies of power at various levels of society, from the family to the workplace, and from the Church to the nation-family.

Within these chains of hierarchy exist other elements of individual identity such as class, gender and ethnicity. The teenage jukebox musical firmly positions stars in the narratives via their identities, casting Aunor as the dark, suffering servant who perseveres under the persecution of the unjust superior; Cruz as the *mestizo* fortunate son who struggles with parental expectations of his future, rebelling in the form of his love for a lower-class woman; Santos as the good girl of a good family who performs emotional labour for the sake of others; and Mortiz as the stereotypical ardent and earnest lover who devotes himself to the women in his life. The teenage jukebox musical's stars and films are sometimes regarded as neo-colonial bad influences in their use of Taglish and English, a phenomenon tied to class and the *bakya*, and a site of struggle between nationalists in favour of a pure native language and the youth of the 1970s who mixed and matched readily the tongues of their nation's history. The resulting hybrid of Taglish does not ignore the histories of the languages involved and, in fact, codes them with elements of class and moral judgement, leading to a hierarchy of languages that indicate a wide range of clues and social messages about characters and individuals in 1970s Philippine society.

In this manner, love teams were able to walk the line between modernity and tradition, primarily through the strategy of appearing modern but promoting traditional values. These include modest and wholesome courtships that respect the traditional Philippine and Catholic values of their society, up to and including taking on gendered roles of subservience, sacrifice and redemption on behalf of their men and family. In this celebration of establishment values, even the more threatening star image that Aunor possessed was tamed and made safe through repetitive narratives of 'marriage' to Cruz's upper-class *mestizo* image and the fulfilment of a national Cinderella–Prince Charming fantasy of hypergamy and family roles. Other struggles between tradition and modernity such as a move to protect Tagalog as the relatively new national language against the perceived English assault that love teams represented show that Aunor was particularly targeted in the expectation to safeguard and carry the local culture in her body and personhood due to her more 'native' (Lim 2004: 66) appearance.

Conclusion

Love team legacies

The teenage love teams of this research were short-lived, not lasting very long before they aged out of the teenage category and into different paths in their careers. It is worth noting that the women did not leave love teams behind entirely but, in fact, continued to rely on love teams in making their transition to a more mature star image. Aunor would occasionally revisit her love team with Cruz throughout her career. Of the two, Guy and Pip had the longest-lasting career, appearing together in films sporadically over the years, including a made-for-television film *When I Fall in Love* released for Valentine's Day in 2014 (dir. Joel Lamangan) on TV5, twenty-five years after their last film together, *Bilangin ang Bituin sa Langit* (dir. Elwood Perez 1989). As the decade went by, the female stars of the love team proved to be much more durable and able to adapt to the changing nature of the industry. Aunor and Santos moved on to work with several of the auteurs of Philippine cinema, starring in various key films of the Second Golden Age of Philippine Cinema (discussed below).

In her personal life, Aunor joined her star image to that of Christopher de León, her co-star in *Banaue* (dir. Gerry de León 1975) through their marriage between 1975 and 1980. De León was a younger, *mestizo* star whose parents were both stars of 1940s and 1950s cinema working primarily with LVN Pictures. De León started earning a reputation as a dramatic performer in the mid-1970s working with auteur directors and was even paired with Aunor in the critically acclaimed *Tatlong Taong Walang Diyos* (dir. Mario O'Hara 1976). Through her marriage with de León, Aunor's star image shifted away from the narrative of teenage puppy love to a mature woman, wife and mother of five children. In linking their star images, both stars also reinforced the quality performances that each represented, making them a formidable match of stars – the darling of the masses and the scion of the film industry (also replicating the same 'taming' dynamic Aunor had with Cruz). In another typically Philippine show business twist symbolic of the intertwining stardom of the two women, de León's most enduring love team partner was none other than Vilma Santos, with whom he made a total of twenty-two films between 1976 and 2004. Their work with auteur directors produced such critically acclaimed films as their debut film *Tag-Ulan sa Tag-Araw* (dir. Celso Ad. Castillo 1975), *Relasyon* (dir. Ishmael Bernal 1982), *Sinasamba Kita* (dir. Eddie Garcia 1982), *Paano Ba ang Mangarap* (dir. Eddie Garcia 1983) and *Broken Marriage* (dir. Ishmael Bernal 1983). The pairing remains iconic, translating even into news coverage of politics such as an article titled 'Vilma–Boyet Love Team: From Movies to the Political Arena?' (Santiago 2007) that discusses their political aspirations in the Batangas province, when Santos successfully ran for Governor while de León ran an unsuccessful campaign for Vice-Governor under another political party. A key point is that once the two female stars began working in auteur films, the titles of the films mostly shifted to Tagalog or consisted of only a character's name.

Working with auteur directors radically reshaped the star images of the women while maintaining a kernel of their origins in the teenage love team. Aunor would become a far more subversive figure in the hands of the auteurs, with her unique membership of the lower class allowing her to channel an authenticity in roles that called for a downtrodden woman of the masses. Her sufferance reached peak levels in films such as *Atsay* (dir. Eddie Garcia 1978), where she plays a poor woman from the countryside who goes to the city to find work as a housemaid and is ill treated by multiple employers; *Bona* (dir. Lino Brocka 1980), where she plays a version of her fans – a woman obsessed with a bit player, casting herself into servitude to him only to have him pursue other women and eventually plan to leave her, inciting her to pour boiling water on him in a rage; and *Himala*, where she is killed because of the threat that her fervent religious-based following poses to the patriarchal status quo of her community. These roles all capitalise on her representativeness of the poor, dark masses, while *Bona* and *Himala* directly reference her quasi-religious fan following earned in her teenage love team career in the early 1970s. At present, Aunor is strongly associated with independent cinema, appearing in two films by Brillante Mendoza, *Thy Womb* (2012) and *Taklub* (2015) that did well internationally. Her 'golden voice', the instrument that launched her stardom, was damaged in a cruel twist of fate during a botched cosmetic surgical procedure in 2010 that left her unable to sing.

Vilma Santos made a decision to differentiate herself from Aunor by accepting edgier roles that required her to bare some skin, including the skimpily costumed (but family-friendly) Philippine superhero Darna, which she played in three films between 1973 and 1975, marking the beginning of her transition away from love team films; and, in *Burlesk Queen* (1977), a young woman who works as a dancer at a burlesque club to support her disabled father, and who suffers a miscarriage and dies as she dances on the stage in a final performance that marked a stark change from her chaste teenage love team films. Santos's first screen kiss came only a year before in *Makahiya at Talahib* (dir. Emmanuel H. Borlaza 1976). Her role in *Sister Stella L.* (dir. Mike de Leon 1984) sees her playing a nun who gets involved with the labour movement after becoming aware of their oppression. The role is somewhat prescient, ultimately reflected in the involvement of religious people in the People Power Revolution (also known as the EDSA Revolution) that would overthrow President Marcos two years later in 1986. Santos was an active politician in the Philippines between 1998 and 2022, having largely moved away from filmmaking for some years. She is associated with Star Cinema, the filmmaking arm of the ABS-CBN studio, and occasionally releases a film to express her gratitude to fans, including a deglamourised role as a lower-class woman who is a film extra in *Ekstra* (dir. Jeffrey Jeturian 2013), a role that exposes the power imbalance inherent in the labour of extras under the studio. Prior to this semi-retirement, Santos earned a reputation as a dramatic performer in the studio, often cast as the matriarch of a family during difficult times.

Eclipsed by the fan devotion of the female stars, the male stars of the love team struggled to find a new foothold in the evolving industry, with Mortiz returning to his roots in television comedy and variety programmes and Cruz making films and records on a much smaller scale than at the height of his fame. Both men would go through a renaissance of sorts working with contemporary studio ABS-CBN in the 1990s and 2000s, with the now mature Cruz becoming a strong character actor who often played roles that cast him as the head of the family in films featuring much younger love teams, while Mortiz would turn to directing young stars and love teams in several comedy and variety shows. Cruz's son appeared in 2007 on the reality television show *Pinoy Big Brother* and brought Maria Leonora Teresa out for an appearance with him in a direct effort to evoke the hysteria of his father's love team fandom and Maria Leonora Teresa's own popularity. It was her most recent appearance and one that came after many years of absence from the public eye, featuring in a segment when Elmo 'Bodie' Cruz discussed the fame of his father and the impact that the Guy and Pip tandem had on his life, including fans believing that his family was responsible for preventing Aunor and Cruz from being in a real relationship. Maria Leonora Teresa would also later inspire a horror film in 2014 titled *Maria Leonora Teresa* (dir. Wenn V. Deramas), which featured three murderous dolls named after her. Reflecting his continued involvement in the film industry, Tirso Cruz III was appointed by President Ferdinand Marcos Jr as the chairperson of the Film Development Council of the Philippines in 2022.

Cruz and Mortiz along with another love team partner and ex-husband of Aunor, Christopher de León, appear to have maintained a long-standing and close friendship. In 2019, they performed in a tour that went to the US called the 'Timeless Through the Years' concert, marking a return to their musical variety shows of the 1970s and 1980s. On stage, the three take turns singing the music of their youth, with Mortiz notably performing 'My Pledge of Love' from the love team film with Santos of the same name, with the audience singing along enthusiastically. During publicity for that tour, the three appeared on popular talk show *Tonight with Boy Abunda* in 2019 discussing their 'rivalry', with Mortiz joking that Aunor preferred the two 'tisoy' or 'light-skinned' men, prompting Cruz to laugh openly. When asked about their rivalry in the past, Cruz repeats a sentiment shared by Aunor in a personal interview with the author: it was not they who were rivals, but the people around them that pitted them against each other. De León and Mortiz are long-time colleagues who worked together on the 1980s television show *Goin' Bananas*, working in a team of five male stars known as the Bad Bananas. During the 8th Metro Manila Popular Music Festival in 1985, de León performed 'Maria Leonora Teresa' onstage with a fake doll.

For Valentine's Day in 2023 after a forced disruption to their ability to work together due to the COVID-19 pandemic, a new concert titled 'Some Kind of Valentine: Unlimited Love, Music, and Laughter' added Cruz to make up the modern trio of Bad Bananas, performing the songs of Frank Sinatra, the Beatles and Barry Manilow alongside comedy skits. The three stars who came of age in the era of the jukebox musical, now aged between sixty-six and seventy years old, returned to the stage and the era that made Cruz and Mortiz famous. The three men ribbed each other gently as an intro to a segment titled 'To All the Girls We've Loved Before', consisting of a series of choruses containing the names of women. Mortiz sings 'Maria Leonora Teresa' to tease Cruz, and Cruz responds by singing Mortiz's 'My Pledge of Love', substituting the lyrics 'cannot be broken' with 'cannot Vi broken' to invoke his love team partner. Sitting in the audience, former Governor of Batangas Vilma Santos laughs at their antics. They bring Santos on-stage to dance to a famous song from the 1970s, ending with her hugging and kissing all three men who were her leading men over the years. Notably absent is Aunor, who appears to remain an outsider to this group, a fact that was brought up by Abunda in the 2019 interview in connection with a possible reunion film; de León and Cruz indicate that they are open to such a possibility should the right project arise and fit with their schedules, but also give the impression that this is not likely. Santos reunited with de León in 2023 for a love team film titled *When I Met You in Tokyo* (dir. Rommel Penesa and Conrado Peru), shot in Japan. Cruz also appears in the film in a supporting role.

Influencing contemporary love teams

In my 2013 honours dissertation, I examined a contemporary love team, John Lloyd Cruz and Bea Alonzo of the ABS-CBN studio. The results of my present research have allowed me to reframe some of the aspects of their management, stardom and film narratives. The 1990s marked a shift from film studios to television studios as star-makers. The contemporary television studio recruits and trains stars in very similar ways to the film studios, testing out and developing star combinations on its television channel during the early 2000s after they are auditioned by studio talent management and join what is known as a 'Star Circle Batch', which trains and grooms teenage stars. Unlike the jukebox musical, stars are trained for either dramatic or romantic comedy roles. Once a suitable training period passes and popularity is earned, love teams are given roles in ensemble films with multiple other young stars of the same age to test for good chemistry, similar to the films of 1969 and 1970 for Guy and Pip, and Vi and Bot. Should they prove themselves worthy at the box-office, stars then progress to starring roles in their own love team films. Early films contain themes of puppy love and teenage romance with care taken to ensure star images are clean-cut, wholesome and appealing – good daughters and sons helping their families financially through their unexpected success.

The films of these new love teams follow the 1970s teenage jukebox musical theme of retaining English songs or lyrics as their titles, such as

Close to You (dir. Cathy Garcia Molina 2006) and *Miss You Like Crazy* (dir. Cathy Garcia Molina 2011). Moreover, they retain the singing of the theme song during public appearances to promote the film (even in cases where stars are unable to sing), while a professional singer supplies a cover for the soundtrack. Sometimes original songs are written in English for these films and performed by popular singers or the stars, demonstrating a continuing relationship between music and cinema in the Philippines. Overseas photoshoots and films remain reserved for the very best love teams of the studio, an expense justified by the profit they represent. In the press, the television studio retains its control over the star image through an in-house magazine. The images of teenage love teams in the early 1970s and 2000s are startlingly similar, with the studio ensuring that the stars pose modestly and portray an innocent courtship. Images of kissing and scenes containing kisses remain reserved for the slightly older love team, with hugs, handholding and forehead kisses for the new love team. The magazine features behind-the-scenes images of the love team filming on location, with a photographer following them around to shoot them having a good time together in various foreign locations including Hong Kong and the US. The headlines and speculation are similar to those discussed in Chapter 4 in relation to Santos and Mortiz, for example, 'John Lloyd and Bea: Getting Closer than Ever', 'Does Reel Become Real?', 'The Truth about John and Bea'.

Overall, an impression of sameness takes hold: that lining up John Lloyd Cruz and Bea Alonzo next to Nora Aunor and Tirso Cruz III, and Vilma Santos and Edgar Mortiz and the themes of their respective love team films would not be incongruous. They diverge, of course, in terms of their broader genre, with John Lloyd and Bea's films relying more heavily on narrative rather than song, though both have in common the love team as the spectacle. Both sets of love teams work in the heavily derided popular cinema – still low-culture and compared unfavourably with contemporary independent cinema. Parental authority and approval are still central to the narratives of the early teenage love team films, often acting as the source of conflict between the young lovers. Alonzo continues to suffer as the *babaeng martir*, while John Lloyd Cruz's masculinity exists along the continuity of Edgar Mortiz as a modern and emotive one, permitting him to cry on-screen. And the fans still support a favourite love team and pray for a real relationship, though with nowhere near the quasi-religious fervour of Santos's and Aunor's fans of the 1970s. The modern love team represents a return to the more remote star, with access to them limited and restricted to public appearances controlled by the studio. Till today, it is possible to encounter both Santos and Aunor easily and on a one-to-one basis through their fans (as I was able to in December 2016 at a Vilmanian Christmas party and at a press conference for the release of Aunor's film *Kabisera*, dir. Real Florido and Arturo San Agustin), while the stars of ABS-CBN can mostly only be encountered in a crowd at an official event from a distance enforced by security personnel. Thanks to the cross-media conglomerate reach of ABS-CBN, contemporary stars have success internationally through online platforms and cable channels, often resulting in international tours to cities with a high number of overseas Filipino workers. The new stars also have some transnational appeal within Southeast Asia, particularly as their *teleserye* (television series) travel well and play in countries such as Indonesia, Myanmar, Thailand, Cambodia, Vietnam, Brunei, Singapore and Malaysia.

Each successive batch of teenage love teams has given the impression of modernity perhaps through the aesthetics of their era's modernity, but not through their images and film narratives, which remain largely traditional and bound by the same set of rules as the stars launched in the 1970s: good moral conduct and character; obedience to and sacrifice for the family; playful and chaste teen courtships; respect for the dominant religion and culture. The suggestion of a rebellious nature is introduced through the conflict with older characters in the narrative, but at every iteration so far, the teenage love team continues to work to reinforce hierarchies of power within the studio and society, giving the impression of change without achieving or advocating any meaningful change. The iconic love teams of the 1970s remain the standard for fame and love team success in the multimedia reach of Philippine studios, with successive love teams citing them as inspirations and working to achieve their stature.

Years later in 2015, a modern love team would invoke Guy and Pip in their television performance on a variety show called *Eat Bulaga!* on the GMA channel, rival star-maker to ABS-CBN. AlDub (Alden Richards and Maine Mendoza) is a love team that was discovered and developed on the show, known for musical performances and their strong chemistry and popularly associated with viral dubsmash or lip synch performances. Unlike the usual love teams that are carefully matched and tested to ensure a successful product, their love team was an accident, brought about coincidentally on the show and without the two even interacting in person during the initial stage of their success. The perceived authenticity of the pair drove a social media campaign to get the two together, at several points trending globally on Twitter. Such was the magnitude of their success that the BBC covered the love team in an article discussing the genesis of their fame and success (Chen 2015). At the peak of their early success, the new love team of the moment chose to invoke the memory of one of the most popular love teams of all time.

Their performance appropriately featured Richards first lip synching to Cruz's song 'Maria Leonora Teresa' with a blonde doll tucked under his arm to mimic Cruz's carrying of the doll in their films, followed by Mendoza's lip synch of Aunor's 'Tiny Bubbles' while wandering around a digitally created garden with a prop bridge installed for them to walk across and a bench to sit on. It culminates in Cruz and Aunor's duet of 'Together Again' from their 1971 film *Guy and Pip* which their garden set imitates. The attention to detail of the love team included appropriate 1970s costumes and digitally recreated garden backdrop, Aunor's prominent mole on her cheek, and Cruz's trademark hairstyle with his long curls for sideburns (see Figure C.1). On digital screens suspended over the set, images of Cruz and Aunor made to look like a scrolling film reel played. In Aunor and Cruz, they were emulating what is perhaps one of the most popular love teams of all time with the most devoted fan following in the Philippines. Not coincidentally, Mendoza's character, Yaya Dub, is described as 'a young and innocent companion (half caretaker, half housemaid)', which coincides with the kinds of roles Aunor often played (Pertierra 2016). Sociologist Br. Clifford Sonita says that the AlDub love team resonated with Philippine society because of her Cinderella complex, something she has in common with Aunor (Paglicawan 2015). Imitation is the sincerest form of flattery and the influence of the teenage love teams of the 1970s still looms large in Philippine popular culture.

Writing in 2022 (on Valentine's Day), Andrea Panaligan of CNN Philippines took stock of the current state of love teams. Panaligan flags up AlDub as gradually dissolving after 2017, KathNiel as choosing to work in projects with other stars, and JaDine as announcing their split in 2020. Love teams took a hit during the pandemic and, aside from an online pandemic series from KathNiel, had not returned to the cinema at the time of the article (ibid.). Exacerbating the situation was the shutdown of the ABS-CBN franchise in 2020 under the Duterte administration, severely affecting its dominant grip on the industry as long-standing talent began looking for work elsewhere, including with rival studio GMA. One effect

Figure C.1 Richards and Mendoza play Guy and Pip on *Eat Bulaga!* in 2015 on a set that recreates the set of 'Together Again' from the film *Guy and Pip*. Source: GMA Integrated News YouTube channel

of this disruption has been the creation of new talent agencies helmed by stars who used to be managed by ABS-CBN's Star Magic, such as Maja Salvador's Crown Artist Management Inc. and James Reid's Careless, which may signal an evolving change in the industrial conditions of the love team moving forwards. Panaligan's interview with Bolisay (ibid.), however, suggests that the love team is not dead, merely that the prevailing industrial and societal conditions have seen the formation and circulation of love teams move to the arena of social media, as demonstrated by AlDub, KathNiel and JaDine in addition to newer pairings.

But Panaligan's article identifies another arising issue of concern, listing three incidents where the female stars of love teams have spoken out against various restrictions they face as part of a love team (ibid.). In 2017, Maine Mendoza of the AlDub pairing wrote an open letter to fans asking for freedom and their understanding. In it, she clarifies that she is merely friends with Alden Richards, and recalls the earlier days of their love team when 'everyone was taking things lightly and we were all just so happy', going on to add:

> But I need to be honest, I am at this point where I feel like I live in a box. I have not been able to do what I want and say what I feel

> because every time I try to express my thoughts and feelings, some of you tend to misapprehend and invalidate them in so many ways. (Mendoza 2017)

A few days later, actress Solenn Heussaff also wrote an open letter to fans on her blog, writing:

> I've spoken to a few friends who have been in love teams or are in one, and of course they're super grateful for all the work that a successful love team can bring in. But what the world doesn't always see is that being in a love team can be hard'... when your love team is too strong and you get a job where you have to act with someone else or you have to be the love interest of a different person, someone gets attacked... Let's love the couple on-screen, but also respect them as individuals off-screen. We can love the work that they do as actors, and still support their individual lives. (Quoted in Bigtas 2017)

In February 2023, in a vlog episode, young *mestiza* star Liza Soberano of the popular LizQuen love team spoke out in what was perhaps the most overt rejection of love teams and the fan culture built around them, sparking heated debate in the Philippines about the value of love teams in modern Philippine society. In an interview with Bea Alonzo, Soberano said:

> To be honest, love teams are a phenomenon only created in the Philippines, only existing in the Philippines. And to box a woman like that is so dangerous actually for their mental health and also for their growth, not just as a professional but as an individual. So I stay away from that. (Soberano 2023)

Her comments were made in reference to working with 'one main co-star [Enrique Gil, with whom she is also in an off-screen romantic relationship], with the same production company, rotating around the same three directors' and without feeling like she had any creative control or input over her life and work (ibid.). As a case in point, 'Liza' is the screen name derived from her middle name of 'Elizabeth' that was given to her by her management at Star Magic when she was launched, and she is currently rebranding herself outside the mainstream studio environment in James Reid's Careless agency as 'Hope Soberano', her given name.

The subsequent debate led some to question whether her comments and the resulting uproar she faced about the love team would mark a cultural turning point on love teams (Gutierrez 2023). The most startling aspect of the three women's comments is how similarly they read to Aunor's own recollections of her teenage years, a sentiment echoed by Cruz in the 2019 Abunda interview on rivalry discussed above, and Mortiz in a 2008 interview that included his thoughts on his fans and their reaction to the love team break-up (Carballo 2008). As love teams have moved online and gained access to the ability to publish their thoughts directly – whether through X (formerly Twitter), blogs, vlogs or other kinds of social media – the young female stars of the modern love team are reckoning with the toxic side of love team fandoms and studio management, another instance of the events of fifty years ago still having lasting effects on the stars and the entertainment industry of today.

Future avenues

There are three main reasons why love teams remain a star-making force in Philippine cinema. Firstly, the industrial: the fact that love team films are easy to make if a basic formula for success is adhered to. If popular stars with clean star images and sufficient chemistry are continually cast together, audiences will come. This is a guaranteed profit that is difficult to resist from a business angle, and one of the key reasons that love team films remain the primary product of the filmmaking industry in the Philippines. This guarantee and stable formula also precludes innovation, making love team films a very simple matter to produce. Innovative plots are less vital than showcasing the couple appropriately with suitable gaps between projects and a solid professional relationship in place. An added bonus is if the love team are in a real-life relationship or able to sustain the will they/won't they speculation that drives interest in their union.

From the aspect of the studio's economic investment in the couple, love teams also make sense. Stars are contracted exclusively to their studio in a similar manner to the Classical Hollywood studios, and at a price renegotiated at set periods, so they are a controllable investment. Where the cost of reuniting Julia Roberts and Richard Gere or Tom Hanks and Meg Ryan in the present Hollywood context would be possibly one of the (if not the largest) expenses of a film's budget, the cost of reuniting stars in Philippine mainstream cinema is not a concern as long as their labour is still exclusive to the studio; and with stars working as part of the studio family rather than individuals with their own agents and profit margins, studios only have to pay their star enough to keep them happily working with them rather than a rival studio. This is another compelling reason to maintain the couple and the romance genre as a key attraction in Philippine cinema, though this may evolve in the aftermath of the disruption of ABS-CBN's dominance.

A final consideration is that of the deeply ingrained cultural centrality of love in the Philippines. Appearing in literature, songs, television commercials and government offices, love features in the daily life of the Philippines, no doubt helped along by the ever-present love teams and entertainment industry that promotes romance as a genre and a way of life. A hand-drawn monthly planner I saw in the office of the Mayor of Sagada for the month of February 2014 featured administrative tasks and appointments, but the 14th was left blank but for a drawing of a heart pierced by an arrow for Valentine's Day. Facing the whiteboard were the Mayor's staff at their desks, hard at work to keep the municipality running smoothly. Love teams too are central to the culture, used in everything from referring to a long-running romantic relationship to a strategy for running for political office by comparing oneself to a popular love team. As long as the Philippines has been making films, the Philippines has had love teams.

The research in this book builds on Dyer's work on the star by looking at film couples and considering what they say about concepts like individuality and authenticity in the star image. It departs from Nochimson's pioneering methods of analysis of the film couple by eschewing any ranking of a couple's ability to transcend the status quo and instead considers couples in terms of their appeal to the audience and the unique dynamics of their joint image. In addition, it contributes to the study of film couples by introducing terms designed to explore the joint image at various levels of couple identity and performance. This study of love teams contributes to the literature on Philippine cinema particularly in terms of the popular cinema of the 1970s, a routinely dismissed aspect of cinema immediately prior to the Second Golden Age of Philippine Cinema as well as before and during the Martial Law era. The study of love teams exposes the role of the popular in the normalisation of authoritarian ideology towards its target audience of the youth and the masses Marcos sought to control.

During the course of this research, one question that came up is: how would star studies respond to the idea of the couple as an industrial standard practice (as love teams are in the Philippines) and how would our understanding of the star as an individual be impacted? The images of the stars of this research and other stars of popular love teams have in their narrative (either in the past or present) being part of a team – of being more than an individual, one of two. This aspect of stars' work as being collaborative is explored in work like Dyer's and McDonald's which looks at the studio structure and the role of the vast teams built around star production. But couple collaboration is elevated to a higher level by being indivisibly and indisputably part of a pair, a relationship formalised by the word 'and' that either precedes or follows their own name, linking them to their cinematic (and sometimes romantic) other half. A fruitful avenue of further research would be to examine the role of the couple in other national cinemas and see how the notion of the star as individual stands in each, a concept that has the potential to shift our understanding of the star as a whole.

This research focuses on a popular youth genre of the 1970s: the teenage jukebox musical, a phenomenon that Wright explores in her examination of Elvis Presley and his unique version of the musical two decades earlier. These musicals are representative of their eras and often swept aside in favour of more serious genres that privilege narratives of social concerns or change. The central concern of freedom versus authority is omnipresent in teenage genres worldwide and makes unlikely allies of Nora Aunor and Elvis Presley in their 'rebel' images that challenged the status quo of stardom and their individual societies at the time. Both remain standout stars who represented the zeitgeist of a particular era and ideology, looming large over their national industries, singers who found success in the film industry and shook up the industry by virtue of their outsider status. An examination of youth genres, transmedia stars and agency is another interesting avenue of study for future research beyond the dominant cinemas of the West.

Similarly, a cross-cultural examination of the couple outside the Hollywood context to investigate ideas about love, courtship, individuals and stardom would go a long way towards enriching the fields of star studies and national screen cultures and society. The industrial aspect of cinema and stars also can be investigated by considering how various studio systems and national cinemas have addressed the couple in the romance genre in their specific contexts. Another aspect to consider is post-colonial national cinema, particularly in the case of the Philippines by looking at other Spanish Catholic ex-colonies and their influence on each other's art forms (in particular, the *teleserye* or television series) and how the couple, ideas of freedom, authority, ethnicity and romance are treated. Within the Philippine context itself, future work that takes into consideration the work of the love teams in television would enrich the understanding of the love team. Television is the root of their fame, particularly musical variety programmes that helped launch and keep teenage stars in the public eye. Modern love teams also have a measure of international stardom through their television series that are exported to Southeast Asia and beyond, where they are consumed by audiences outside their national context, a particularly interesting phenomenon in a region where Catholicism is a minority religion. Another avenue that bears exploration is fan narratives of the era to help reveal specific attractions and lived historical context for the era, giving voice to the audience that first loved the love teams and made its teenage female stars lasting icons of Philippine cinema.

Conclusion

In 2005, professor, celebrated screenwriter of key films of the Second Golden Age of Philippine Cinema, and director Clodualdo del Mundo Jr made a film that dealt directly with the *masa*'s love for film, stars and all things entertainment, *Pepot Artista* (Pepot Superstar). Del Mundo Jr's film is narrated by a writer who is typing out a story about Pepot, a young boy from a background of poverty who is obsessed with stars and with a dream to become famous which he pursues throughout the film, uncovering similar forgotten desires in others around him. In fact, the hidden dream about seeking superstardom is a running joke, with nearly every character in Pepot's world dreaming about becoming a star. Such a film made wholly around the obsession for 'superstars' (itself a clear reference to Aunor, Superstar of the Philippines) could only be set in one era – the 1970s – and the massive fandom and regular cinema visits built around the stars of the 1970s love teams and Fernando Poe Jr. *Pepot Artista* brings together many of the themes of this research: the popular teenage love teams and jukebox musicals of the era; the dream of success and escape from difficult circumstances that Aunor represented; the national obsession with stars, cinema and song; Noranians, Vilmanians and the deeply entrenched divide between their supporters; class and inequality in the Philippines; and the divergence in the interests of the audience of popular cinema and academic and critical discourse on Philippine cinema.

Pepot sells *komiks* magazines on a street with editions featuring Cruz and Aunor, and Santos and Mortiz. One day he attempts to sell a *komiks* featuring on its cover Santos and Mortiz to a present-day (2000s) Tirso Cruz III, who tells him that Cruz is more handsome and manly, and winks conspiratorially at Pepot, who recognises him, which is conveyed in the film by a brief burst of the song 'Together Again' and its accompanying visuals from *Guy and Pip*. Cruz and Aunor also appear in footage from *Guy and Pip*, which Pepot and his friend watch in the cinema featuring the scene in which Aunor and Cruz have an argument by proxy through Maria Leonora Teresa, followed by the song 'Maria Leonora Teresa' and accompanied by a montage of the pair running through the garden. For modern audiences who have never seen a teenage jukebox musical, the sequence (and the film as a whole) serves as a crash course in the stars, genre and obsession that made the love teams of the 1970s iconic (Lim 2010). The love teams of Cruz and Aunor, and Santos and Mortiz are very much present in the film, either through archival footage or through the spectre of their fame in extra-filmic materials such as the *komiks*, symbolic of a bygone era of superstars. In the case of Aunor and Cruz, their presence extends to a pair of impersonators who work at a local fairground, complete with trademark mole for her, and long sideburns for him.

The film has many such moments in which it knowingly and affectionately plays on the star and cinema obsession of the 1970s: in the name of Pepot's younger sister, Vilma; and in extended scenes where Pepot fantasises about his favourite stars, dancing like Aunor and Cruz in front of a painted *Guy and Pip* poster at a cinema with his two friends in one extended fantasy sequence that lovingly sends up the musical numbers of the teenage jukebox musical. In the background as Pepot schemes about a way to raise money for an audition, a young woman pastes up a sign that reads 'Marcos Tuta' (Marcos Lapdog). He dreams of Aunor and Cruz in his sleep, and when awake, fantasises about playing Maria Leonora Teresa in a dress, make-up and wig after insinuating himself into the household of the couple who impersonate Aunor and Cruz (see Figure C.2).

Pepot turns to the impersonators as being a poor simulacrum of the love team he wishes to be close to and perceives to be the ideal couple after running away from home. At home, his parents have a difficult relationship and quarrel over money, and his father ultimately cooks Pepot's pet pigeons and goes drinking after returning disappointed, cheated and in debt from an attempt to go to work in Saudi Arabia. The irony of the matter is that the impersonators themselves (whose one-room shack is

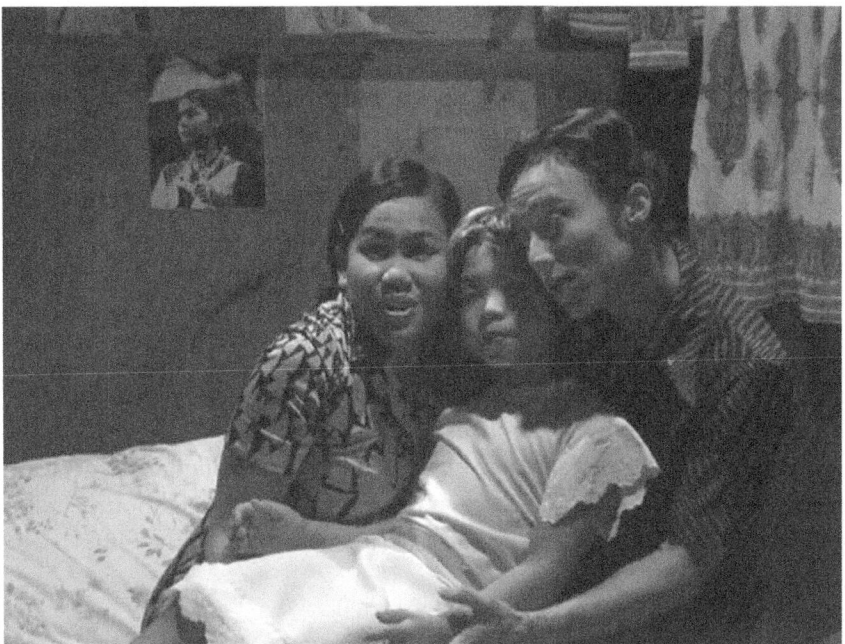

Figure C.2 Pepot dressed as Maria Leonora Teresa with the fairground impersonators of Guy and Pip in *Pepot Artista*

a shrine to Guy and Pip) are arguing about money and luck when Pepot encounters them, proving to be a more accurate simulacrum of his disillusioned parents than the stars they impersonate.

Del Mundo Jr's film does this often, juxtaposing the dreams of 'luck' and success with the sorry reality that the dreamers face instead. The narrative is sprinkled with frequent flights of fantasy for Pepot, demonstrating a rich inner world that is constantly thwarted by the real-world events that take place. The film is a love letter to the cinema and stars of a bygone era but also examines the difficult lives of the *masa* who loved those stars and sought the fantasy of the love teams to help them cope with 'bad luck', a recurring theme in the film. Pepot's dream of becoming a star is ultimately thwarted by his scheming friend and a comically cruel director at an audition he fought to be at, in perhaps the most cruel irony of the film: Pepot struggles to put together enough money to wear the smartest clothes that he can afford, and aided by the impersonators at the fairground, he arrives at the audition dressed as closely to his idol Cruz as possible in a shiny, long-sleeved shirt and pants complete with patterned bolero. However, the director rejects Pepot because he intended to cast a poor Filipino boy instead. This accurately represents the conflicting desires of the poor, whose primary dream is to better their circumstances, and the modern film industry that first builds an image of sophistication and glamour for the poor in their favourite stars but ultimately chooses to feature the poor as caricatures of abject poverty, an accusation levelled against independent cinema in the Philippines, which is often labelled 'poverty porn', with films destined for international film festivals (Ramoran-Malasig 2018).

The end of the film takes place in the present day (the 2000s) and shows the writer/narrator's wife taking their son to an audition at ABS-CBN in the hopes of turning him into a star. The narrator is revealed to be the adult version of Pepot, and his childhood dream of being a star is but a distant memory. Pepot symbolises the hopes and dreams of the poor and the downtrodden, the fantasies of the *masa* of achieving fame and leaving behind their poverty in every talent contest and neighbourhood, a philosophy imparted by the narrator/writer at the end of the film:

> Inside and outside of my miserable nation;[1]
> Where many suffer from grief;
> Pepot Artista is very alive;
> Singing the song of the hopeless.

The first line is quoted from *Florante at Laura*, considered one of the most famous nineteenth-century Tagalog poems and therefore an example of high culture taught to Filipino children in schools. The delineation between high culture in the quote from the poem and the popular culture of love team films crucially does not exist for Pepot, who is as excited to play the role of Florante in a school staging of *Florante at Laura* as he is to play Maria Leonora Teresa. Del Mundo Jr's film does not judge the *masa* harshly for their love of superstars, nor does it condemn them as unappreciative of literature and high culture. In *Pepot Artista*, *Florante at Laura* and *Guy and Pip* exist harmoniously together, two narratives in different media about lovers facing challenges that Pepot encounters.

The film is based on del Mundo Jr's first screenplay, written as a student in the 1970s, and is also the first film he directed. The writing of *Pepot Artista* is unique in that it was able to see something that many academic criticisms against the stars and genre of the era were not able to, just as Lacaba's defence of the *bakya* did: that popular films and the people who love them are not to be viewed as inferior. Pepot's narrative opens with a title card that speaks to the fantasy of superstardom and success: 'Hindi masama ang mangarap' (It's not bad to dream). This is the fantasy that raised the love teams of the 1970s to extraordinary heights: the hope of something better in the fantasy offered by the cinema, a fantasy peopled by representative figures such as Aunor and Mortiz and aspirational figures such as Cruz and Santos, joined together in their respective love teams to marry representation and aspiration in love songs and happily ever afters.

Note

1. *Sa loob at labas ng bayan kong sawi*, sometimes translated as 'There, hapless state, and even 'yond'. The translation given above is taken from the English subtitles of the film.

Bibliography

Abunda B. (2007) 'Unforgettable silent films', *Philstar.com*, 1 June, accessed 9 December 2023. https://www.philstar.com/entertainment/2007/06/01/3465/unforgettable-silent-films

Affron C. (1977) *Star acting: Gish, Garbo, Davis*, Dutton, New York.

Airhernaez (2011) 'Noranians', *Airhernaez*, 23 August, accessed 9 December 2023. https://airhernaez.wordpress.com/tag/nora-aunor/

Alberoni F. (1972) 'The powerless "elite": theory and sociological research on the phenomenon of the stars', in McQuail D (ed) *Sociology of mass communications*, Penguin, London.

Almajose K and Ramos J. V. (2013) *Kakaibang tingin, kakaibang titig: an appreciation of the Golden Period in Philippine Cinema*, La Abuela Publishing House, Batangas City.

Altman R. (1987) *The American Film Musical*, Indiana University Press, Bloomington.

Amurao P. O. (1970) 'Vilma & Tirso: at the top of the ladder', *Republic Weekly*, 24 July.

Ancheta M. R. G. (2006) 'The "king" of Philippine comedy: some notes on Dolphy and the functions of Philippine cinematic humor as discourse', *Humanities Diliman: A Philippine Journal of Humanities*, 3(2):74–117.

'The appeal of Nora' (1972), 26 May.

Asia-Philippines Leader (1971) 'If Vilma comes, can Edgar be far behind?', *Star For All Seasons*, 9 July, accessed 9 December 2023. https://starforallseasons.com/tag/articles/page/42/

Asilo R. P. (2019) 'Gabby explains why his love team with Sharon continues to fascinate fans', *Philippine Daily Inquirer*, 1 September, accessed 9 December 2023. https://entertainment.inquirer.net/343892/gabby-explains-why-his-love-team-with-sharon-continues-to-fascinate-fans

Aunor N. (2016) Author interview with Nora Aunor.

Babao-Guballa C. (2011) 'Marcos and "Iginuhit ng Tadhana," FPJ and serendipity', *Inquirer.net*, 13 November, accessed 9 December 2023. https://lifestyle.inquirer.net/22093/marcos-and-%E2%80%98iginuhit-ng-tadhana%E2%80%99-fpj-and-serendipity/

Balbuena V. A. (2010) 'Veteran star Tirso Cruz muses about the past, present, and future of show business', *Philstar.com*, 31 December, accessed 9 December 2023. https://www.philstar.com/cebu-entertainment/2010/12/31/643752/veteran-star-tirso-cruz-muses-about-past-present-and-future-show-business

BFI (British Film Institute) (2015) 'The greatest screen couples of all time unveiled', *British Film Institute*, 18 December, accessed 13 January 2018, accessed 9 December 2023. http://www.bfi.org.uk/news-opinion/news-bfi/announcements/greatest-screen-couples-all-time-unveiled

Bigtas J. A. (2017) 'Solenn Heussaff speaks the truth about love teams', *GMA News Online*, 30 November, accessed 9 December 2023. https://www.gmanetwork.com/news/showbiz/showbizabroad/635006/solenn-heussaff-speaks-the-truth-about-love-teams/story/

Bolisay R. (2016) 'The good and the bad: AlDub in film', *Plaridel*, 13(2):246–250.

Bolisay R. (2019) '"Yes, you belong to me!": Reflections on the JaDine love team fandom in the age of Twitter and in the context of Filipino fan culture', *Plaridel*, 16(2):41–61.

Brillantes A. B. (1987) *Dictatorship & Martial Law: Philippine authoritarianism in 1972*, Great Books Publishers, Quezon City.

Cabbuag S. (2021) 'Striving for authenticity: the foundation and dynamics of the AlDub nation fandom', *Plaridel*, 20(1):133–162.

Campos P. F. (2006) 'Looming over the nation, uneasy with the folks: locating Mike de Leon in Philippine cinema', *Humanities Diliman: A Philippine Journal of Humanities*, 3(2):35–73.

Campos P. F. (2016) *The end of national cinema: Filipino film at the turn of the century*, University of the Philippines Press, Quezon City.

Capino J. B. (2010) *Dream factories of a former colony: American fantasies, Philippine cinema*, University of Minnesota Press, Minneapolis.

Carballo B. M. (2008) 'Direk Bobot rolls with the punches', *The Philippine Star*, 8 September, accessed 9 December 2023. https://www.philstar.com/entertainment/2008/09/08/399008/direk-bobot-rolls-punches

Carballo B. M. (2010) *Filipino directors up close: the golden ages of Philippine cinema, 1950–2010*, Anvil, Mandaluyong City.

Celoza A. F. (1997) *Ferdinand Marcos and the Philippines: the political economy of authoritarianism*, Praeger, Westport, CT.

Centina III, G. L. R. (n.d.) 'Periscoping the Philippine cinema', *Now*.

Chen H. (2015) '"AlDub": a social media phenomenon about love and lip-synching', *BBC News*, 28 October, accessed 5 January 2024. https://www.bbc.com/news/world-asia-34645078

Cobb S. and Ewen N. (eds) (2015a) *First comes love: power couples, celebrity kinship, and cultural politics*, Bloomsbury Academic, New York.

Cobb S. and Ewen N. (2015b) 'Love', in Cobb S. and Ewen N. (eds) *First comes love: power couples, celebrity kinship, and cultural politics*, Bloomsbury Academic, New York.

Cordero-Fernando G. and Chaves M. G. (2001) *Pinoy pop culture*, Bench/Suyen Corporation, Manila.

Dasmarinas V. O. (1970) 'Edgar Mortiz: success at sixteen', *Republic Weekly*, 24 July.

David J. (1990) 'A Second Golden Age: an informal history', in *The national pastime: contemporary Philippine cinema*, Anvil, Mandaluyong City.

David J. (2008) 'Awake in the dark: Philippine film during the Marcos era', in Patajo-Legasto P. (ed) *Philippine studies: have we gone beyond St. Louis?*, University of the Philippines Press, Quezon City.

David J. (2015) 'On Nora Aunor and the Philippine star system', *Kritika Kultura*, 25, pp. 248–284.

David J. (2018) 'Book texts – critic in academe', *Ámateurish!*, 16 April, accessed 9 December 2023. https://amauteurish.com/2018/04/16/book-texts-critic-in-academe/

de Guzman N. (2005) *Si Nora Aunor sa mga Noranian: mga pagunita at pagtatapat* [Nora Aunor to the Noranians: memories and confessions], Milflores, Quezon City.

de Manila Q. (1970) 'Nora Aunor Golden Girl', *Philippines Free Press*, 11 July.

de Manila Q. (1977) *Joseph Estrada and other sketches*, National Book Store, Manila.

de Manila Q. (1990) 'Vilma, the Glad Girl', *Graphic*, 5 November.

del Mundo Jr C. A. (1998) *Native resistance: Philippine cinema and colonialism 1898–1941*, De La Salle University Press, Manila.

del Mundo Jr C. A. (1999) 'Philippine cinema: an historical overview', *Asian Cinema*, 10(2):29–66.

Deocampo N. (2011a) *American influences on Philippine cinema*, Anvil, Mandaluyong City.

Deocampo N. (2011b) *Cine: Spanish influences on early cinema in the Philippines*, Anvil, Mandaluyong City.

Diaz V. (2015) '"Brad & Angelina: and now . . . Brangelina!": a sociocultural analysis of blended celebrity couple names', in Cobb S and Ewen N (eds) *First comes love: power couples, celebrity kinship, and cultural politics*, Bloomsbury Academic, New York.

Dolan R. E. (1993) *Philippines: a country study*, Library of Congress, Washington DC.

Dolor C. (2016) Author interview with fans.

Dyer R. (1979) *Stars*, British Film Institute, London.

Dyer R. (2004) *Heavenly bodies: film stars and society*, 2nd edn, Routledge, London.

Esguerra E. (1968) 'The President and the First Lady as parents – an ordinary mommy and daddy', *Kislap*, BLG 163, 29 November.

Espiritu T. (2017) *Passionate revolutions: the media and the rise and fall of the Marcos regime*, Ohio University Press, Athens.

Esteban E. M. (1970) 'Bakit lalong tumatamis ang tambalang Vilma Santos–Edgar Mortiz?', *Liwayway*, 3 August.

Evora E. (1970a) 'The Nora–Tirso romance goes PFFFT?', *Graphic*, 13 May.

Evora E. (1970b) 'Nora Aunor's problem', *Graphic*, 24 June.

Ewen N. (2015) 'The good, the bad and the broken: forms and functions of neoliberal celebrity relationships', in Cobb S and Ewen N (eds) *First comes love: power couples, celebrity kinship, and cultural politics*, Bloomsbury Academic, New York.

Fernandez M. B. (2013) *A tribute to the movie queen Carmen Rosales: ang tangi kong pag-ibig*, DLD Publishing, Makati City.

Ferrer N. D. (2015) *Sisikat din ako!: your guide to making your mark in show business*, Anvil, Mandaluyong City.

Fischer L. and Landy M. (2004) *Stars: the film reader*, Routledge, New York.

Flores P. (2000) 'The dissemination of Nora Aunor', in Tolentino RB (ed) *Geopolitics of the visible: essays on Philippine film cultures*, Ateneo de Manila University Press, Quezon City.

Flores P. (2001) 'The star also suffers: screening Nora Aunor', *Kasarinlan*, 16(1):71–96.

Francisco B. (n.d.) 'Nora Aunor: changing the taste of Filipino moviegoers', Manunuri ng Pelikulang Pilipino (MPP), accessed 13 February 2019. http://www.manunuri.com/nora_aunor_changing_the_taste_of_filipino_moviegoers

Francisco B. (2004) 'Nora & Tirso's Maria Leonora Theresa', *Philstar.com*, 1 May, accessed 9 December 2023. https://www.philstar.com/entertainment/2004/05/01/248296/nora-amp-tirso146s-maria-leonora-theresa

Francisco B. (2017) 'Toast of the Manunuri on 40th year is brilliant actress and unfading star', *Facebook*, accessed 9 December 2023. https://www.facebook.com/groups/vilma-santos-3-the-last-philippine-movie-queen-standing-325848381114107/permalink/461925240839753/

Frith S. (2002) 'Look! Hear! The uneasy relationship of music and television', *Popular Music*, 21(3):277–290.

Fuentes E. C. (1970) 'The End of the Glamour Stars', *Graphic*, 5 August, pp. 28–32.

Garcia J. B. (1984) *Queen Vi: an intimate biography*, n.p., Bacolod City.

Glasius M. (2018) 'What authoritarianism is … and is not: a practice perspective', *International Affairs*, 94(3):515–533.

Gledhill C. (1991) *Stardom: industry of desire*, Routledge, London.

GMA News (2012) 'Veteran Filipino actor Luis Gonzales passes away', *GMA News*, 16 March, accessed 6 January 2024. https://www.gmanetwork.com/news/showbiz/content/251663/veteran-filipino-actor-luis-gonzales-passes-away/story/

Gonzalez A. B. (1982) 'The Philippines: identification of languages in the country', in Noss R. B. (ed) *Language teaching issues in multilingual environments in Southeast Asia*, Anthology Series 10, SEAMEO RELC, Singapore.

Gorospe D. (2018) 'Which star sparkles brighter: Nora Aunor or Vilma Santos?' (video), Carl E. Balita Facebook page, accessed 6 January 2024. https://www.facebook.com/watch/?v=1873391132691527

Graphic (1970) [Untitled], 16 December.

Griffin S. (2011) *What dreams were made of: movie stars of the 1940s*, Rutgers University Press, New Brunswick, NJ.

Gutierrez D. (2023) 'Liza Soberano and love teams, cultural turning point?', *Inquirer.net*, 23 March, accessed 9 December 2023. https://entertainment.inquirer.net/491781/liza-soberano-and-love-teams-cultural-turning-point

Hernando M. A. (ed) (1993) *Lino Brocka: the artist and his times*, Sentrong Pangkultura ng Pilipinas, Manila.

Hernando M. A. (2011) 'Nora Aunor: an appreciation', *Inquirer.net*, 1 October, accessed 9 December 2023. https://lifestyle.inquirer.net/16469/nora-aunor-an-appreciation/

Holmes S. (2005) '"Starring … Dyer?": re-visiting star studies and contemporary celebrity culture', *Westminster Papers in Communication and Culture*, 2(2):6–21.

Inton M. N. (2018) 'Exploring the Dolphy bakla: queerness in Philippine cinema', in Magnan-Park A. H. J., Marchetti G. and Tan S. K. (eds) *The Palgrave handbook of Asian cinema*, Palgrave Macmillan, London.

James D. E. (2015) *Rock 'n' film: cinema's dance with popular music*, Oxford University Press, Oxford.

Jaucian D. (2016) 'Two hours in traffic with Nora Aunor', *CNNPhilippines*, 1 July, accessed 9 December 2023. http://cnnphilippines.com/life/entertainment/film/2016/07/01/nora-aunor-interview.html

Jimenez B. K. (1983) *Ang true story ni Guy* [The true story of Guy], Mass Media Promotions, Quezon City.

Jimenez-Varea J. and Expósito-Barea M. (2015) '*Tears of the Black Tiger*: the western and Thai cinema', in Higgins M. E., Keresztesi R. and Oscherwitz D. (eds) *The western in the Global South*, Routledge, London.

Juan B. R. (1971) 'Vilma at Edgar: ang pinakatanyag na love team ng 1971', *Liwayway*, 24 May.
Juan B. R. (1972) 'Vilma at Edgar: tutuloy na rin sa altar?', *Liwayway*, 7 February.
King B. (1985) 'Articulating stardom', *Screen*, September.
Knapp R., Morris M and Wolf S (eds) (2013) *The Oxford handbook of the American musical*, Oxford University Press, Oxford.
Lacaba J. F. (1970) 'Notes on bakya: being an apologia of sorts for Filipino masscult', *The Philippines Free Press*, 31 January.
Leavold A. (2014) 'Bamboo gods and bionic boys: a brief history of the Philippines' B films', *Plaridel*, 11(1):129.
Lent J. A. (1996) 'Lino Brocka as filmmaker, dissident, and constitutional commissioner', *Asian Cinema*, 8(1):71–82.
Leonard S. (2015) 'The return of Liz and Dick', in Cobb S. and Ewen N. (eds) *First comes love: power couples, celebrity kinship, and cultural politics*, Bloomsbury Academic, New York.
Lim B. C. (2004) 'Cult fiction: *Himala* and bakya temporality', *Spectator*, 24(2):61–72.
Lim B. C. (2010) 'Pepot and the archive: cinephilia and the archive crisis of Philippine cinema', *Flow*, 12(3), 2 July.
Lim B. C. (2012) 'Fandom, consumption and collectivity in the Philippine New Cinema: Nora and the Noranians', in Kim Y. (ed) *Women and the media in Asia: the precarious self*, Palgrave Macmillan, London.
Lim B. C. (2015) 'Sharon's Noranian turn: stardom, race, and language in Philippine cinema', in Bandhauer A. and Royer M. (eds) *Stars in world cinema: screen icons and star systems across cultures*, I.B. Tauris, London.
Liwayway (1970a) 'The most popular movie, radio, TV loveteam of 1970', 1 June.
Liwayway (1970b) 'Torino's fashion house', 30 March.
Liwayway (1970c) 18 May.
Liwayway (1970d) 'Tirso cannot defeat Manny?', 16 November.
Liwayway (1970e) 'What chaos will result if Nora and Tirso reconcile?', 16 November.
Liwayway (1970f) 'Ernie Ma. Santiago designs', 20 December.
Liwayway (1971a) 15 February.
Liwayway (1971b) 'Coronation of 1971 Box Office King and Queen', 21 November.
Liwayway (1972a) 'Is 1972 still the year of the Nora–Tirso "love team"?', 3 January.
Liwayway (1972b) 10 January.
Liwayway (1972c) 3 April.
Liza Jr J. V. (1969) 'Lansag na ang Tirso Cruz III–Nora Aunor–Edgar Mortiz triangle', *Kislap*, 5 September.
Liza Jr J. V. (1970a) 'Edgar Mortiz talks . . . sino ang da best Kina Nora at Vilma', *Kislap*, 6 March.
Liza Jr J. V. (1970b) 'Bakit ko iniibig si Vilma Santos? – Edgar Mortiz', *Liwayway*, 4 May.
Liza Jr J. V. (1970c) 'Vilma Santos "sixteen", at ganap nang bituin', *Liwayway*, 1 June.
Llanes R. (2008a) 'Superstar Nora Aunor's urban legends, part 2: the legend of the "Lucky 12" and "Operation: Kumbento"', *PEP.ph*, 18 July, accessed 8 December 2023. https://www.pep.ph/lifestyle/16518/superstar-nora-aunors-urban-legends-part-2-the-legend-of-the-lucky-12-and-operation-kumbento
Llanes R. (2008b) 'Superstar Nora Aunor's urban legends, part 3: the Superstar phenomenon', *PEP.ph*, 1 August, accessed 9 December 2023. https://www.pep.ph/lifestyle/16624/superstar-nora-aunors-urban-legends-part-3-the-superstar-phenomenon

Llanes R. (2008c) 'Vilma Santos's urban legends part 2: the men in Vilma's life', *PEP.ph*, 19 September, accessed 9 December 2023. https://www.pep.ph/lifestyle/17033/vilma-santoss-urban-legends-part-2-the-men-in-vilmas-life

Lo R. (2003) 'Ate Luds, "queen of showbiz intrigues," laid to rest', *Philstar.com*, 3 October, accessed 9 December 2023. https://www.philstar.com/headlines/2003/10/03/222880/ate-luds-145queen-showbiz-intrigues146-laid-rest

L'OFFICIEL Vietnam (2022) 'Hyun Bin and Son Ye Jin's timeline of love', accessed 9 December 2023. https://www.lofficielph.com/fashion/8-dau-an-tinh-yeu-co-tich-cua-hyun-bin-va-son-ye-jin

Lumbera B. (1989) *Pelikula: an essay on Philippine film*, Cultural Center of the Philippines, Manila.

Lumbera B. (1997) *Revaluation 1997: essays on Philippine literature, cinema and popular culture*, University of Santo Tomas Publishing House, Manila.

Lumbera B. (2011) *Re-viewing Filipino cinema*, Anvil, Mandaluyong City.

McCoy A. W. (ed) (2009) *An anarchy of families: state and family in the Philippines*, University of Wisconsin Press, Madison.

McDonald P. (2000) *The star system: Hollywood's production of popular identities*, Wallflower Press, London.

McLean A. L. (ed) (2011) *Glamour in a golden age: movie stars of the 1930s*, Rutgers University Press, New Brunswick, NJ.

Malasig J. (2018) 'Most popular YouTube video commercial digs deep into Filipinos' hearts and past', *InterAksyon*, 29 August, accessed 9 December 2023. https://interaksyon.philstar.com/breaking-news/2018/08/29/132924/popular-youtube-video-commercial-filipinos-hearts-past-sharon-cuneta-gabby-concepcion/

Medina B. T. G. (2001) *The Filipino family*, 2nd edn, University of the Philippines Press, Quezon City.

Mendoza A. (1970) 'Vilma Santos talks . . . ang pagkakaiba Nina Tirso at Edgar', *Kislap*, 6 March.

Mendoza M. (2017) 'An open letter to our fans', *mainemendoza.com*, 26 November, accessed 9 December 2023. https://mainemendoza.com/an-open-letter-to-our-fans/

Mercado M. A. (1970) 'This Nora thing', *Graphic*, 15 July.

Mercado M. A. (1977) *Doña Sisang and Filipino movies*, A. R. Mercado Management, Manila.

Mijares P. (1976) *The conjugal dictatorship of Ferdinand and Imelda Marcos*, Union Square Publications, San Francisco, CA.

Morin E. (1972) *Les stars* [1957], Seuil, Paris.

Morota R. L. (1971a) '"Over-exposed" na nga kaya ang Vilma–Edgar love team?', *Liwayway*, 14 June.

Morota R. L. (1971b) 'Nora Aunor walang pagmamahal sa awiting Pilipino?', *Liwayway*, 11 October.

Mueller J. (1984) 'Fred Astaire and the integrated musical', *Cinema Journal*, 24(1):28–40.

Naremore J. (1988) *Acting in the cinema*, University of California Press, Berkeley.

Navarro W. (2017) 'Walter Navarro – Filipino actor – posts', *Facebook*, 11 January, accessed 9 December 2023. https://www.facebook.com/589595664517662/posts/the-1970s-era-proved-to-be-a-difficult-time-for-philippine-movies-as-president-m/1091129904364233/

Negra D. (2015) 'The making, unmaking and re-making of Robsten', in Cobb S and Ewen N (eds) *First comes love: power couples, celebrity kinship, and cultural politics*, Bloomsbury Academic, New York.

Nochimson M. (2002) *Screen couple chemistry: the power of 2*. University of Texas Press, Austin.

Ocarizawa J. (1971) '"Kung hindi kami magkatuluyan ni Edgar . . ." – Vilma Santos', *Liwayway*, 22 November.

Office of the President of the Philippines (1987) Executive Order No. 209 The Family Code of the Philippines, 6 July, Presidential Management Staff, Manila.

Official Gazette (1972) 'Letter of Instruction No. 13, s. 1972', *Official Gazette*, 29 September, accessed 6 January 2024. https://www.officialgazette.gov.ph/1972/09/29/letter-of-instruction-no-13-s-1972/

Orsal C. D. (2000) 'Vilma reads her fans', *Pelikula: A Journal of Philippine Cinema*, 2(2):53–56.

Orsal C. D. (2007) *Movie queen: pagbuo ng mito at kapangyarihang kultural ng babae sa lipunan* [Construction of myth and cultural power of women in society], New Day Publishers, Quezon City.

Paglicawan M. C. R. (2015) 'Sociologist explains popularity of AlDub tandem', *LionhearTV*, 13 August, accessed 9 December 2023. https://www.lionheartv.net/2015/08/sociologist-explain-why-aldub-hits/

Palmer R. B. (2010) *Larger than life: movie stars of the 1950s*, Rutgers University Press, New Brunswick, NJ.

Panaligan A. (2022) 'Are we in a new era of Filipino love teams?', *CNNPhilippines*, 14 February, accessed 9 December 2023. https://www.cnnphilippines.com/life/entertainment/2022/2/14/a-new-era-of-Filipino-love-teams.html

Paredes A. (2012) 'Behind the magic, 20 years of star magic', *YES!*, July.

Pascual W. O. (2005) 'Devotion', *Philippine Studies*, 53(2/3):300–318.

Pertierra R. (2016) 'Anthropology and the AlDub nation entertainment as politics and politics as entertainment', *Philippine Studies: Historical & Ethnographic Viewpoints*, 64(2):289–300.

Polotan K. (1969) 'The men, the method', *The Philippines Free Press*, 5 April.

Press Trust of India (2013) 'Shah Rukh Khan, Kajol voted Most Romantic Bollywood couple', *ndtv.com*, 14 February, accessed 9 December 2023. https://www.ndtv.com/entertainment/shah-rukh-khan-kajol-voted-most-romantic-bollywood-couple-631786

Quirino J. A. (1971) 'Politicos join big crowd to welcome back Tirso, Nora', *The Daily Mirror*, 1 November.

Rafael V. L. (1995) 'Taglish, or the phantom power of the lingua franca', *Public Culture*, 8(1):101–126.

Rafael V. L. (2000) *White love and other events in Filipino history*, Duke University Press, Durham, NC.

Ramoran-Malasig C. (2018) 'Philippine cinema is growing fast, and is moving away from typical themes of poverty and violence', *Forbes*, 1 March, accessed 9 December 2023. https://www.forbes.com/sites/cmalasig/2018/03/01/philippine-cinema-more-than-poverty-porn-violence/

Ramos E. (1970a) 'Nora marks a birthday', *Graphic*, 10 June.

Ramos E. (1970b) 'All that Tirso wants for Christmas', *Graphic*, 16 December.

Realuyo B. A. (2014) 'Dear Nora Aunor, greatest Filipina actress, brown and beautiful', *Huffington Post*, 24 June, accessed 9 December 2023. https://www.huffpost.com/entry/dear-nora-aunor-greatest-filipina-actress_b_5519642

Redmond S. and Holmes S. (2007) *Stardom and celebrity: a reader*, Sage.
Reyes G. R. (1969) 'Dialogue: middle aged cynic and young idealist on the Philippine condition', *The Philippines Free Press*, 11 October.
Rodrigo R. (2006) *Kapitan: Geny Lopez and the making of ABS-CBN*, ABS-CBN Publishing, Quezon City.
Rodrigo R. (2010) *Undaunted: the Lopez legacy, 1800–2010*, Lopez Group Foundation, Pasig City.
Rojek C. (2001) *Celebrity*, Reaktion Books, London.
Salazar O. (1970) '400 at Awit Awards – pulls films, radio', *Billboard*, 29 August.
San Diego Jr B. (2012) 'Actor Luis Gonzales dies; 81', *Philippine Daily Inquirer*, 16 March, accessed 6 January 2024. https://entertainment.inquirer.net/33605/actor-luis-gonzales-dies-81
San Diego Jr B. (2017) 'Home body: the Superstar Nora Aunor lives here', *Inquirer.net*, 2 January, accessed 9 December 2023. https://entertainment.inquirer.net/211164/home-body-superstar-nora-aunor-lives
Santiago A. M. V. (2006) *Imaging the Filipino woman: a critical discourse analysis of melodramatic films made by Filipino Mainstream woman directors from 1990–2000* [Thesis], College of Mass Communication, University of the Philippines, Diliman, Quezon City.
Santiago E. (2007) 'Vilma–Boyet love team: from movies to the political arena?', *PEP.ph*, 29 March, accessed 5 January 2024. https://www.pep.ph/lifestyle/12162/vilma-boyet-love-team-from-movies-to-the-political-arena
Santiago E. (2009) '(Updated) Talent manager Douglas Quijano passes away at 64', *PEP.ph*, 13 June, accessed 9 December 2023. https://www.pep.ph/news/22100/updated-talent-manager-douglas-quijano-passes-away-at-64
Santos L. A. (1971) 'Katangi-tangi ang pagsasamahan ng mga magulang Nina Vilma at Edgar', *Liwayway*, 23 August.
Sebastiampillai C. (2022) 'One more second chance: love team longevity and utility in the era of the television studio', in Driskell J (ed) *Film stardom in Southeast Asia*, Edinburgh University Press, Edinburgh.
Shingler M. (2012) *Star studies: a critical guide*, Palgrave Macmillan, Basingstoke.
Sioson-San Juan T. (1999) *Pinoy television: the story of ABS-CBN*, ABS-CBN Broadcasting Corporation, Quezon City.
Smith I. R. (2013) '"You're really a miniature Bond": Weng Weng and the transnational dimensions of cult film stardom', in Egan K and Thomas S (eds) *Cult film stardom: offbeat attractions and processes of cultification*, Palgrave Macmillan, Basingstoke.
Soberano L. (2023) 'This is me', *YouTube*, 26 February, accessed 9 December 2023. https://www.youtube.com/watch?v=roLGm8vkIpg
Star For All Seasons (2015) 'Iginuhit ng Tadhana (1965)', *Star For All Seasons*, 7 September, accessed 9 December 2023. https://starforallseasons.com/2015/09/07/iginuhit-ng-tadhana-1965/
Tadiar N. X. M. (1997) 'Domestic bodies of the Philippines', *Sojourn: Journal of Social Issues in Southeast Asia*, 12(2):153–191.
Tadiar N. X. M. (2000) 'The Noranian imaginary', in Tolentino RB (ed) *Geopolitics of the visible*, Ateneo de Manila University Press, Quezon City.
Tadiar N. X. M. (2002) '*Himala* (Miracle): the heretical potential of Nora Aunor's star power', *Signs: Journal of Women in Culture and Society*, 27(3):703–741.
Tan M. V. (n.d.) 'Edgar Mortiz 1970's most promising recording star', *Kislap*.
Taylor M. (2016) *Musical theatre, realism and entertainment*, Routledge, London.

Teodoro Jr L. V. (1970) 'In quest of the Pilipino movie', *Graphic*, 1 July.
Teodoro Jr L. V. (1981) *Out of this struggle: the Filipinos in Hawaii*, University of Hawai'i Press, Honolulu.
The Philippine Daily Star (1970) 16 July.
The Philippines Free Press (1970) 'Ed Finlan and Hilda Koronel Valentine's special', 14 February.
Thompson R. M. (2003) *Filipino English and Taglish: language switching from multiple perspectives*, John Benjamins, Amsterdam.
Tiongson N. G. (1983) *The Urian anthology, 1970–1979: selected essays on tradition and innovation in the Filipino cinema of the 1970s by the Manunuri ng Pelikulang Pilipino, 1970–1979*, ML Morato, Manila.
Tiongson N. G. (2000) 'The imitation and indigenization of Hollywood', *Pelikula: A Journal of Philippine Cinema*, 2(1):22–31.
Tiongson N. G. (2001) *The Urian anthology, 1980–1989: film essays and reviews by the Manunuri ng Pelikulang Pilipino with a filmography of Philippine movies, 1980–1989*, AP Tuviera, Manila.
Tiongson N. G. (2008) 'Four values in Filipino drama and film', in Aguila A. A. A., Arriola J. L. and Wigley J. J. G. (eds) *Philippine literatures: texts, themes, approaches*, University of Santo Tomas Publishing House, Manila.
Tolentino J. L. (1970) 'Ang pagtatapat ni sarhento Aunor, ang umapon kay Nora Aunor', *Liwayway*, 16 February.
Tolentino R. B. (2000) *Richard Gomez at ang mito ng pagkalalake, Sharon Cuneta at ang perpetwal na birhen at iba pang sanaysay ukol sa bida sa pelikula bilang kultural na texto* [Richard Gomez and the myth of masculinity, Sharon Cuneta and the perpetual virgin and other essays regarding movie stars as cultural texts], Anvil, Mandaluyong City.
Tolentino R. B. (2001) *National/transnational: subject formation, media and cultural politics in and on the Philippines*, Ateneo University Press, Quezon City.
Tolentino R. B. (2009) 'Globalizing national domesticity female work and representation in contemporary women's films', *Philippine Studies*, 57(3):419–442.
Torre Jr N. U. (1970) 'Sing-sing, brawl-brawl, strip-strip', *Manila Chronicle*, n.d.
Trinidad J. L. (1971) 'Ang "Valentine" ni Edgar', *Liwayway*, 15 February.
Turner G. (2004) *Understanding celebrity*, SAGE, London.
Umerez R. M. (1970) 'Tirso Cruz III, in the eyes of his father', *Kislap*, BLG 197, 20 March.
Valdez (1969) 'Sizzling scoop (kissing cousins)', *Kislap*, BLG 190.
Velasco J. (2008) '"Feminized" heroes and "masculinized" heroines: changing gender roles in contemporary Philippine cinema?', in Patajo-Legasto P (ed) *Philippine studies: have we gone beyond St. Louis?*, University of the Philippines Press, Quezon City.
Velasco J. (2009) *Huwaran/Hulmahan atbp.: the film writings of Johven Velasco* [Modelling/Moulding etc.: the film writings of Johven Velasco], University of the Philippines Press, Quezon City.
Video 48 (2008) 'Video 48: Nora Aunor circa 1970: Nora–Manny de Leon love team', *Video 48*, 16 April, accessed 9 December 2023. http://video48.blogspot.com/2008/04/nora-aunor-circa-1970-nora-manny-de.html
Video 48 (2009) '"Guy and Pip" tops them all!', *Video 48*, 2 April, accessed 9 December 2023. http://video48.blogspot.com/2009/04/guy-and-pip-tops-them-all.html
Walsh T. P. (2013) *Tin Pan Alley and the Philippines: American songs of war and love, 1898–1946: a resource guide*, Scarecrow Press, Lanham, MD.

Williams L. R. (2015) 'Jane Fonda, power nuptials and the project of ageing', in Cobb S and Ewen N (eds) *First comes love: power couples, celebrity kinship, and cultural politics*, Bloomsbury Academic, New York.

Williams M. (2015) '"Gilbo-Garbage" or "the champion lovemakers of two nations": uncoupling Greta Garbo and John Gilbert', Cobb S and Ewen N (eds) *First comes love: power couples, celebrity kinship, and cultural politics*, Bloomsbury Academic, New York.

Wright J. L. (2018) *Crossover stardom: popular male music stars in American cinema*, Bloomsbury Academic, New York.

Yambot I. (1965) 'Movie on Marcos suspended – palace body defends action', *The Manila Times*, 3 September.

Yeoh A. and Begum M. (2014) 'Malaysia's first celebrity power couple, P. Ramlee and Saloma', *The Star*, 30 August, accessed 9 December 2023. https://www.thestar.com.my/lifestyle/uncategorized/2014/08/30/remembering-our-idols

Filmography

50 First Dates. Dir. Segal, Peter. Columbia Pictures, Happy Madison Productions, Anonymous Content, 2004. Film.
A Gift of Love. Dir. Holmsen, Danny, and German Moreno. Sampaguita Pictures, VP Pictures, 1972. Film.
Aloha My Love. Dir. Borlaza, Emmanuel H. Tagalog Ilang-Ilang Productions, 1972. Film.
Always in My Heart. Dir. Torres, Mar S. Sampaguita Pictures, 1971. Film.
Anak, ang Iyong Ina!. Dir. Torres, Mar S. Sampaguita Pictures, 1963. Film.
And God Smiled at Me. Dirs. Holmsen, Danny, and Mar S. Torres. Sampaguita Pictures, VP Pictures, 1972. Film.
Ang Pagsilang ng Mesiyas. [The Birth of the Messiah]. Dir. Tolosa, Carlos Vander. Lebran, 1952. Film.
Ang Tangi Kong Pag-ibig. [My Only Love]. Dir. Mar S. Torres. Sampaguita Pictures, 1955. Film.
Atsay. [Maid]. Dir. Garcia, Eddie. Ian Film Productions, 1978. Film.
Banana Split. Dir. Mortiz, Edgar. ABS-CBN, 2008. Television.
Banaue. Dir. de León, Gerry. NV Productions, 1975. Film.
Bilangin ang Bituin sa Langit. [Count the Stars in Heaven] Dir. Perez, Elwood. Regal Films, 1989. Film.
Blended. Dir. Coraci, Frank. Gulfstream Pictures, Happy Madison Productions, Karz Entertainment, 2014. Film.
Blue Hawaii. Dir. Taurog, Norman. Hal Wallis Productions, 1961. Film.
Bona. Dir. Brocka, Lino. NV Productions, 1980. Film.
Broken Marriage. Dir. Bernal, Ishmael. Regal Films, 1983. Film.
Burlesk Queen. [Burlesque Queen]. Dir. Ad. Castillo, Celso. Ian Film Productions, 1977. Film.
Close to You. Dir. Molina, Cathy Garcia. ABS-CBN Film Productions, Star Cinema, 2006. Film.
Crash Landing on You. Dir. Lee Jeong-hyo. Studio Dragon, 2019–2020. Television.
D' Musical Teenage Idols!. Marquez, Artemio. Tower Productions, 1969. Film.
Dalagang Bukid. [Country Maiden]. Dir. Jose Nepomuceno. Malayan Movies, Nepomuceno Productions, 1919. Film.
Darling. Dir. Marquez, Artemio. Tower Productions, 1970. Film.

Dear Heart. Dir. Danny L. Zialcita. Sining Silangan Productions, 1981. Film.
Drakulita. Dir. Osorio, Consuelo P. Barangay Productions, RJF Bros. Pictures, 1969. Film.
Eat Bulaga!. Dir. various. GMA, 2015. Television.
Edgar Loves Vilma. Dir. Garcia, Leonardo L. Jela Productions, 1970. Film.
Ekstra. [The Bit Player] Dir. Jeturian, Jeffrey. Cinemalaya Foundation, Quantum Films, 2013. Film.
Eskwelahang Munti. Perf. Edgar Mortiz. GMA, 1961–1970. Television.
Eyes Wide Shut. Dir. Kubrick, Stanley. Warner Bros., Stanley Kubrick Productions, Hobby Films, 1999. Film.
Fiesta Extravaganza. Dir. Osorio, Consuelo P. JBC Pictures, 1969. Film.
Ging. Dir. Santiago, Cirio H., and Teodorico C. Santos. People's Pictures, 1964. Film.
Goin' Bananas. Dir. Quinn, Al. Intercontinental Broadcasting Corporation, 1986–1991. Television.
Goin' Bulilit. Dir. Mortiz, Edgar, and Frasco Mortiz. ABS-CBN, 2005–2019. Television.
Gone with the Wind. Dir. Fleming, Victor. Selznick International Pictures, Metro-Goldwyn-Mayer, 1939. Film.
Guy and Pip. Dir. Moreno, German. Sampaguita Pictures, VP Pictures, 1971. Film.
Himala. [Miracle]. Dir. Bernal, Ishmael. Experimental Cinema of the Philippines, 1982. Film.
Iginuhit ng Tadhana: The Ferdinand E. Marcos Story. [Destined by Fate: The Ferdinand E. Marcos Story]. Dir. Conde, Conrado, Jose De Villa and Mar S. Torres. Sampaguita Pictures, 777 Films, 1965. Film.
Ithaca. Dir. Ryan, Meg. Co-Op Entertainment, The Exchange, Apple Lane Productions, 2015. Film.
Joe Versus the Volcano. Dir. Shanley, John Patrick. Warner Bros., Amblin Entertainment, 1990. Film.
Kabisera. [The Seat]. Dir. Florido, Real, and Arturo San Agustin. Firestarters Productions, Silver Story Entertainment, 2016. Film.
Leron-Leron Sinta. [Leron, Leron, My Love]. Dir. Emmanuel H. Borlaza. Tagalog Ilang-Ilang Productions, 1972. Film.
Love Letters. Dir. Cruz, Abraham. Tagalog Ilang-Ilang Productions, 1970. Film.
Makahiya at Talahib. Dir. Borlaza, Emmanuel H. Goodwill Productions, 1976. Film.
Maria Leonora Teresa. Dir. Deramas, Wenn V. ABS-CBN Film Productions, Star Cinema, 2014. Film.
Memories of Our Love. Dir. Holmsen, Danny. Sampaguita Pictures, 1975. Film.
Miss You Like Crazy. Dir. Molina, Cathy Garcia. ABS-CBN Film Productions, Star Cinema, 2011. Film.
My Blue Hawaii. Dir. Holmsen, Danny, and German Moreno. Sampaguita Pictures, VP Pictures, 1972. Film.
My Little Brown Girl. Dir. Holmsen, Danny. Sampaguita Pictures, VP Pictures, 1972. Film.
Nora in Wonderland. Dir. Marquez, Artemio. Tower Productions, 1970. Film.
Notting Hill. Dir. Michell, Roger. Polygram Filmed Entertainment, Working Title Films, Bookshop Productions, 1999. Film.
Oh, Delilah. Dir. Osorio, Consuelo P. JBC Pictures, 1969. Film.
Paano Ba ang Mangarap. Dir. Garcia, Eddie. Viva Films, 1983. Film.
Pepot Artista. [Pepot Superstar]. Dir. del Mundo Jr, Clodualdo. Buruka Films, 2005. Film.

Pinagbuklod ng Langit. [Heaven's Fate]. Dir. Garcia, Eddie. Sampaguita Pictures, United Brothers Productions, 1969. Film.
Pinoy Big Brother. Dir. various. ABS-CBN, Endemol Entertainment, 2007. Television.
P.S. I Love You. Dir. Garcia, Eddie. Viva Films, 1981. Film.
Relasyon. [Affair]. Dir. Bernal, Ishmael. Regal Films, 1982. Film.
Remembrance. Dir. Borlaza, Emmanuel H. Tagalog Ilang-Ilang Productions, 1972. Film.
Ricky Na, Tirso Pa!. Dir. Wenceslao, Jose. Cruz Brothers Productions, 1970. Film.
Sinasamba Kita. [I Worship You]. Dir. Garcia, Eddie. Viva Films, 1982. Film.
Sister Stella L. Dir. de Leon, Mike. Regal Films, 1984. Film.
Sleepless in Seattle. Dir. Ephron, Nora. TriStar Pictures, 1993. Film.
Tag-Ulan sa Tag-Araw. [Summer Rains]. Dir. Ad. Castillo, Celso. Archipelago Films, 1975. Film.
Taklub. [Trap]. Dir. Mendoza, Brilliante. Centerstage Productions, 2015. Film.
Tatlong Mukha ni Rosa Vilma. [Three Faces of Rosa Vilma]. Dir. Suzara, Romy. Roma Films, 1972. Film.
Tatlong Taong Walang Diyos. [Three Years without God]. Dir. O'Hara, Mario. NV Productions, 1976. Film.
The Crown. Dir. various. Left Bank Pictures, Sony Pictures Television Production UK, 2016–2023. Television.
The Mummy. Dir. Kurtzman, Alex. Universal Pictures, Alphaville Films, 1999. Film.
The Negotiation. Dir. Lee Jong-seok. JK Film, CJ E&M, 2018. Film.
The Princess Bride. Dir. Reiner, Rob. Act III Communications, Buttercup Films Ltd, The Princess Bride Ltd, 1987. Film.
The Wedding Singer. Dir. Coraci, Frank. Juno Pix, New Line Cinema, Robert Simonds Productions, 1998. Film.
The X-Files. Dir. various. Ten Thirteen Productions, 20th Century Fox Television, 1993–2002, 2016, 2018. Television.
The Young at Heart. Dir. Holmsen, Danny. Sampaguita Pictures, VP Pictures, 1970. Film.
Thy Womb. Dir. Mendoza, Brilliante. Centerstage Productions, Film Development Council of the Philippines, 2012. Film.
Trudis Liit. Dir. De Villa, Jose. VP Pictures, 1963. Film.
When I Fall in Love. Dir. Lamangan, Joel. TV5, 2014. Television.
When I Met You in Tokyo. Dir. Peru, Conrado, and Rommel Penesa. JG Productions, 2023. Film.
Winter Holiday. Dir. De Villa, Jose. Sampaguita Pictures, VP Pictures, 1972. Film.
YeYe Generation. Dir. Marquez, Artemio. VP Pictures, 1969. Film.
Young Love. Dir. Cayado, Tony. Sampaguita Pictures, VP Pictures, 1970. Film.
You've Got Mail. Dir. Ephron, Nora. Warner Bros., 1998. Film.

Index

Note: *italics* denote a figure. n denotes a note The index is organised by letter-by-letter format.

ABS-CBN, 4, 16, 21n, 34, 36–7, 82, 94, 202, 204, 206–8, 211
Abunda, B., 203–4, 210
Acting in the Cinema (Naremore), 8
Adorno, Theodor W., 37
Affron, Charles, 5
agency, 66, 75, 102–18, 154, 169, 171, 180–1, 191–4, 212
Agoncillo, Teodoro, 183
'Alaala', 92
Alberoni, Francesco, 5
AlDub love team, 15, 206–8
Almajose, Kathy, 15–16, 33, 45–8, 51, 63–4
Aloha My Love, 121–4
'Aloha Oe', 121
Alonzo, Bea, 1, 37, 204–5, 209
'Alphabet Song (A You're Adorable)', 141, *142*
Altman, Rick, 143–5
Always in My Heart, 154, 171–2, 174, 192
American popular music, 121–2, 144, 147, 159, 183
Amoranto, Norberto S., 97, 107
Anak, ang Iyong Ina!, 77
And God Smiled at Me, 173, 179–80
Ang Pagsilang ng Mesiyas, 84, 133
'Ang Tangi Kong Pag-ibig', 34
Ang True Story ni Guy (Jimenez), 14
'Articulating Stardom' (King), 5
Atsay, 201
audience, 3, 17, 27–8, 31–2, 35, 40–1, 55–64, 67, 76, 105, 107, 122, 128, 131, 144, 157, 159–60, 166, 170, 176–7, 181, 203–4, 211, 213–14
class, 148, 184
diegetic, 138, 146–8, 157
Aunor and Cruz love team, 1, 4, 18–19, 32–3, 35, 40, 51, 85–90, *87*, 95–111, *101*, *106*, 115, 117–25, 129–36, *130*, 138, 140–54, 157–61, 165–6, 170–6, 179–81, 189, 191–6, 203–7, *208*, 214
Aunor, Nora, 1, 4–5, 7, 13–14, 17–20, 32–3, 35, 44, 50–2, *52*, 54, 62, 66–77, 70, 74, 79, 81–90, *87*, 92, 95, 95–6n, 97, 99–119, *101*, *106*, *109*, 121–5, 129–54, *130*, 136n, *142*, *151*, *153*, 156–7, 159–61, 165–6, 169–71, 174–6, *175*, 183, 191–201, 203–7, 212–14, 217
fandom, 13–14, 67, 73–7, 97–8, 102–8, 178–81, 185–6, 189, 193–5
musicality, 68–72, 100–1, 113, 178
performance style, 71, 83, 178–81, 201
recording career, 100, 121, 186
relationships with leading men, 102–8
use of English, 20, 147, 185–6
auteur cinema, Philippine, 4, 13, 20, 45, 82, 138, 200–1
authenticity, 2–3, 15–16, 20, 22, 31, 39–40, 42, 53, 75–6, 99, 114–18, 122–7, 135, 145, 148, 154, 160, 164, 169, 172, 201, 206–7, 211
real or reel (constructed), 2, 18–19, 22, 28, 42, 99, 103–4, 122–7, 129–30, 148, 167, 195, 205

authoritarianism, 2–3, 16, 19–20, 44–5, 51, 64, 138, 168–9, 178–81, 186–9, 198, 211
authoritarian values
  internalisation of, 187–9
  transmitted through media, 179–81, 211
authority, 20, 168, 178–82, 184, 198, 212–13
  Church, 20, 173–74, 190
  parental, 150–1, 154, 179–80, 187–9, 190–3, 196, 205
  respect for, 46, 80, 134, 145, 175–82, 187–9, 206
  resistance to, 3, 11, 178–81, 184
  studio, 45–47, 108, 150, 179–81

babaeng martir characters, 20, 76, 174–8, 205
Badiday, Inday, 105–7, 119, *150–1*
bakya, 73, 89, 129, 183, 186, 199, 216
Balagtas, Francisco, 216
'Ballad of Nora and Tirso, The', 119–20
Baretto, Claudine, 37
Beams, Dovie, 62
Belmonte, Ricky, 85, 88, 101–2, 129, 170
Bernal, Ishmael, 4, 13, 201
Bernardo, Kathryn, 1, 37; *see also* KathNiel love team
'Beyond the Reef', 121
Biancaflor, Norma, 84
Bilangin ang Bituin sa Langit, 200
Blanca, Nida, 1, 34, 69
Blended, 29
Blue Hawaii, 122
'Blue Hawaii' (Aunor), 121–2
'Blue Hawaii' (Presley), 122
Bolisay, Richard, 15, 37, 208
bomba cinema, 44, 51, 62–3, 69, 137
Bona, 201
Borlaza, Emmanuel H., 56
Brillantes, Alex B., 186
Brocka, Lino, 4, 13, 36
Broken Marriage, 201
Burlesk Queen, 80, 202

Cabbuag, Samuel, 15
Capino, José B, 121
Carballo, B.M., 15
Castillo, Celso Ad, 4
Catholicism/Catholic Church, 3, 7, 20, 32, 38, 93–4, 134, 145, 154, 168, 172–8, 180–81, 185, 190, 192, 194, 199, 212–13
Celebrity (Rojek), 5

celebrity
  achieved, 17, 42, 66–75, 137, 170, 178–9, 193
  ascribed celebrity, 17, 42, 66, 77–81, 84–9
  attributed celebrity, 137
celebrity couples, 2, 8, 12, 22–42, 44, 53, 60, 148, 189
  fictionalisation of, 28–9, 52–63, 178–99
Celoza, Albert F., 186
censorship, 4, 16, 44–5, 59, 62–64, 187
Chaibancha, Mitr, 26
Chaowarat, Petchara, 26
child stars, 17, 44, 77–9, 81–2, 90–1, 114, 116, 196
Cinderella, 17, 54, 67–72, 76, 82, 95, 207
Cinderella-Prince Charming narrative, 88, 107, 124, 191–3, 199
class, 4, 14, 17–18, 20, 32, 48, 51–2, 57, 61–2, 66–91, 110, 128–9, 135, 139, 145, 148, 150–2, 155–6, 168–70, 176–99, 201–2, 213
  privilege, 48–9, 77–8, 86, 170, 176, 184–6
  struggle, 178–81, 213
Close to You, 205
Cobb, Shelley, 12, 25, 28
colonialism, legacy of, 13, 33, 37, 48, 86–8, 120–2, 143–5, 147, 168, 180–1
  American, 13, 17, 33, 48–9, 66, 79, 86, 91, 98, 120–2, 143–5, 147, 159, 180–8
  Spanish, 33, 48–9, 86, 90, 180–6, 212–13
colorism, 48–9, 67, 69, 86, 145
Concepcion, Gabby, 1, 35–6
concerts, 24, 86, 88–9, 140, 203–4
Conjugal Dictatorship of Ferdinand and Imelda Marcos, The (Mijares), 60
Conroy, Kevin, 27
coupledom, 6, 22–43, 53–62, 64, 140, 149–99
  chemistry, 8–12, 18–19, 27–32, 60, 102, 145, 204, 206, 210
  triangulation, 115–18
courtship, 3, 7, 11–12, 39, 58, 152–54, 168–72, 174, 190, 194, 205–6, 212
Crash Landing on You, 27–8
Crisol, Jose Ma, 188
Crossover Stardom (Wright), 144
Crown, The, 28–30
Cruz, Jesus *see* Belmonte, Ricky
Cruz, John Lloyd, 1, 37, 88, 204–05
Cruz, Tirso III, 1, 4, 14, 17–19, 32–33, 35, 44, 66, 73, 75, 84–92, 87, 95, 97–115, *101*, *106*, *109*, 117–19, 121–5, 129–31, *130*, 133–8, 136n, 140–8, *142*, 150, *151*, *152*, *153*,

155, 157, 159–61, 165–6, 169–71, 175–6, 181, 183, 186, 189, 191–6, *195*, 199–200, 202–5, 207, 210, 214–15, 217
   fandom, 97–8
   masculinity, 18, 90–4
   musicality, 17–18, 84–9, 101, 112
   recording career, 85–9, 121, 186
Cuneta, Sharon, 1, 35, 185
cultural purity, 168–87

'Dahil Sa'yo', 58
Dalagang Bukid, 24, 32, 116
dancing, 8–9, 34–5, 41–2, 50, 80, 141, 159–60, 164, *164*, 166, 214
Darling, 104
Darna film trilogy, 52, 127, 202
David, Joel, 14, 32, 35
Dear Heart, 35
de Guzman, Nestor, 14, 51
de la Rama, Atang, 21n, 32–3
de la Rosa, Rogelio, 1, 33–4, 47, 49
de la Rosa and Rosales love team, 33–5
de León, Christopher, 200–1, 203–4
de León, Doña Narcissa, 34, 47, 150; *see also* Sisang, Doña
de León, Gerry, 116
de León, Manuel 'Manny', 48, 73, 88, 100, 102–5, 117, 123, 129, 133, 157, 194
de León, Mike, 4, 13
de Manila, Quijano, 68; *see also* Joaquin, Nick
del Mundo, Clodualdo Jr, 33, 213, 215–16
del Rosario, 'Bos Vic' Vicente Jr, 35
del Rosario, Rosa, 1, 33
del Sol, Mila, 33
Deocampo, Nick, 32–3
de Villa, Nestor, 1, 34
'Devotion' (Pascual), 193
Diaz, Vanessa, 28
discipline, 3, 17, 19–20, 45–7, 62, 162, 189
dissent, suppression of, 187–99
D' Musical Teenage Idols!, 85, 101
Dolor, Danny, 48
Dolphy, 13, 69, 78, 88
Drakulita, 113
duets, 54, 148, 160, 207
Duran, Tita, 49
Dyer, Richard, 2, 5–6, 8–9, 11, 22, 31, 38, 66–7, 123, 144, 211–12

Eat Bulaga!, 206, *208*
Eddie-Nora Show, The, 100

Edgar Loves Vilma, 94, *111*, 138, 152, 155–6, 161–6, *163*, *164*, 171, 185, 196
Eisenberg, Susan, 27
Ekstra, 202
English language
   fluency in, 51–2, 88, 176, 183–6
   in Philippine popular culture, 20, 52, 57–8, 71, 73, 79, 128, 147, 176, 182–6, 199, 204
Eskwelahang Munti, 90, *91*, 111
Espiritu, Talitha, 56–7, 60–2
Estrada, Joseph, 69, 88, 116
ethnicity, 1, 13, 17, 66–7, 145, 168, 198, 212; *see also* mestizaje/mestizos
Ewen, Neil, 12, 25, 28
extra-filmic materials, 4, 9, 12, 19, 37, 98–134, 168, 172, 189–98, 210, 214

Fabon, Esperanza, 130
family, heteropatriarchal, 19–20, 32, 38–9, 46, 54, 187–99, 201–2, 205
fandom, 3, 13–16 19, 24, 31, 37–42, 48–49, 51–3, *52*, 68, 71, 75–6, 80–1, 89, 97–136, 144, 183
fatherhood, 187–8
female martyr characters *see* babaeng martir characters
femininity, normative, 54–6, 65, 80–1, 134, 150–7, 174–9, 187–99, 201–2, 208–10
   resistance to, 180–1, 201–2
Fernandez, M.B., 34, 43n
Ferrer, Noel, 16
Fiesta Extravaganza, 101
5th Manila Film Festival, 104–5, 160, 182–3, 194
50 First Dates, 29
filial obedience, 46, 55, 63–4, 80, 134, 145, 150–1, 154, 168–72, 175–89, 196, 204–6
Filipino language *see* Tagalog language
Filipino Directors Up Close: The Golden Ages of Philippine Cinema, 1950–2010 (Carballo), 15
Filipino Family (Medina), 168–9
Film: American Influences (Deocampo), 33
film studios, 137–8, 204
   family dynamic of, 45–53, 187
   independent star-owned, 51–2, 126
   television network studios, 16, 30, 35–8, 204–5
   see also studio system
Finlan, Ed, 88, 128, 130
First Comes Love (Cobb and Ewen), 12, 25

First Golden Age of Philippine Cinema, 3, 32–4, 45–51, 63
First Quarter Storm, 62, 178, 198
Fischer, Lucy, 5
Florante at Laura (Balagtas), 216
Flores, Patrick, 13, 76, 180
forbidden, 7, 149, 152–5, 162
Francisco, Butch, 98, 103–4, 116
Frith, Simon, 144
Fuentes, Amalia, 53, 67–9
Fuentes, Eduardo C., 49
Functional Couples, 10, 12, 25, 41

Garcia, Freddie M., 36
Garcia, J.B., 14
gaze, 8, 56–8, 60, 76, 146, 159–60, 173, 181
gender, 14–15, 18, 54–5, 65–94, 80–1, 88, 91–4, 93, 134, 150–7, 168, 174–9, 187–99, 201–2, 205, 208–10
Gledhill, Christine, 5
Ging, 79, 82
Gomez, Richard, 1, 85
Gonzalez, A.B., 186
Gonzales, Luis, 56, 59–61, 77–9
Graphic, 52, 71
Guy and Pip, 4, 97, 100–8, 118–20, 138, 141, 142, 154, 157–61, *158*, 165, 170–6, 179, 193–5, 206–7, *208*, 214, *215*, 216
'Guy and Pip', 119–20, 150, 157–61
Guy and Pip love team *see* Aunor and Cruz love team

Hawaii, 97, 108, 120–2, 124, 131
Hawaiian Souvenirs (Cruz), 121
'Hawaiian Wedding Song, The', 121
'Hear My Plea (O Lord)', 92
Heavenly Bodies (Dyer), 5–6, 66–7
heteronormativity, 7, 11, 32, 166–72, 190
Heussaff, Solenn, 209
hierarchy, 3, 17, 46, 55, 150, 168, 178–81, 184, 186–90, 198–9
high culture, 139, 216
Himala, 4, 13–14, 71, 181, 201
Hollywood, 2, 9–10, 22, 28–31, 38, 86, 128, 166, 210
 influence on Philippine television and film, 33, 37, 48, 86, 121, 147
Holmes, Su, 5
homogamy, 192–3
Huwaran/Hulmahan Atbp.: The Film Writing of Johven Velasco (Velasco), 14–15

hypergamy, 191–3, 199
hypogamy, 193, 199
Hyun Bin, 27–8

Iconic Couples, 10, 25, 30, 41
ideolect, 8, 80, 83
Iginuhit ng Tadhana: The Ferdinand E. Marcos Story, 17, 53, 56–7, 78, *78*, 82
'Ikaw', 160
Ilagan, Hermogenes, 115
Ilagan, Jay, 92, 94, 115–17, 126, 176
Ilagan, Marcelino, 32–3, 116
Ithaca, 29

JaDine love team, 15, 207–8
James, David E., 139–40, 148
Jimenez, Baby K., 14, 100
Joaquin, Nick, 68, 82–3, 103–4
joint image, 2, 6, 16, 18, 26, 53–61, 64, 67, 97–136, 148, 168, 172, 189, 191, 196, 211

Kajol, 26
Kakaibang Tingin, Kakaibang Titig (Almajose and Ramos), 15–16
Kampanang Ginto, 34
KathNiel love team, 37, 207–8
kayumanggi, 69, 73, 86, 101, 110, 113
Khan, Shah Rukh, 26
King, Barry, 5
Kislap Graphic, 91, 128–9, 187–8
Knapp, Raymond, 139
*komik*s, 24, 127, 214
Koronel, Hilda 88, 128, 130

labour, 3, 6, 9, 35–6, 46–53, 61, 71, 102, 107, 120, 152, 154, 156, 178, 184, 192, 198, 199, 202, 210
Lacaba, Jose F., 129, 216
Landy, Marcia, 5
language, 20, 64, 168, 199
 as marker of class, 181–8
Lapuz, Romy, 105
Laurel, Victor, 88, 133
Laxa, Espiridion, 52, 98
Leary, William, 79, 91, 98
Leavold, Andrew, 35
Lee, Cornelia 'Angge', 116
Leonard, Suzanne, 31
Leron-Leron Sinta, 170–1
Les stars (Morin), 5
Letter of Instruction No. 13, 63–4

Ligaw na Bulaklak, 33
Lim, Bliss C., 13–14, 35, 185
linguistic diversity, 182–7
linguistic purity, 168, 184–5
'Little Grass Shack', 121
Liwayway, 81, 93, 98, 111, 124–5, 128–34, *130*, 131, 133–4, 174, *175*
Love Letters, 143, 152, 154–6, 171, 173, 185
'Love Story (Where Do I Begin?)', 159
love teams, 138–67
  definition, 23–5
  history of, 32–7
  naming conventions of, 39–40
  neo-colonial, 182–87
  performance styles, of 157–66
low culture, 2, 18, 139, 205
Lozada, Ike, 105–7, 118–20, 150, *151*, 195
Lumbera, Bienvenido, 32, 35, 51, 137–9
Lustre, Nadine, 15; *see also* JaDine love team
LVN Pictures, 32, 34, 45–8, 150, 200

Macapagal, Diosdado, 59
McDonald, Paul, 9, 212
Maceda, Ernesto, 56, 97
Ma. Santiago, Ernie, 130
maid, 58, 93, 192, 201, 207
Makahiya at Talahib, 202
Malasig, Jeline, 35
Manahan Johnny, 36
Manunuri ng Pelikulang Pilipino, 81, 98, 103
Marcos, Ferdinand, 3, 16–19, 30, 53–64, 168–9, 178, 186–91, 198
  sex scandal, 62
Marcos, Imee, 78, 82
Marcos, Imelda, 17, 30, 44, 53–62, 64, 78, 178, 187–91
Marcos regime, 3, 51, 53–65, 168–9, 186–99, 202, 211
  student protests against, 3, 44, 51, 61–2, 64, 138, 156, 178–81, 198
  use of mass media, 3–5, 16–17, 53–64, 178–99, 203
Maria Leonora Teresa, 19, 75, 98, 103–5, 107–8, 119, 136n, *142*, 154, 160, 171, 189, 193–6, *195*, 198, 202–3, 207, 214–16, *215*
marriage, 3, 7, 38–41, 53–9, 119–20, 124–6, 151, 169–73, 190, 192–200
Martial Law era, 3–5, 20, 43–5, 53, 62–4, 166, 187–8, 198, 211
Martinez, William, 35
Marquez, Artemio, 102, 105

Mary, devotion to, 93–4, 161, 172–4, 176, 194
masa ('masses'), 17, 48, 54, 67–9, 71–2, 75–6, 95, 113, 138, 149, 178, 191–2, 196, 198, 200–1, 211, 213, 215–16
masculinity
  gentle, 88, 91–4, *93*, 205
  hypermasculinity, 88
  normative, 18, 55–6, 65, 151–7, 187–99
May Bukas Pa, 43
Medina, Belen T. G., 168–9, 171–3
melodrama, 17, 57, 60–2, 64, 75–6, 78, 83, 139–40, 187
Memories of Our Love, 107
Mendoza, Brillante, 201
Mendoza, Maine, 15, 206–9, *208*; *see also* AlDub love team
Mercado, Monina A., 47, 49, 71
mestizaje/mestizos, 17–18, 48–9, 67, 82, 86–8, 101, 110, 116, 128, 181–2, 192, 199–200
Mijares, Primitivo, 60
Miss You Like Crazy, 205
modernity, 19–20, 133, 166, 168–72, 190, 199, 205–6
Monteverde, 'Mother' Lily, 35, 85
'Moonlight Becomes You', 72, 141, 143, 147
moral gatekeeping, 50–1, 63–4, 149
morality clauses, 17, 47–8, 50
Moreno, German, 75, 100, 105, 107, 119, 147, 150, *151*
Morin, Edgar, 5, 34, 67
Morris, Mitchell, 139
Mortiz, Edgar, 1, 3–5, 18–19, 33, 52, 66, 79–83, 85, 88–95, *91*, *93*, 98–100, 102–3, 108–22, *109*, *111*, 124–7, 129–30, 133–5, 137–8, 140, 148–9, 152, 154–6, 161–6, *163*, *164*, 170, 173–4, 176, 181, 186, 189, 195–6, 199, 202–5, 210, 214, 217
  musicality, 18, 92, 112, 115
motherhood, 187–8
Movie Queen: Pagbuo ng Mito at Kapangyarihang Kultural ng Babae sa Lipunan (Orsal), 15
Mueller, John, 141, 143
Muhlach, Aga, 85, 88
music, 3, 18, 33, 42, 55, 58, 66–7, 92, 138–67, 205
  love team music, 118–22, 127
musical, 19–20, 24, 28, 32–3, 53, 59, 65, 69, 73, 79–80, 107, 137–67, 206–7, 212–14
  integrated, 141–3
  unintegrated 143–5
musician biopic, 138–40

My Blue Hawaii, 97, 121–2, 131, *132*
My Little Brown Girl, 152, *153*, 155, 192
'My Pledge of Love', 92, 203–4

Naremore, James, 2, 8, 25
nationalism, 182–99
Navarro-Pedrosa, Carmen, 54
Navarro, Walter, 90
Negotiation, The, 27
Negra, Diane, 32
New Society initiative, 3, 20, 45, 63–4, 188–9
Noble, Corazon, 33
Nochimson, Martha, 2, 10–12, 25, 30–2, 41, 211
Nora in Wonderland, 105
'Nora My Love', 119

Oh, Delilah, 85, 113
open nature spaces, 56, 79, 141, 149, 154, 160, 162
Operation Kumbento, 106–7
Oras ng Ligaya, 100
ordinariness, 26, 49, 68–75, 89
Original Pilipino Music (OPM), 92, 147
Orsal, Cesar D., 15
Overseas Filipino Worker (OFW), 14, 15, 206
Oxford Handbook of the American Musical, The (Knapp, Morris and Wolf), 139

Paano Ba ang Mangarap, 201
Padilla, Daniel, 1, 37; see also KathNiel love team
Panaligan, Andrea, 207–8
Paraluman, 33, 49
parenting, 187–9, 194–8
Pascual, Piolo, 15, 37, 88
Pascual, Wilfredo, 193
patriarchy, 19–20, 32, 38–9, 46, 54, 152, 187–99, 201–2, 205
  threats to, 13, 178–81, 201
Passionate Revolutions (Espiritu), 56
Pepot Artista, 213–17, *215*
Perez, Doc Jose, 46–7, 50, 56, 64, 70, 77–8, 97, 100, 102, 105, 107, 150
Peregrina, Eddie, 85, 88, 100, 130
personhood, 16, 22, 31, 38–9, 189, 190, 199
Philippine theatre, 24, 32–4, 45, 47, 83, 115–16
piety, 76, 92, 133–4, 145, 172–4, 179–81, 189
Pilipino language see Tagalog language
Pinagbuklod ng Langit, 61, 78, 82
Poe, Fernando Jr., 1, 13, 53, 68–9, 88, 213
political couples, 17, 53–62
pornographic films see bomba cinema

poverty, 13, 17–18, 54, 68–9, 72, 90, 95, 170, 173, 178–80, 191, 193, 213
  caricatures of, 216
power hierarchies, 3, 9, 17, 53–66, 73–5, 166, 178–81, 184–99, 202, 206
  threats to, 13, 202
P. Ramlee, 28
Presley, Elvis, 122, 138, 143–5, 212
proximate star, 18, 77, 84–9
P.S. I Love You, 35

Queen Elizabeth II, 28–30
Queen Vi: An Intimate Biography (Garcia), 14
Quezon, Manuel L., 182
Quijano, Douglas, 85
Quirino, Jose A., 97

radio, 3, 5, 18, 24, 34, 50–1, 66, 71–3, 88, 95, 100, 106, 113, 116, 120, 140, 146, 150, 190
Rafael, Vicente L., 53–5, 178, 183–4
rags-to-riches narrative, 14, 68, 95, 144–5, 191–4, 213; see also poverty
Ramos, J.V., 15–16, 33, 45–8, 51, 63–4
Redmond, Sean, 5
Regal Films, 35–6, 85
Reid, James, 15, 208–9; see also JaDine love team
relatability, 17, 53, 57, 66, 79, 81, 88, 122, 166, 179
Relasyon, 201
religion, 14, 32, 168, 172–8, 192, 206, 213; see also Catholicism/Catholic Church and piety
Remembrance, 92, 94, 116–17, 156, 184
Richard Gomez at ang mito ng pagkalalake, Sharon Cuneta at ang perpetwal na birhen at iba pang sanaysay ukol sa bida sa pelikula bilang kultural na texto (Tolentino), 15
Richards, Alden, 15, 206–10, *208*; see also AlDub love team
Ricky Na, Tirso Pa!, 85, 129
Roces, Susan, 1, 53, 67–9, 78, 85, 88, 102
Rock 'N' Film (James), 139
Rodriguez, Lolita, 77
Rojek, Chris, 5, 41–2, 66
Roman Catholicism see Catholicism/Catholic Church
Romero, Gloria, 47, 56, 59–61, 78
Romero and Gonzales love team, 59–61
Romualdez, Daniel, 57
Rosales, Carmen, 1, 33–34, 47, 77
Rosales, Jericho, 15

St Teresa, 154, 172, 174
Salcedo, Leopold, 1, 50
Saloma, 28
Salvador, Maja, 208
Sampaguita Pictures, 4, 16–17, 34, 44–7, 50, 55–6, 64, 74–5, 77, 85, 88, 97–8, 100, 102–8, 118–20, 134, 146, 150, 173, 181, 194–6
Santiago, Ciriaco, 150
Santos and Mortiz love team, 1, 3, 5, 18–19, 33, 40, 52, 91–5, 108–27, 129–30, 134–5, 138, 140, 161–6, *163*, 173–4, 176, 189, 195–6, 205, 214
Santos-Concio, Charo, 36
Santos, Judy Ann, 15, 37
Santos, Simon, 4
Santos, Vilma, 1, 3–5, 14, 17–19, 33, 44, 52, 66–8, 73, 77–95, *78*, 98–100, 108–22, *109*, *111*, 124–30, 133–5, 137–8, 140, 152, 156, 161–4, *163*, *164*, 166, 170–1, 173–4, 176–7, 181, 189, 195–6, 199–206, 214, 217
  dancing, 80, 82, 95, 163–4, *164*, 202, 204
  fandom ('Vilmanians'), 81, 83, 134, 213
  musicality, 79–80, 114–15
  performance style, 78–9, 83
  political career, 201–2, 204
  recording career, 79, 118–19, 186
sarsuwela, 24, 32–4, 47, 57, 83, 115–16, 187
screen couple, 2, 8, 10–12, 22–31, *26*, 38–9, 41–2, 59–60, 102, 148, 189
Screen Couple Chemistry (Nochimson), 10
Second Golden Age of Philippine Cinema, 4, 20, 45, 76, 82, 84, 94, 127, 200, 211, 213
self-sacrifice, 174, 178, 189, 199, 206
set, or setting *see* space
Shingler, Martin, 5
Sinasamba Kita, 201
Sinderella figure, 67–8, 72, 76, 124, 192; *see also* Cinderella-Prince Charming narrative
singing contests, 17–18, 67, 69, 71–3, 90, 95, 112–13, 143, 145, 147–8, 179, 192
Si Nora Aunor sa Mga Noranian: Mga Pagunita at Pagtatapat (de Guzman), 14
Sisang, Doña, 34, 150; *see also* de León, Doña Narcissa
Sisikat Din Ako!: Your Guide to Making Your Mark in Show Business (Ferrer), 16
Sister Stella L., 202
'Sixteen' (Santos), 79, 118–19
slippage, 19, 22, 31–2, 37–8, 41, 123, 145, 149, 195

Soberano, Liza, 209
Son, Ye-jin, 27–28
'Song of My Life, The', 159
Sonita, Clifford, 207
Sonora, Rosemarie, 85, 101–02, 170
Soriano, Maricel, 35
space, 19, 141, 149–57
  bedroom, 149, 152–4, 161
  church, 58–9, 154, 161, 172–4, 193
  domestic spaces, 141, 149–52, 162
  forbidden, 149, 152–55, 162
  garden, 56, 59, 112, 154, 160, 162, 165–6, 195, 207, 214
  outdoor, 56, 141, 146, 148, 154–6, 160, 162–5
  park, 79, 154–5, 160
  studio sets, 19, 141, 145–50, 157–61, 165–66, 207
  university, 156
Spanish language, 181–6
Star Acting (Affron), 5
'Star also Suffers: Screening Nora Aunor, The' (Flores), 76
star couples, 2, 8, 22, 25–32, *26*, 38–9, 41–2, 59–61, 148, 189
Stardom (Gledhill), 5
Stardom and Celebrity (Redmond and Holmes), 5
star images, 6–20, 35, 53–136, 204–5, 210–11
Stars (Dyer), 5–6, 66
Stars: The Film Reader (Fischer and Landy), 5
star persona, 8, 17, 35, 39, 42, 53–4, 56, 60–1, 68–69, 75–6, 79–80, 88, 92, 127, 131–2, 147, 179–81
Star Studies (Shingler), 5
Star System, The (McDonald), 9
star vehicle film, 3, 6, 9, 19, 42, 138, 144, 147
studio boss character, 150, 175–6, 179–81
studio system, 3–4, 6, 9–10, 15–18, 32–7, 44–53, 66, 99–118, 202, 204–10
Subido, Danny, 91
submissiveness, 20, 64, 80, 139, 150, 152, 174, 178–81, 189, 196, 199, 201–2; *see also* femininity, normative
sufferance, 13, 17, 35, 54–5, 60–1, 67, 75–6, 108, 152, 174–81, 189, 198–9, 201–2, 205, 215–16
Synergistic Couples, 10–11, 25, 41

Tadiar, Neferti, 13, 71
Tagalog language, 15, 33, 52, 58, 92, 128, 160, 169, 181–7, 199, 201, 216
  role of cinema in popularising, 182

Tagalog Ilang-Ilang Productions (TIIP), 52, 91, 98, 117, 134
Taglish language, 20, 182–6, 199
Tag-Ulan sa Tag-Araw, 201
Taklub, 201
Tan, Robbie, 35
Tatlong Mukha ni Rosa Vilma, 94, 116, 155–6, 176, 185
Tatlong Taong Walang Diyos, 200
Tawag ng Tanghalan, 71–3, 90, *91*, 113, 141, 147
teenage consumer market, 3, 61, 138, 144, 168–72, 183–4, 196–7
teenage jukebox musical, 2–3, 66, 69, 79–83, 137–67, 169, 183, 190, 198–9, 204–5, 212–14
  cinematography, 145–9
  definition, 138–45
  semi-biographical, 19, 138, 140, 143, 145, 147, 157, 179, 181, 193
teleserye, 206, 212
television, 3, 10, 16–18, 29–30, 34–8, 50–2, 64, 66–7, 71–6, 79–80, 82, 87–91, 94–5, 100, 105, 108, 113, 145, 190, 200, 202–6, 212–13
  variety shows, 5, 18–19, 27, 73, 111, 127, 137–8, 140, 143–5, 206
Teodoro, Luis V. Jr, 182–4, 186
'Then I Met You Edgar', 118
Thompson, R.M., 183, 186
Thy Womb, 201
Tiongson, Nicanor, 32–3, 180
'Together', 160
'Together Again', 108, 160, 207, *208*, 214
Tolentino, Rolando B., 14–15, 35
Torres, Mar S., 56
'Towards the Restructuring of Filipino Values', 188
Tower Productions, 74–5, 102–6, 119–20, 123, 157, 173, 191, 194–5
'To You Sweetheart, Aloha', 121
tradition/traditional values, 19–20, 50, 133–4, 160, 166, 168–72, 190, 199, 204–6
  promotion through media, 179–81, 211

Trudis Liit, 77, 82
'true love', 41, 169, 171–2, 190
Turner, Graeme, 5

Understanding Celebrity (Turner), 5
university students, 51–2, 61–3, 128, 156, 178–81, 198–9, 211

Vasquez, Romeo, 53, 68
Velasco, Johven, 14
Vera, Dolores Honrado, 9, 46
Vera-Perez Maceda, Marichu, 50, 56, 64
Vi and Bot love team *see* Santos and Mortiz love team
'Vilma', 118
Vilma, Rosa 185
voice, 17–18, 27, 34, 54, 57, 59, 62, 67, 69–72, 76, 79, 92, 101, 112, 150, 162–3, 173, 193, 201, 213

'Walk With Faith in Your Heart', 92
Weng Weng, 13
When I Fall in Love, 200
When I Met You in Tokyo, 204
Williams, Linda Ruth, 40
'Windmills of Your Mind', 72
Winter Holiday, 131
Wolf, Stacy, 139
work ethic, 17–18, 46–7, 50, 66, 117, 125, 179, 193
working class, 35, 67–75, 89, 178–81, 198, 201, 211, 215
Wright, Julie Lobalzo, 144, 212

Yan, Rico, 37
YeYe Generation, 85
Young at Heart, The, 85, 101, 104–5, 141, 147–52, *151*, 170–1, 176, 179, 192, 193
Young Love, 107–8, *109*, 131, 133, 143, 149, 152, 170–1, 179, 192–3
youth culture, 19, 24, 44, 51–2, 67, 72–95, 105, 128, 137–99, 212

Zulueta, Dawn, 1

EU Authorised Representative:
Easy Access System Europe Mustamäe tee 50, 10621 Tallinn, Estonia
gpsr.requests@easproject.com

Printed and bound by CPI Group (UK) Ltd, Croydon, CR0 4YY

02/03/2026

02063627-0008